∟ windows root→ Sy

MW01177801

Craig Witherspoon
Coletta Witherspoon

SAMS
Teach Yourself
Linux®-Mandrake™
in 24 Hours

SAMS

A Division of Macmillan USA
201 West 103rd St., Indianapolis, Indiana, 46290

Sams Teach Yourself Linux-Mandrake in 24 Hours

Copyright © 2000 by Sams Publishing

International Standard Book Number: 0-672-31877-6

Library of Congress Catalog Card Number: 99-67583

Printed in the United States of America

First Printing: March, 2000

01 00 99   4   3   2   1

Trademarks

Warning and Disclaimer

ASSOCIATE PUBLISHER
Mark Taber

ACQUISITIONS EDITOR
Neil Rowe

DEVELOPMENT EDITOR
Tony Amico

MANAGING EDITOR
Lisa Wilson

PROJECT EDITOR
Dawn Pearson

COPY EDITOR
Kezia Endsley

INDEXER
Greg Pearson

PROOFREADER
Katherin Bidwell

TECHNICAL EDITOR
Jim Westveer

TEAM COORDINATOR
Karen Opal

MEDIA DEVELOPER
Dan Scherf

INTERIOR DESIGNER
Gary Adair

COVER DESIGNER
Aren Howell

COPYWRITER
Eric Borgert

PRODUCTION
Lisa England
Steve Geiselman
Brad Lenser
Louis Porter Jr.

Contents at a Glance

Contents

PART IV Putting Linux-Mandrake to Work   157

HOUR 11 Getting on the Internet   159

HOUR 12 Document Processing with KLyX   181

About the Authors

Craig and **Coletta Witherspoon** are freelance authors who have been writing for the computer industry since the 1970s producing training and promotional materials for multinational corporations and small businesses. They are the authors of 16 computer books and the technical editors of dozens of others.

Dedication

To Marlene Hoffmann

Acknowledgments

We want to express our thanks to everyone at Macmillan Computer Publishing for the support and assistance we received throughout this entire book project. In particular we would like to thank Karen Opal for recommending us to Neil Rowe. We want to thank Neil Rowe for providing the opportunity and all the support we ever asked for. Many thanks to Tony Amico for keeping the manuscript flowing and to Jim Westveer for making sure we kept the facts straight. Our special thanks to Kezia Endsley for doing such a great job of making our words sound right and to Dawn Pearson for keeping this project on the right track.

Coletta would also like to thank Sleepy for the years of loyal and dependable service as our test computer. Sleepy has survived numerous beta testing programs, hard drive crashes, and other abuse caused by late working hours and frustrated writers.

And, of course, to our roosters for getting us up early in the morning so that we could start our workday bright-eyed and bushy-tailed.

Tell Us What You Think!

As the reader of this book, *you* are our most important critic and commentator. We value your opinion and want to know what we're doing right, what we could do better, what areas you'd like to see us publish in, and any other words of wisdom you're willing to pass our way.

As an Associate Publisher for Sams, I welcome your comments. You can fax, email, or write me directly to let me know what you did or didn't like about this book—as well as what we can do to make our books stronger.

Please note that I cannot help you with technical problems related to the topic of this book, and that due to the high volume of mail I receive, I might not be able to reply to every message.

When you write, please be sure to include this book's title and author as well as your name and phone or fax number. I will carefully review your comments and share them with the author and editors who worked on the book.

Fax: 317-581-4770

Email: opsys@mcp.com

Mail: Mark Taber
            Associate Publisher
            Sams
            201 West 103rd Street
            Indianapolis, IN 46290 USA

Introduction

Why All the GNU/Linux Hype?

Linux is a free UNIX clone that runs on personal computer systems. It provides users with an operating system that supports true multitasking, a multi-user environment, TCP/IP networking, the X Windows system, and much more. Linux is a small, friendly version of UNIX that comes with all the tools you need to learn system administration, programming, networking, and all the other things that computing is about. You can install Linux on virtually every personal computer made since the introduction of the Intel i386 family of processors. Linux can also be ported to 64-bit RISC processor systems like DEC Alpha and Sun Sparc workstations.

Lots of older equipment like Commodore Amigas and low-end Pentium machines, and even a large number of Apple Macintosh and Power PC platforms, will benefit greatly from the installation of a Linux operating system. Linux normally provides some measurable improvement in the operation of every piece of hardware where it is installed. But perhaps most importantly, Linux provides a popular platform for ordinary people to have access to the astounding volume of open source software available from the GNU project and others, and distributed under the GPL (GNU Public License).

Reasons for Giving GNU/Linux a Spin

If you have been wondering what it would be like to have a faster computer and all those dream applications to do just about anything you can think of, from playing games to running a professional Hollywood movie studio, without spending any money, then you need to look into GNU/Linux.

If you want a real platform for learning UNIX at home in an environment with built-in help for the commands and open access to all the functions of your computer, then you need to look into GNU/Linux.

If you have an ongoing business that requires a stable platform for running your business/scientific applications, managing your organization's intranet, or maybe even running your TV station, you need to look into GNU/Linux.

What Makes Linux-Mandrake Different?

The Linux-Mandrake distribution found on the CD in the back of this book has been carefully organized to provide the easiest path to install and configure Linux on your computer. It is particularly well organized for those who need networking and easy configuration of the Linux machine. The best utilities for configuring, upgrading, and modifying your Linux-Mandrake installation have been selected and are included in the installation package. Documentation for Linux and additional documentation for special features are also included on the distribution CD. The Linux community has named Linux-Mandrake as the easiest Linux distribution to install and configure. Support for installation related problems and other problems users may incur with the distribution is provided online.

Who Should Read This Book?

This book is aimed at the computer user who is familiar with other operating systems (like DOS/Windows or Apple Macintosh systems) who needs a good introduction to Linux, and Linux-Mandrake in particular. Although the book is written with the Mandrake user in mind, the general information about Linux and all the application software we discuss in the book applies to all Linux users.

This book is directed toward the Linux beginner to intermediate user, and those with existing knowledge of Windows, Macintosh, or other computer operating systems. The focus of the book is to make as much use as possible of the existing knowledge of the user and build on that to create a good understanding of Linux-Mandrake and give the reader a great introduction to its use with open source software from the GNU project and others.

How This Book Is Organized

We designed the book to be read and used, along with the included lessons, workshops, and tests, over a total of 24 one-hour working sessions. The chapter/hours are arranged to take the reader from the basic installation of Linux-Mandrake through a logically ordered progression from the simplest tasks to the more complex techniques, and to provide introductions to applications that most effectively utilize the power of Linux-Mandrake to provide a sophisticated and powerful tool to accomplish myriad tasks.

In Part I, Installing Linux-Mandrake, we take you through the process of planning your Linux installation including the gathering of the information about your computer and peripherals that you will need to have a successful installation. Then we guide you through the installation itself in detail, followed by a discussion of troubleshooting information and techniques for anything that might not have automatically worked for you.

In Part II, An Interface for All Occasions, you learn to work in a graphical user environment (GUI). This will be a good introduction to Linux-Mandrake for users of Microsoft Windows or other operating systems who have limited command line experience. You will even get to use more than one graphical user interface here.

In Part III, Understanding the Filesystem, you will explore the directory structure, learn to manage files with both command line input and with the file managers included with the graphical user interfaces. Here you will learn the system administration tasks that you must perform to manage your system, how to back up your system, and how to plan for networking your enterprise with Linux-Mandrake.

In Part IV, Putting Linux-Mandrake to work, you will learn how to get on the Internet and we will introduce you to some of the production applications that come in the Linux-Mandrake distribution and some others that you can download. You will learn about KLyX (a word processor), how to manage your checkbook with the Check Book Balancer (CBB), and how to print and fax documents. You will also meet a really SCREEMing HTML editor and site manager.

In Part V, The Beginner's Guide to Emacs, you will meet the most powerful application found in Linux distributions, Richard Stallman's Emacs text editor. Emacs can be anything you want it to be. It is complex and it can be used to write applications, edit files, and lots of other things. You can use Emacs to write a whole operating system, but it might take you a while to learn how to use it that effectively. You will learn how to use Emacs for text processing, and how to use the very nice calendar and other time management tools.

Part VI, Going for the Graphics, is your introduction to The Gimp, KIllustrator, video and animation applications, and many of the graphics viewers and utilities included with the distribution.

Part VII, Sit Back and Have Some Fun, introduces you to the multimedia players and games that come with Linux-Mandrake to round out your Linux education.

Conventions Found in This Book

This book uses special typefaces and other graphical elements to highlight different types of information.

Notes

We use notes to mention places where more information can be found (such as program help and the Internet), reminders, and references to information in other chapters of the book.

Tips

These talk about ways in which programs can be used more efficiently, and areas that can be explored to increase your skills.

Cautions

We use cautions to point out places in programs where caution needs to be exercised to avoid potential difficulties.

New Terms

 This is the book's on-the-fly glossary. It defines terms that may be unfamiliar as they are used.

Lessons

In the lessons for each chapter we take you through step-by-step demonstrations of the concepts being explained.

Q&A

The Questions and Answers section highlights items of particular importance and provides more information about how to use features covered in the chapter.

Exercises

These show how to use features not covered in the chapters or where to find programs that are similar to the ones discussed.

What's on the CD-ROM?

At the back of this book, you'll find a CD-ROM with the Macmillan Complete Linux distribution, which is based on the Linux-Mandrake distribution. You'll find everything you need on this CD to get you up and running with Linux (except maybe for a few programs that you can download off the Internet).

PART I

Installing Linux-Mandrake

Hour

HOUR 1

Preparing for the Installation

Congratulations! Your adventure with Linux-Mandrake is about to begin and you may be in for the ride of your life. While you're taking the ride, you'll be seeing some new sights as Linux-Mandrake powers you along the trail. But, be a smart rider and plan your trip. This preparation will help you avoid the trail hazards and stay on track to the scenic viewpoints. With the right preparation, you can map out those areas with loose rocks, blind corners, and cliff hazards and avoid the major problems as you move along.

It'll be fun; you'll probably want to stop and enjoy the view along the way. There are some secrets to discover and a few hidden surprises along the road to a successful installation. But you don't need to worry; you are beginning the trip in the best of company with Linux-Mandrake. Linux-Mandrake is one of the easiest GNU/Linux distributions to install and configure. During the next hour, you'll work through the Linux trail guide and learn the secrets

to successfully installing Linux-Mandrake on your computer. During the
following hour, you'll prepare for the installation by

- Determining whether your computer meets the minimum system requirements
- Deciding where Linux-Mandrake will reside on the computer
- Selecting which applications and services you want to install
- Making sure that your equipment is compatible with Linux-Mandrake

Before You Begin

There are many ways to work with Linux-Mandrake and we can't cover them all in one
book. This book concentrates on using the distribution on a standalone workstation and
introduces a selection of applications that you might use at home or at work. Home users
will enjoy the assortment of Internet and personal management applications. If computer
graphics are your gig, you'll find a powerhouse of graphics applications to fit any art
project. Programmers will find every programming environment imaginable. And, of
course, the strong suit of GNU/Linux is its networking capabilities.

At a minimum, you should run Linux-Mandrake on a computer with the following configuration:

- Pentium-class or compatible CPU
- 32MB RAM
- 500MB hard disk drive space minimum, 1.6GB is recommended
- Keyboard, mouse, sound card, and video card (with 2MB VRAM)
- Floppy disk drive, and an IDE or SCSI CD-ROM
- Modem (for Internet access) or Ethernet card (if connected to a network)

> Linux-Mandrake is optimized for Pentium-class computers. This means that,
> while other GNU/Linux distributions run on i386 and i486 computers, Linux-
> Mandrake does not. Visit http://mcpsupport.linuxcare.com/ to obtain a
> special version that works with i386 and i486 computers.

If you'll be running any commercial applications, such as Corel WordPerfect or StarOffice,
you need to reserve hard disk space for these applications. You also want to check what
processor speed the application needs and the minimum amount of RAM required.

Graphics work such as Web graphics and similar small image files can be done comfortably on a Pentium 133MHz computer with 32MB RAM. But if you need to do

higher-end graphics, pre-press and large format photographs, or other high-resolution images, a Pentium 200 with 64MB RAM and 500MB free on the hard drive will make a killer workstation—one that can handle large files easily.

Deciding How to Install Linux-Mandrake

The best Linux-Mandrake installation method is the one that accommodates your specific needs. If you have an old machine that's not a good Windows machine anymore, chances are that it might make a good Linux standalone workstation. If you have only one computer and you don't want to mess with its hard drive or operating system, you might want to install Linux-Mandrake on a second hard drive. If you need to install Linux and another operating system on the same drive, you create new partitions for Linux and install Linux-Mandrake on the hard drive. There are several options to consider, but before you attempt to install Linux-Mandrake, you have to make a few decisions and do a little detective work.

Using Linux-Mandrake as the Sole Operating System

Linux-Mandrake can be installed as the only operating system on a computer. A good reason to do this is to restore an old Windows machine to service. For example, our business has an old Compaq Presario P133 that we have been using for several years as a Windows beta machine. It had become so cranky and undependable that we had to restart it a half-dozen or more times a day. Its 1.6GB hard drive ran constantly, sounding like a chattering set of teeth. We really thought it was finished. We decided to give it one last chance and loaded Linux-Mandrake to see whether we could use it as a GNU/Linux machine. It has run for months now without a glitch—we've returned it to service again as a Web graphics workstation.

Installing Linux-Mandrake on a Separate Hard Drive

Installing Linux-Mandrake on its own hard drive offers several advantages. You can operate your computer as a dual-boot machine without having to do anything to any other hard drive on the system or having to make room on the Linux drive for any other operating system files. Since Linux-Mandrake is small, it fits comfortably along with its application software on a 1.6GB hard drive with room to spare. Yes, one of those old hard drives from yesteryear will work just fine for GNU/Linux.

Running Windows and Linux-Mandrake Together

This is the most complex of the methods for installing Linux-Mandrake. It is more complex because it involves altering a single hard drive to allow it to contain different operating systems. Since the advent of large format hard drives (above 2GB), most computer manufacturers install a single large format hard drive in the machines that they build. In order to install Linux-Mandrake on one of these machines, this large drive must be partitioned to make room for Linux files.

During the Linux-Mandrake installation, the Mandrake automated setup tool DrakX guides you through the job of partitioning, re-sizing, and formatting the hard drive with graphical aids to help you make the right choices to fit your particular Linux installation. If you want it to, it can even automatically partition the drive for you. Once this was a complex job and made the installation of Linux quite daunting to the newcomer. The new DrakX installation program makes it a snap to install Linux-Mandrake on just about any modern PC.

Selecting Applications to Install with Linux-Mandrake

When you begin your installation of Linux-Mandrake, you are given an option to choose one of three classes of installation:

- The Recommended option is for those who are brand-new to Linux.
- The Customized option is for those familiar with Linux and who want to specify the types of application programs to be installed on the system.
- The Expert option is for the truly experienced and fluent GNU/Linux guru (and you know who you are).

It is strongly recommended that you accept the defaults when installing Linux-Mandrake for the first time, so if you decide to install something else later, you can use Mandrake's tools to install other packages.

Choosing Installation Packages

You are shown a list of package groups to be installed. You can deselect package groups to configure your machine with the software you want, but it is strongly suggested that you accept the defaults the first time through. The package groups to be installed are listed in the installation program display, and the recommended ones are already selected.

The applications components shown in Table 1.1 represent a reasonable setup for an all-purpose workstation.

TABLE 1.1 Customize a Multi-Purpose Workstation

Component	Description
Graphics Manipulation	Adds graphics applications to the installation such as The GIMP and XMorph.
KDE	Installs the KDE graphical user interface and an assortment of applications designed for the K Desktop Environmnet.
GNOME	Installs the GNOME graphical user interface and a number of GLP software applications.
Other Window-managers	Installs kdm, enlightenment, fvwm, fvwm2, and so on.
Mail/WWW/News tools	Required if you want to send and receive email, surf the Web, and participate in Usenet newsgroups.
Communication facilities	Provides a number of programs that are needed to use the system to send and receive faxes, provide voicemail services, and use telnet facilities.
Office	Applications that are part of Koffice such as the KLyX word processor and the KIllustrator drawing program.
Multimedia Support	Provides multimedia support for the X Window system and on text consoles.
Games	Installs games that run on a text console and games that run under the X Window system.
System Configuration	Sets the daemons that are controlled depending on how the system is configured.
Web Server	Allows the machine to be set up as an Apache Web server.
Network Management Workstation	Enables the workstation to monitor traffic on a network to which it is connected and to make changes to the network configuration.
Documentation	Installs information from the Linux Documentation Project, along with important HOWTOs and other information.
Databases	Installs databases such as MySQL and PostgreSQL, which are both based on the Structured Query Language database language.
Miscellaneous	Selects packages that are not included in the list above.

Sorting Out the Daemons

NEW TERM   During the installation, DrakX selects the *daemons* (or system servers) to run on the computer system based on the choices you make during setup. Daemons run system processes automatically in the background. The user does not have to execute these processes before they can be performed. DrakX loads only the necessary system services. By doing this, DrakX helps you avoid system overload, security problems, and conflicts. But nothing is perfect and you may find that you want to load a Daemon to perform a service not included in your original installation. The information in Table 1.2 will give you some help with choosing others.

Table 1.2 helps you decide which daemons you want to run on your system.

TABLE 1.2   Choose Your Daemons

Daemon	Description	Service Performed
apmd	Advanced Power Management BIOS Daemon	Select this daemon if your computer runs on a battery.
atd	At Daemon	Required. Manages scheduled jobs.
crond	Cron Daemon	Required. Manages repeated tasks.
gpm	General Purpose Mouse Daemon	If you will be working within a GUI, do not use this daemon.
inet	Internet Super-Server	Handles dial-in services like ftp, smtp, and asf. If you only dial out (for connecting to the Internet), turn it off! In its default setting, it essentially invites anyone who knows your IP address to launch an attack at your box.
keytable	Generic service	Required. Loads the selected keyboard map as set in /etc/sysconfig/keyboard.
linuxconf	Linux Configuration	Required. You will be using linuxconf to configure your system in later hours.
lpd	Line Printer Spooler Daemon	Required if you will be attaching a printer to the computer.
netfs	Network Filesystem Mounter	Needed for mounting NFS, SMB, and NCP shares.
network	Generic service	Required to activate network interfaces when the system is booted.
nfs	Network filesystem	Provides shared files across a network.
pcmcia	Generic service	Use this service if you are using a laptop.
random	Random Number Generating Daemon	Required.
routed	Network Routing Daemon	If you use a dial-up connection to the Internet, do not use this service.

1

Daemon	Description	Service Performed
sendmail	Mail Transport Agent	If your mail client is capable of sending and receiving mail on its own (Netscape Mail, kmail, Pine), you may disable this service. In a workstation configuration, a mail transport agent is not generally needed, but if you are managing a permanent Internet connection and mail for several users with permanent IP addresses (an Intranet), then you will need to keep sendmail.
syslog	System Message Logger	Required.
ypbind	NIS Binder	Needed only if your computer is part of a NIS (Network Information Service) domain (yp for its old name *yellow pages*). May cause trouble on a dial-up workstation.

Making Sure You Have the Right Equipment

Successful installations happen when your computer's hardware is compatible with the GNU/Linux operating system. In order for you to determine whether your hardware is compatible, you must know some things about your computer before proceeding. If your computer hardware is compatible, chances are good that Linux-Mandrake will install easily on your computer, and you can begin enjoying your new Linux operating system and the applications included with the distribution. If your equipment is not compatible, you're only setting yourself up for trouble.

What You Need to Know About the Computer

As you begin your exploration into the world of operating system changes, there are many pieces of information that you need to start keeping in a logbook. You can begin with an inventory of devices and the system information about them. Table 1.3 lists each device and the information about it that you need to know.

TABLE 1.3 System Information You Need to Collect

For This Device...	You Need to Know:
CPU	Type (Pentium, Pentium II)
RAM	Amount of system RAM
Hard drives	Number of hard disk drives, how they are numbered, size of each drive, partitions, hard drive controller (IDE or SCSI), amount of space to be dedicated to Linux-Mandrake

continues

TABLE 1.3   continued

For This Device...	You Need to Know:
Keyboard	Keyboard language, number of keys
Mouse	Type of mouse (PS/2, serial mouse, number of buttons)
CD-ROM drives	Manufacturer, model number, controller type (ATAPI, IDE, SCSI, or other)
Monitor	Manufacturer and model, maximum resolution, vertical and horizontal refresh rate parameters
Video card	Manufacturer and model, type of graphics card and chipset, video memory, color depth (256 color, 16-bit color, 24-bit color)
Sound card	Manufacturer and model, type (SoundBlaster, ESS), IRQ address
Serial ports	Number of serial ports, port assignments (COM1, COM2), IRQ addresses
Modem	Manufacturer and model number, speed, communications port (COM port), fax support
Printer	Manufacturer and model, type of printer (PostScript, HPCL)
Network interface cards	Manufacturer and model
SCSI controllers	Manufacturer and model

Use an external modem. Your chances of getting Linux-Mandrake to recognize an internal modem are slim. And, if it's a Winmodem, there's no chance it will work. External modems, on the other hand, work like a charm.

Finding System Information

Finding out the necessary information about your computer can entail some detective work. If Microsoft Windows is installed on the same computer that you are going to install Linux-Mandrake on, you can use the tools in Windows to find out about your hardware. If you have any manuals or books that came with your computer, you can also find information there. Even if you don't have the manuals, you can probably download the information from the equipment maker's site.

During the installation, you will find that Linux-Mandrake is very good at probing and determining things about your hardware. In many cases the proper choice will already be highlighted in the Installation program. However, there are times when the probes don't return accurate information and you have to enter the correct information manually. For this reason, it is very important to take the time to find out all you can about your equipment.

Checking System Properties in Microsoft Windows

The easiest way to collect most of the information you need about the computer system is with the aid of Microsoft Windows. You can view the list of system devices and make a note of them one by one, but there is a more efficient method for collecting this information. Try these steps:

1. Open the System Properties dialog box. You can use one of two methods. Right-click on the My Computer icon and select the Properties command. Or, click on Start, Settings, Control Panel. In the Control Panel, double-click on the System icon.

2. Click on the Device Manager tab. A list of the devices installed on the computer is displayed in a list.

3. Click on the plus sign next to a device type to expand the list and show all the devices of that type.

4. Click on the Print button to display the Print dialog box as shown in Figure 1.1.

> Check the printer settings. You can change the printer and the print options by clicking on the Setup button.

5. Click on the All devices and system summary option button. This will print a summary of the entire system including IRQ and IO port summaries, memory and DMA usage, and disk drive information. A report of all the system devices follows.

6. Click OK to send the report to the printer.

Collecting Your Computer User Manuals

Our business has a raggle taggle assortment of computers, each with its own peculiar set of attachments, video cards, monitors, CD-ROMs, ZIP drives, network cards, CPUs, user manuals, and everything else. In order to keep track of what's installed or configured on each machine, we keep logbooks and files containing all the manuals, directions, and warranties that came with the machine. It makes changing the operating system on the computer more manageable by keeping the information all in one place.

We have a three-ring binder for each machine into which entries are made whenever anything is changed. With the speed at which technology is changing, you need to hold on to all the documentation supporting each machine and component to be able to span a gap of a couple of years and maintain compatibility between older and newer equipment.

These three-ring binders are also a good place to record configuration changes, computer problems and associated solutions, and mistakes you'd like to avoid in the future. We know this may seem like extra work, but someday you'll be glad you have a paper trail.

FIGURE 1.1

FIGURE 1.1

The System Properties dialog box contains most of the system information you need.

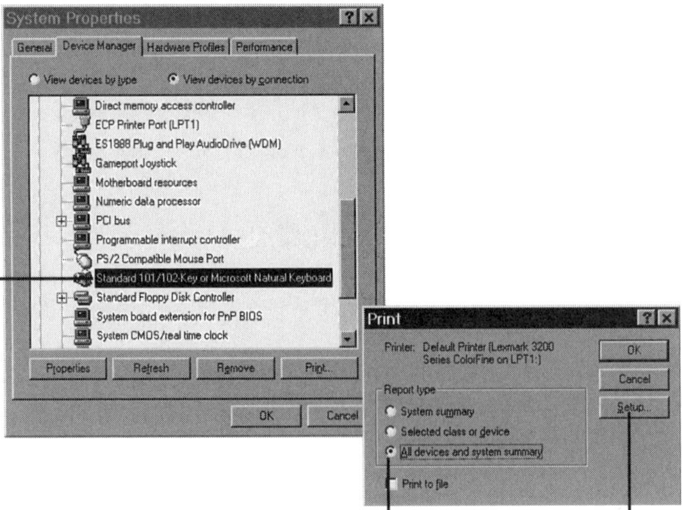

View device information

Print a system and device report

Change printer settings

Determining Hardware Compatibility

Determining the compatibility of your hardware is a matter of checking the hardware compatibility FAQ to see whether your hardware is listed there. You can find the hardware compatibility list on the Linux-Mandrake Web site at
`http://www.linux-mandrake.com/en/fhard.php3`. There's also the Linux Hardware Compatibility HOWTO at `http://www.linuxdoc.org/HOWTO/Hardware-HOWTO.html`.

You can also seek information from the distribution support page. For current information on hardware that Linux-Mandrake supports, see the Macmillan support Web page at
`http://www.linuxcare.com/mcpsupport/comp_linux.epl`.

Getting Ready for the Installation

Now that you have collected information about your hardware and thought about how you will be using your Linux-Mandrake machine, it is time to decide how you want to install Linux-Mandrake on your system. The following is a description of three suggested ways that you can install Linux-Mandrake:

1

- As a standalone GNU/Linux machine
- As a dual-boot machine with Linux-Mandrake installed on a separate hard drive
- As a dual-boot machine with Linux-Mandrake installed on a shared hard drive

The tasks to be performed for each of the three methods of installation are listed in Table 1.4.

TABLE 1.4   Installation Tasks

Task	Linux Only	Separate Drive	Shared Drive
Back up files	x	x	x
Create boot disks	x	x	x
Create rescue disks	x	x	x
Defragment hard drive			x
Install Linux-Mandrake	x	x	x

Summary

During this hour, you learned how to prepare your computer for installing Linux-Mandrake. You found out where to obtain needed information to ensure that Linux supports your hardware components. You learned where sources of information about your computer and components could be found and what specific installation tasks need to be done to load Linux-Mandrake on your computer in three different ways.

Q&A

Q I'd like to learn more about Linux-Mandrake before I begin the installation. Where can I go?

A You should start with the Linux-Mandrake home page at www.linux-mandrake.com and Macmillan Software support at mcpsupport.linuxcare.com. Other good sources of information are InformIT at www.informit.com and MandrakeUser.Org at www.mandrakeuser.org. If you lurk the Usenet newsgroups, try alt.os.linux.mandrake.

Q Are there any sources of information about GNU/Linux for newbies on the Web?

A Try the beginners page at the Linux portal site, Linux Links (www.linuxlinks.com/Beginners). There are several links to information that is of interest to those just beginning with GNU/Linux. There are also some good tutorials at Linux Planet (www.linuxplanet.com/linuxplanet/tutorials).

Q What is the easiest way to install Linux-Mandrake on a computer?

A The easiest way is to use Linux-Mandrake as the sole operating system. The installation is easy because there is no second hard drive to set up and no resizing and non-Linux partitions to create. You just put the Linux-Mandrake CD into the CD-ROM drive and restart the computer. The disk drive is wiped clean and replaced with Linux-Mandrake and a cool assortment of applications.

Workshop

This past hour was spent deciding how you want to install Linux-Mandrake and making sure that your computer's hardware devices are compatible. It's time to test your knowledge and give you a few extra-credit assignments to boost your confidence before you begin the installation process.

Quiz

1. What does it mean that Linux-Mandrake is optimized for Pentiums?
2. What is a daemon?
3. What kind of modem is best for Linux-Mandrake to connect to the Internet?
4. Can you use a ZIP drive with Linux-Mandrake?

Exercises

1. Keep a journal for each computer on which you've installed Linux-Mandrake. A small ring binder might work best. Use this journal to record the computer system devices you collected in this past hour. Keep up the journal by noting the steps you followed during the installation, configuration changes made after the installation, problems encountered and solutions found, and users and peripherals attached to the system.

2. It's always a good idea to research a subject before you dive into a task. You can read the user documentation on the Linux-Mandrake CD-ROM from your Windows computer. Navigate to the DOC directory on the CD. You'll find the Linux-Mandrake installation guide and the user guide. There are also several manuals for the K Desktop Environment. You can read these files with your favorite Web browser or with a text editor such as WordPad. You may find it useful to browse through these files before you get involved in the installation.

Hour 2

Installing Linux-Mandrake

In this hour, you finish the last pre-installation tasks and install Linux-Mandrake on your computer. To get started, you may need to make an installation boot disk, if you don't already have one. This installation boot disk starts the Linux-Mandrake installation if your computer boots from the floppy drive. There are several tools on the CD-ROM that will create an installation boot disk. We'll show you the old-fashioned DOS method. From there, you'll need to do a little housekeeping so that the computer is cleaned up and ready for Linux-Mandrake's visit.

Then, you'll use DrakX to help load Linux-Mandrake on your computer. DrakX walks you through the Linux-Mandrake installation. It provides instructions for each screen in the installation process. You may have heard some Linux installation horror stories. DrakX makes it easy to follow this complicated installation process and helps you make installation choices by automatically detecting information about your computer system. Even though DrakX simplifies the installation task, you may still want to read this chapter and the Linux-Mandrake Install Guide before you begin. While you are installing Linux on your computer, we'll go step by step through each DrakX installation screen and help you make the right choices. Once Linux-Mandrake is installed, you'll learn how to log in and out of your new Linux system, and how to shut it down properly. Today, you accomplish the following:

- Create an installation boot disk
- Prepare your hard drive
- Make the right choices during installation
- Set up your computer to dual-boot

Locating the Boot Disk

NEW TERM The Linux-Mandrake installation program on the CD is self-booting, that is if you have a computer that can boot from the CD-ROM. However, if your computer doesn't boot from the CD-ROM, you need an *installation boot disk*. This is a 3.5-inch disk that can be used to boot the installation program on the CD. The disk image for the installation boot disk, along with the program to create the disk with the boot image on it, can be found on the Linux-Mandrake distribution CD in the back of the book.

If you purchased Linux-Mandrake in the boxed set, you may already have an installation boot disk. If you do not have one, you need to make one. Even if your computer does boot from the CD-ROM, if you don't have an installation boot disk, we recommend that you make one. The program that you use to make this disk is the `rawrite` program found in the \dosutils directory on the Linux-Mandrake Installation CD. The `rawrite` program can be run from inside Windows in a DOS Window or from DOS.

Lesson 2.1: Creating the Installation Boot Disk

To make the installation boot disk, you need a blank 3.5-inch disk, and the `rawrite.exe` program and its documentation. `Rawrite` and the documentation are located in the \dosutils directory of the CD in the back of this book. You may want to read the file named README before you begin. If you want to use the `rawrite` program in DOS, follow these steps:

To get to the DOS prompt from Microsoft Windows, click the Start button and select Shutdown. Use the Restart in MS DOS Mode option.

1. Change to the CD-ROM drive by typing **D:** and pressing Enter (Where **D:** is your CD-ROM drive).

2. Change to the directory where the rawrite program is stored on the Linux-Mandrake CD by typing **cd dosutils** and pressing Enter.

> If your screen prompt doesn't display the directory, but shows only the drive, type **prompt pg** and press Enter.

3. Type **rawrite** and press Enter. The rawrite program interface will appear and ask you for information.

4. The first thing rawrite needs is the disk image source filename. Enter the path to this file by typing **D:\images\cdrom.img** and then press Enter.

5. Next, you need to specify the target disk drive, which is your floppy drive. Type **A:** and press Enter. You'll then be asked to place the disk into the drive. The files will be copied to the disk.

6. When the copy process is finished, remove the disk. Be sure to label the disk: Linux-Mandrake 7.0 Installation Boot Disk.

Preparing the Hard Drive

If you want to boot into different operating systems residing on a single hard drive, perhaps letting Linux and Microsoft Windows share one drive, you need to resize the partition that Windows is in and create a new partition for your Linux files to occupy.

There are several methods for partitioning your hard drive. The DOS fdisk program can be used to make space on your hard drive, but an unfortunate side effect of using fdisk is the destruction of all the data on the hard drive. If you want to use fdisk or another drive partitioning program (such as PartitionMagic), you will need to partition the drive before you install Linux-Mandrake.

Your other option is to let the DrakX installation program do the partitioning automatically after you supply some basic information. And it will safely create and format space on your Windows hard drive for Linux-Mandrake without causing damage to your Windows installation.

Before you begin the Linux-Mandrake installation and partition your hard drive, you need make sure that the drive is free from errors and defragmented. Both of these chores can be done in Windows with the Disk Defragmenter.

If you cannot find the Disk Defragmenter, try Start, Programs, Accessories, System Tools.

The Disk Defragmenter rearranges everything on your hard drive into a nice tidy organized file system again. You may even gain some more space on your hard drive in the process. When the Disk Defragmenter finishes its task, you are ready to begin making room on your hard drive for your Linux-Mandrake system.

Installing the Distribution

Once your computer is ready for the installation, place the Linux-Mandrake CD in the CD-ROM drive and place the installation boot disk, if needed, in the floppy drive. Then, restart the computer. When the computer restarts, the installation process takes over your computer. The Windows operating system start up process is bypassed.

The Linux-Mandrake graphical installation program, DrakX, contains several tools to guide you through the installation:

- The panel on the left of the screen lists all the installation steps and the indicator buttons change color to show the status of each step as the installation progresses. Red indicates a step not yet performed, orange shows the step that is currently processing, and green indicates that the step is completed.
- You may click on any of the steps in the list that are available (hold the mouse cursor over them to determine availability) and go back to make changes even if you have already completed the step.
- You can customize the installation screens if you want. The three button bars at the bottom left of the screen will change the colors used in the installation screens. If you want a different look, you can click any one of these buttons at any time during the installation.

Choose Your Language

The first screen you'll see is the choose a language screen. You are asked to select a language to use during the installation. English is the highlighted default but if English isn't your preferred language, use the scroll bar to move through the list and click to highlight the language that you want to use. Then click the OK button. Once you have finished with each screen you will be automatically moved to the next one.

Select Installation Class

On this screen you may choose from three different skill levels for the class of installation you want. In this book we concentrate on installing and configuring Linux as a workstation for small business and the home. In order to have some control over the installation and customization process you need to select the Customized installation class. You will then be prompted to specify your usage of the system. For this discussion, select the Normal usage in the screen that follows.

> The Linux-Mandrake Install Guide (which is on the Installation CD in the back of the book in /doc/en/mdkinstallguide/index.html) is directed toward those users who want to use the Recommended class to install Linux-Mandrake.

Setup SCSI

The screen that comes up next asks whether you have any SCSI adapters. If you do, Select Yes and then the type of SCSI card you have. If you don't have any SCSI adapter cards, select No.

Choose Install or Upgrade

The next screen asks whether you want to Install a new Linux-Mandrake system or upgrade an existing one. There are a few considerations here. You can update another Linux-Mandrake version that you have installed on your computer. But, it's a tedious task that may require some previous knowledge of Linux operating system files and dependencies.

You cannot use Linux-Mandrake at all to upgrade any other Linux distributions you may have installed. Your best bet is to install from scratch. Luckily, installing Linux-Mandrake from the CD is pretty straightforward, so we are going to do it that way. Click the Install button.

Choose Your Keyboard

The next screen asks about your keyboard. This choice is made automatically from the language selection. Typically, if you choose English, the US keyboard will be selected. Highlight the type you have. To make this easier, the choice for the US-QWERTY keyboard is already highlighted. But if you're French, perhaps you might prefer the FR-AZERTY keyboard. If this is the case, scroll down the list to the FR-AZERTY keyboard and click to highlight it as the choice. Then click the OK button.

Setup Filesystems

The DrakX setup tool wants you to provide some information about how you want the drive to be partitioned and where the filesystems will be mounted on the hard drive. If you are installing onto a Windows drive the DrakX screen will display a graphical representation of the device (hda for the first IDE hard drive, hdb for the second, and so on) that shows the type of filesystem installed, size of the drive, and any partitions that may already be installed.

To begin click on the partition at the top of the hda tab to select it and the display will change to show the device statistics in the right pane and the left pane will display the four Linux partitions that need to be configured:

```
/boot
/
/swap
/home
```

Clicking on any of the items in the above list brings up a dialog that helps you provide the needed data to DrakX so that it can make a partition on the hard drive with adequate room for Linux-Mandrake and then format the Linux native and swap partitions to get ready for the system installation.

If you are installing a new system on a Windows drive for the first time it would probably be best to allow DrakX to automatically allocate space for your Linux installation by selecting Auto allocate. The DrakX setup program will then create the new partitions that you need and size and format them for you.

If you are not satisfied with the way that DrakX wants to partition things then you can go back and specify the sizes that you want by just clicking Undo. Once you are satisfied with the partitioning, click Done.

The Linux operating system is a *filing system* (as are all computer operating systems). Whenever you want to attach another filing system to Linux (such as an ext2 or a vfat filesystem on a floppy disk, or an iso9660 filesystem on a CD-ROM), you must tell Linux where you want to look, in the Linux filesystem, to see the contents of the filesystem you are attaching. This is called the mount point.

The *mount point*, or attachment point, for the floppy drive filesystem is /mnt/floppy for Linux-Mandrake systems. The mount point for the CD-ROM filesystem is /mnt/cdrom.

Format Partitions

The next screen is the Partitions to Format screen, which asks which partitions you want to format. The Linux native partitions will be highlighted; /swap, /boot, /, and /home.

The defaults will be the right choice unless you have another Linux partition already on the drive that you don't want to format, like a partition with another version of Linux on it perhaps. When you are sure you have what you want, then click the OK button at the bottom of the screen.

It might take a while for Linux to format large partitions and if yours is a slow computer, this might take some time. So just relax and get a cup of coffee to fortify yourself for the rest of the installation.

Install System

The next screen gives you a list of package groups to be installed. All the package groups are selected. If you know that you will not be using the service that a particular package group supports and you want to free up some space in your Linux partition, you may deselect that package group from the list. In other words, if you know what you are doing and you are customizing your installation for a specific purpose, you can pick and choose. These applications and services will fill most of your needs in the beginning. All you need to do here is to select the defaults. Later on you may want to add or remove packages to allow more flexibility than the defaults provide; you can do this easily with Mandrake's tools after it is installed.

Once your decisions are made, click the OK button.

Install Status

Now (after a quick trip to do something about all the coffee) you can relax and enjoy watching as Linux unpacks all your new toys and installs them. There is a nice progress screen with a graphic slider to represent the progress of the installation as you go along. And, if you can read very fast, a list of what is being installed is displayed as each package installation proceeds.

Network Configuration

Here you are asked if you want to configure dial-up networking (we cover this extensively in Hour 11, "Getting on the Internet"), or your other network adapters. If you have network adapters, select Yes. Your network card should have been detected automatically. If it wasn't, you have to select your adapter from the list and then manually input the information you collected about it before the installation.

Configure Timezone

The system clock needs to be set to your geographical location. Scroll down the list to the name of the city closest to you, click to highlight it, and click the OK button.

Configure Printer

You are next asked if you want to set up a printer. If you have a printer attached to the computer, click Yes and select the printer from a list of options. If you don't want to perform this step right now, click No. You'll have a second chance to configure a printer in Hour 15, "Printing and Faxing Documents."

Set Root Password

You are asked to assign a password to the root, or system administrator, account. The root account, or the superuser, is the administrator account and it has no restrictions. This account is only for performing system maintenance and should not be used for your everyday work or for storing files.

Add a User

Creating a normal user account is an important thing to do at this point because if you don't you will have to do everything logged in as root. This could be potentially damaging. So, create a non-privileged user account where you can log in and not have to worry while you look around and get used to Linux.

Type in a login name for the account, the name of the user, and a password. When you type in the password, nothing is displayed.

A bit of strategy for choosing passwords. Linux is case-sensitive so it sees a difference between upper- and lowercase letters. A good password needs to be at least six characters long and you should try for a mix of upper- and lowercase letters, numbers, and symbols.

Create a Bootdisk

You are asked whether you want to create a start-up disk. Choose Yes and place a blank 3.5-inch disk in the A: drive. Follow the directions onscreen. The files will be transferred to your disk and a window will open when it is finished. Remove the Start-up Disk and label it: Linux-Mandrake 7 Start-up Disk.

Install Bootloader

The next screen asks where you want to install the Linux boot loader lilo. Follow these guidelines:

- If you are going to make this a dual-boot machine and use a boot disk for Linux, select the First sector of the partition.

- If you are going to be using the machine as a Linux only machine, select the First sector of boot partition.

- If you use lilo on a dual boot system, instead of a boot disk or another bootstrap loader program (such as BootMagic), select the MBR.

There are some cases in which it is not possible to use either lilo or another bootstrap loader because of the presence of some manufacturer's proprietary application or data taking up space on the hard drive at the wrong place. (Compaq computers come to mind.) In these cases, you will use the Start-up Disk you made to boot Linux.

Configure X

The installation program runs an X Window configuration utility called Xconfigurator. Xconfigurator probes your computer to determine which video card you have. If the test is successful, the installation program will select and install the proper X Window server for your card. If the test fails, you are shown a list of cards from which to pick, and given the option to manually configure the server.

If your card is not listed but you have the necessary information and can configure the server correctly, go ahead and do so now. It is not essential that you get X Window configured to install Linux. If you can't manage it, you can continue with the installation. We come back later in Hour 3, "Troubleshooting the Linux-Mandrake Installation," and fix it.

You'll now be presented with a list of monitors with the suggested monitor highlighted. The probes don't always return the correct information and if the suggested monitor isn't yours, try and select your monitor from the list. If you don't see it, select the Custom option and use resolution and refresh rates found in your monitor's user guide to configure a monitor.

After you have selected the monitor, Xconfigurator will again probe your video card and check the monitor settings to determine a default color depth and resolution. You may want to just use the default settings for now. We'll show you how to adjust the video display in Hour 3.

Now that Linux thinks that it has your video display configured correctly, it will start X to test the configuration. You should see X Window and a message that says, "Can you see this?". If you can, select Yes. The program will wait some seconds for you to answer but if you don't, it will assume that the test has failed. So you'll want to get to the Yes answer pretty quick.

You'll then see a message that asks whether you want to start X on boot. Answer No. It is a simple matter to type **startx** at boot and if there is a problem with the video, you will need to be at a command line when you start.

Congratulations!

This is the end of the installation. A Congratulations, installation is complete message appears on the last screen. Remove the CD and Installation Boot Disk and press Enter. The computer will now reboot into your Linux-Mandrake operating system.

A bootstrap loader is a program that steps in just after the BIOS loads and offers you a menu of the operating systems installed on the machine. You select the one you want to boot at startup. For many of you that will be a choice between Windows and Linux-Mandrake, but bootstrap loaders, including the Linux Loader (lilo), can load other operating systems as well. There are several variations of Linux you might have loaded on your system, and all these could be sharing your 22GB hard drive with OS2 or Windows NT instead of just WIN9x.

> If you install Linux-Mandrake on a second hard drive, you need to use the Linux-Mandrake Startup Disk you made during the installation process to boot the Linux-Mandrake system.

There are many reasons for having a dual-booting machine. It is great to be able to experiment with Linux, and the Linux-Mandrake distribution has lots of new things to learn and do. But, you may not be the only user of the computer and the others may not be as enthusiastic as you are about Linux in the beginning. Those that want to boot their favorite operating system can do so without hassle and not be bothered by the presence of another operating system at all.

In many cases, it is the function that the computer is being used for that is the determining factor about whether to set up Linux to share the drive with Windows or some other operating system.

Summary

In this hour, you learned how to prepare your computer to install the Linux-Mandrake operating system. You installed the Linux operating system and set up lilo to make yours a dual-boot computer.

In Hour 3, you finish configuring your Linux installation with some information about configuring XFree86 and configuring sound along with an introduction to the Linux man pages where you can find information and help about many of the applications and utilities in Linux.

Q&A

Q How do I turn off my computer?

A After you log off your user interface and are at the command line, type

`shutdown -h now`

The three arguments in the command tell the computer what it needs to know; what=shutdown, how=halt, when=now. The system will shut itself down and you can power off. To get a list of the command options for the shutdown command, type

`shutdown ?`

Q I'm exhausted after installing Linux-Mandrake, but I'm still excited and I want to surf the Web on my Windows machine. Are there some good Web sites I should visit to help me get ready for the next 22 hours?

A If you want to learn more about the graphical interfaces, check out the KDE Web site at `www.kde.org` or the GNOME Web site at `www.gnome.org`. Learn more about Linux-Mandrake from Macmillan's Linux resources at `www.informit.com` or the Linux-Mandrake site at `www.linux-mandrake.com`.

Workshop

We know you worked hard to get Linux-Mandrake installed, so we'll try to go easy on you. Let's test some of the things you learned while installing Linux-Mandrake.

Quiz

1. Which installation class allows you to select the packages that you want installed on your computer?

2. What is the purpose of the startup disk that you created during the installation?

3. How do you change the operating system that will start by default when lilo loads?

Exercises

1. Read the documentation on the CD-ROM. You'll find most of the documentation in HTML format in the doc directory.

2. You've been sitting behind your computer for too long and you may be tense after the long installation. This time we really do want you to get some exercise. Remember to take a break from your computer, walk around, pet your dog, or go two-wheeling down a mountain trail. Enjoy the sunset. You can start back in tomorrow, refreshed and ready.

Hour 3

Troubleshooting the Linux-Mandrake Installation

There are many of you out there who just had a perfect experience the first time loading Linux-Mandrake on your computer. There is something to be said for good fortune and you fortunate ones can shoot on through the first two sections of this hour and get busy right away learning how to find help and the online manuals.

There are a few recurring areas where the Linux installation can go awry, but fear not: Linux has tools to remedy the situation. There are so many video cards and monitors that sometimes the automatic method of probing and configuring the X server during the initial installation doesn't work exactly right, or can't find anything that will work. X Window can be configured to work on almost any combination of hardware you may have. One section of this lesson shows you how to use the Xconfigurator to configure an X server for video on your system and create an optimum screen resolution, refresh rate, and color depth.

The sound setup on the system sometimes isn't automatically handled during the installation either. There are several remedies for configuring sound. If you have an older computer (Pentium 133 or so), it's possible that your card was found and your installation worked. The newer, more complex and feature-rich systems—in particular the ISA/PCI soundcards found on newer multimedia computers—require special handling. There are some good resources and an update on the state of the art in this section of the lesson.

This hour helps you work through these common installation problems and also shows you how to use the command line to wade through the mounds of information available on your Linux system. The hour ends with an introduction to some Linux commands and ways to use them. Today, you learn the following:

- How to configure the X Window system
- Options for configuring sound
- Where to find help
- How to use the command line to find information
- Some useful Linux commands

Adjusting the Video Display

Way back yonder in Hour 1, "Preparing for the Installation," the various installation components were explained. One of the default components is the X Window System (or, as it is also called, X Window). X Window is the program that controls your video display.

Step back a little bit and refresh your memory about the Linux-Mandrake installation. The X Window configuration happened during the last part of the installation. The PCI Probe looked for a video driver and determined the proper X Server. Then you were asked to pick a monitor or select your own settings. Finally, you selected a video mode (that is, the screen resolution and refresh rate). Then, the configuration was tested.

If you were one of the lucky ones, you are now running Linux compatible hardware and the PCI Probe was able to correctly determine your video card. You should be able to continue on to Hour 4, "Living in a Graphical Workspace," and use one of the graphical user interfaces available to you. If you aren't entirely happy with the settings, you can come back here and do a little tweaking.

For those who weren't as fortunate and setup did not automatically configure X Window, here is where you learn how to do it for yourself.

Setting up Xfree86 on your Linux-Mandrake system is a simple matter in most cases, but if you happen to have newer graphics hardware or if you want to tune your X Window installation to get the best performance from your hardware, you will need to know how to write the configuration file (XF86Config) for the X Server that fits your hardware needs.

There is something to be said for knowing how to do this from scratch and one day you may want to try doing it that way. However, since there are probably a large number of people using Linux, and most all other UNIX-like opertating systems, who do not know how to do this from scratch, several configuration programs are available to help you with configuring the X server, as follows:

- XF86Setup is a graphical program provided by the XFree86 team. It is a very useful program that first starts a minimum VGA X server. It allows you to select from lists for your mouse, display type, and other options. The XF86Setup program then writes the XF86Config file for you.

- ConfigXF86 is an older text-based configuration program that asks you questions and then generates the configuration file from your answers. This program sometimes works when others will not for configuring a server.

- Several Linux distributions have added an X configuration tool of their own as a part of their distribution. Red Hat has Xconfigurator (which you will meet in a minute), SUSE has SaX, and Caldera has a more automated configuration for mouse and video that occurs during the initial installation of OpenLinux.

The Linux-Mandrake distribution includes the Red Hat configuration utility for X Window called Xconfigurator. Xconfigurator has its own user interface. So, even if you weren't able to get X working, you can just type **Xconfigurator** on the command line (you must be logged in as the root account) and the graphical user interface for Xconfigurator will appear.

Xconfigurator works much like XF86Setup does. It uses a pre-configured XF86Config file that you modify by selecting hardware and options from lists, and then the program makes a new XF86Config file and saves it to the proper directory. In the Linux-Mandrake distribution, this is the /etc/X11/ directory.

Xconfigurator will overwrite any XF86Config file you have in the /etc/X11/ directory. If you do not want to lose the configuration you have, make a back-up copy of your existing XF86Config file and rename it before you begin. To do this, you must be logged in as root. On the command line, type

```
cp /etc/X11/XF86Config /etc/X11/XF86Config.old
```

Lesson 3.1: Setting Up the X Server

To begin configuring XFree86 on your machine, you need to collect all the data you have on your video card and monitor. You should have all this data from your preparation in the first hour. To open Xconfigurator, you must be logged in as root. Then, perform these steps at the command line:

1. Type `Xconfigurator` and press Enter. The Choose a Monitor screen appears.

   Here you have the opportunity to select your monitor from the list of monitors presented. The important items that you need to know about your monitor are the scan rates and supported resolutions. This information should be available in the monitor's manual.

> If you don't know the refresh rates and resolutions, select a generic monitor from the Monitor list—look for one that most closely resembles yours. Select the monitor description with parameters that you know your monitor can fit into.
>
> In other words, if as a Windows machine, your machine is running a resolution of 1024×768 with 16 bits per pixel color (thousands of colors) and a vertical refresh rate of 70Hz, select the monitor description from the list that does just that.

2. Use the arrow keys to highlight your monitor choice, and then tab to OK and press Enter. The Resolutions screen appears.

   Here is where you select the resolution and color depth that is suitable for your monitor and that fits your needs.

   The graphics used in the book were taken on a 15-inch monitor screen with a resolution of 800×600 and an 8bpp color depth (which is 256 colors). You may find a resolution of 1024×768 and a 16bpp color depth a bit easier to work with.

3. Make your selection of a resolution and color depth, tab to OK, and press Enter. The Test Configuration screen appears.

   This screen informs you that Xconfigurator will need to start X to test the configuration.

4. Select Yes and press Enter. X will start and when the X server has loaded, it will put a small window up asking "Can you see this?". You will need to click Yes in just a few seconds or the server will think that the test has failed and you will have to begin all over again.

It is possible to damage your monitor by selecting parameters outside the capabilities of the monitor. If the settings are obviously not right or nothing appears on your screen after 10 seconds during testing, press Ctrl+Alt+Backspace to kill the X server. You can then run Xconfigurator again and select different settings.

5. The next panel asks if you want to start X automatically the next time you log in. Choose No. You are returned to the command line prompt. To see the results of the configuration, type **startx** at the command line.

If you don't succeed at the first attempt, don't feel too dejected. Just go back and try again. Nearly every X configuration is a little different and most everyone has to run through the configuration a time or two to get it perfect. You should congratulate yourself if you got it right the first time!

3

Wiring the Computer for Sound

Not all computer sound systems are automatically recognized during the installation. Some systems can be reconfigured to work with existing multimedia equipment. The new free sound drivers available and included in the Linux-Mandrake installation are the OSS/Free drivers supplied by the Open Sound System people. Information on these drivers and others can be found at www.linux.org.uk/OSS.

Since the release of the 2.2.x kernel, Linux supports modular sound. This makes the job of configuring sound for your system much easier. Support is provided for ISA PnP cards, and sound is distributed through the system in a way that means you don't have to compile the kernel every time you want to reconfigure options.

Over the past few years, Linux has changed and grown. The job of configuring sound in the past was an often frustrating course of configure and recompile the kernel and test, and then configure and recompile the kernel and test, and repeat for a long time. With the addition of loadable code modules that the kernel uses to provide sound, the job of configuring Linux for sound has become much simpler.

In most cases the PCI plug 'n play soundcard on your machine can be automatically and easily configured. Log into a terminal window as root type **sndconfig** and press Enter.

When the soundconfig introductory panel appears, press Enter to start the probe. Your soundcard will be probed and if one is found then the card will be displayed in the probe results. If there is a card listed, press Enter again. The sound for your system is automatically configured. In most instances this will work quite well.

Because not all sound problems are treated equally, here is a list of Web sites that you can visit to find free or commercial drivers for your sound card:

- 4Front Technologies supports the Open Sound System (OSS). 4Front Technologies provides commercial sound drivers for Linux at `www.4front-tech.com/linux.html`.

  If you are interested in free sound drivers, go to `www.4front-tech.com/ossfree/index.html` where you can download the Open Sound System Free drivers.

- Advanced Linux Sound Architecture (ALSA) at `www.alsa-project.org`. ALSA is the official Linux group that is redesigning the Linux Sound System. The Linux kernel will not be using OSS in the future, but will be using ALSA drivers to control sound.

- If you are looking for a quick reference to the Linux Sound Subsystem, try `www.uk.linux.org/OSS`.

- Creative Open Source page at `opensource.creative.com` provides Linux Soundblaster Live (Emu10k1) device drivers, the driver sources for Dxr2 cards, and the driver and utility sources for AWE32/64 cards.

- Sculpscape information is provided by Ecasound at `www.wakkanet.fi/ecasound`. Ecasound is a multitrack audio processing tool. It can be used to play audio sound, as well as to record and format conversions. But it is more than that, it can also be used to create professional sound effects, and to mix and record audio files.

Getting Help

If you purchased the Linux-Mandrake boxed set, you have a user's manual and several other pieces of documentation that contain lots of good helpful hints, tips, and directions. You can use these to get up and running with Linux. Once you have successfully installed Linux-Mandrake, other truly invaluable sources of information become available for most every application, utility, and command that came with your Linux installation.

There are sources of information available to you from both inside the computer, available as local documentation, or outside the computer on the Internet. Table 3.1 describes where locally available documentation is stored on your computer.

TABLE 3.1   Location of Local (Installed) Documentation

Type of Documentation	Where You'll Find It
Manual pages	/usr/man
Info	/usr/info
HOWTOs	/usr/doc/HOWTO
Frequently Asked Questions (FAQ)	/usr/doc/FAQ
Program documentation	/usr/doc/<program name>

The documentation and help available online includes newsgroups, mailing lists, and books. Of course, there are also printed books like this one, and there may be Linux user groups (lugs) present in your area where you can seek assistance and answers to your questions from other Linux users.

Lots of documentation and help is out there on the Internet if you just go looking. However, the remainder of this hour concentrates on the information available from the Linux man pages. An understanding of how the man pages are organized will help you organize your efforts and save you time when looking for something. Table 3.2 gives you an idea of the contents of the man directories.

TABLE 3.2   How the man Pages are Organized

In This Directory	You Find
/usr/man/man1	Commands you can run from within a shell
/usr/man/man2	Documentation on system calls
/usr/man/man3	Manual pages for libc functions
/usr/man/man4	Information about files in the /dev directory
/usr/man/man5	Details of formats for special files such as /etc/passwd
/usr/man/man6	Games
/usr/man/man7	Descriptions of Linux filesystem and man pages
/usr/man/man8	Pages for root operator utilities
/usr/man/man9	Documentation on Linux kernel source routines

Linux manual pages (usually called *man pages*) are a compilation of the documentation written by the creators and users of the Linux system software. Many of the pages are written by the author(s) of the software, command, or utility discussed in the man page; others are contributions from users. The Linux man pages represent an enormous effort by the people at the Linux Documentation Project (LDP). All those people who make contributions and especially the project founder, Matt Welsh, should not only be commended for their efforts but also assisted if possible.

3

Exploring the man Pages

Although a wealth of information is contained in the GNU/Linux man pages and HOWTOs, and many of the solutions to your problems may be found there, working with the man pages from the command line can be a bit intimidating. This section provides a path through the maze of man pages. It shows you where to go to get the right man page and how to use it once you are there.

Each man page is divided into sections, although not all sections may appear in every page. Table 3.3 lists the different sections of a man page and the contents of each section.

TABLE 3.3   Portrait of a man Page

This Section	Is a Description of
NAME	The name and a brief description of the command
SYNOPSIS	How to use the command and its command-line options
DESCRIPTION	Explanation of the program and its options
OPTIONS	All options with a brief description of each
SEE ALSO	Related man pages
DIAGNOSTICS	Description of the error messages
FILES	List of files used by the command and their locations
BUGS	Known problems
HISTORY	Milestones of program's development
AUTHOR	Program's author and contributors

The manual pages are the built-in online help system that comes with all Linux systems. The man pages won't provide solutions to all problems, but they are a searchable storehouse of information about Linux commands not paralleled by any other source.

But, they still are not all they might be—they are short and they assume a lot of UNIX background that a new Linux user might not have. Moreover, they each focus on a particular command and there is hardly any help available to assist you with even determining whether the command described on the man page is the best one for your needs. One important aspect of the man pages is indispensable. The actions of some commands vary a little between Linux systems and the man pages are the most reliable resource for information about how your system reacts to commands.

When your system's man pages are invoked using the man utility, man searches for a man page on a specified topic, and then sends the output to a pager application. The pager application then prints the man page to the standard output (your display) or to any other display device you may have, such as a printer. Navigation through the man page is dependent on the pager being used. The two most popular pager programs are *more* and *less*, and less is the default choice.

The brief syntax for man is

man [topic]

You call up a man page by passing along the topic you are looking for to the man command. You may modify the response of the man command by specifying which directory or library it should search.

To do this at the command prompt, type

man man

and press Enter to display the man page that describes how the man pages work. It is a good idea to read through this page while you are here.

Here is another example of the way man works; say you are looking for information on the ls command. At the command line, type **man ls** and press Enter. man displays a summary of what the ls command does and its syntax and options. The same is true for all Linux commands.

At the top of each manual page, the first heading is NAME and beneath it is a short one-line description of the command. Using the apropos command, you can search these one-line descriptions. If you don't know exactly what you are looking for, type a keyword and institute a keyword search with the apropos command like so:

apropos print

This command returns a listing of all of the man pages that have *print* in the short description.

In Table 3.4, you'll find a useful short list of Linux commands that you may want to explore on your own. Each command is listed with a short description of what it does. This listing is by no means complete, but you may find some useful tools in it. To find out more about what each command does and how it is used, simply type **man** and the name of the command you are interested in and press Enter.

3

TABLE 3.4   Useful Linux Commands

Try This Command	To Learn How To
alias	Create other names for commands
at	Run programs on a preset schedule
atq	List the programs waiting for **at**
atrm	Remove programs from the **at** queue (list)
cat	Concatenate files (sticks them end to end)
cd	Change to another directory (do not use a backslash)
chfn	Change the **finger** information display
chmod	Change the access permissions for a file or directory
chown	Change the ownership of files and directories
chsh	Change the shell you are using
control-panel	Launch a system administration tool
cp	Copy files
dd	Copy disk images
df	Display available free disk space
dir	List the contents of a directory
dmesg	List the startup messages
du	Display disk space used
dump	Make filesystem backups
export	Set environment variables in bash
find	Find (that is, search for) files
fdformat	Low-level format a floppy disk
finger	Look up information about users on a network
free	Display RAM and swap memory usage
grep	Find lines matching a specified pattern
groupadd	Use groups to manage files and workgroups
groupdel	Delete a group
groups	Display a list of groups
gzip	Compress and decompress files
halt	Shut down the computer system
host	Look up host information
hostname	Display the hostname for the system
ifconfig	Set up network interfaces

Try This Command	*To Learn How To*
init	Change the run level
insmod	Install modules
kill	Abort a system process
less	Launch a pager to view files and directories
ln	Create links between files or directories
locate	Locate files that match a certain pattern
login	Sign on to the system or switch users
logout	Sign out of the current user account
lpc	Manage the printer queue
lpq	Display the printer queue
lpr	Print files
ls	List the contents of a directory
lsmod	Display the loaded modules
make	Compile and maintain programs
makewhatis	Build the **make** database
man	Display the manual pages
mcd	Change to a directory on a DOS disk
mcopy	Copy files to a DOS disk
mdel	Delete files from a DOS disk
mdeltree	Delete directories from a DOS disk
mdir	List the contents of a directory on a DOS disk
mformat	Format a DOS disk
mkdir	Make a new directory
mkswap	Set up a swap device (partition)
more	Launch a pager to view files and directories
mount	Access (mount) a filesystem
mv	Move or rename files
netcfg	Launch a network configuration tool
netstat	Display the status of network connections
passwd	Change a user's password
ping	Check for a host on a network
printtool	Configure a printer

3

continues

TABLE 3.4 continued

Try This Command	To Learn How To
ps	Display the status of running processes
pstree	Display the entire process tree
restore	Restore a backup (see **dump**)
rm	Remove files (permanently)
rmdir	Remove directories (permanently)
rmmod	Remove loaded modules
rpm	Manage RPM packages; install and upgrade packages
set	Temporarily change environment variables
startx	Start the X Window System
su	Switch to the superuser account
tar	Manage archives
top	Display all the running processes
touch	Create a file or change its timestamp
umount	Unmount (un-access) a filesystem
uname	Display information about the system
unzip	Extract compressed files
updatedb	Build the locate database
uptime	Display how long the computer has run
useradd	Add user accounts
userdel	Delete user accounts
usermod	Modify user accounts
whatis	Use commands by reading a brief overview of commands
whereis	Locate a command binary, source, and man page
which	Display the executable path for a program
who	Display a list of users who are logged into the network
whoami	Display the name of the current user

Finding Help on the Internet

There are many sources of information about Linux on the Internet and more are appearing every day. The list that follows describes some of the more useful ones:

- The Linux Frequently Asked Questions list (FAQ). This FAQ is maintained by Robert Kiesling; he can be contacted at `Kiesling@ix.netcom.com`.
- The Linux HOWTO Index. Contains a collection of HOWTO documents, each describing in detail different aspects of Linux. The person currently maintaining the HOWTO files can be reached at `linux-howto@metalab.unc.edu`.
- The Linux META-FAQ. This is a good starting point for new users looking on the Internet for Linux information. It is maintained by Michael K. Johnson. He can be reached at `johnsonm@redhat.com`.
- The Linux Info Sheet. This is a technical introduction to the Linux system. It also lists other sources of information and some of the available software. It is also maintained by Michael K. Johnson.

Summary

During the past hour, you worked on tuning your Linux installation. If your video display was not working correctly, you used Xconfigurator to fix it. If you find that your computer will not make any noise or play your music CDs, you need to search the Internet for a sound driver that will work with your computer's sound system. Finally, you learned how to find helpful information from the command line by using the `man` command.

Q&A

Q I'd like to learn more about how to configure my video display with Xconfigurator. Are there any additional sources of information?

A If you want to know more about the video configuration process, you can read the following documents, found in the Linux directory structure:

- The Xfree86 documentation in /usr/X11R6/lib/X11/doc
- The README file for your chipset (if there is one); also in /usr/X11R6/lib/X11/doc
- The manual page for Xfree86
- The manual page for XF86Config

To access this documentation and the man pages from the command line, refer to the section entitled "Getting Help" in this hour.

Q **I'd like to help create better Linux user manuals. How can I help?**

A The Linux Documentation Project is a volunteer project always looking for good help. If you feel you have something to contribute, let them know. The LDP main site is www.linuxdoc.org. This site, or one of its many mirrors, has all of the online Linux documents, HOWTOs, manuals, and pointers to other sources of information.

Workshop

Fixing computer problems is not any easy task and can at times be very frustrating. But, persevere; some Linux problems take a few attempts before you get them corrected. Here are a few exercises to help you reinforce your Linux troubleshooting knowledge.

Quiz

1. Why do most configuration problems occur in the Linux installation?
2. Which sound standard does Linux support?
3. If you want to read the Linux documentation on your computer, but do not have access to a user interface, how do you do this?

Exercises

1. Run Xconfigurator and change your screen resolution and color depth. Remember to make a copy of the XF86Config file before you begin. If you make a mistake, you can always restore the backup configuration file and return to your original settings.

2. As you progress though this book, you'll find places where we show you how to use a program or utility to perform a task. Some of these tasks can be performed using commands found in Table 3.4. For example, in Hour 7, "System Administration Tasks," you learn how to use Linuxconf to create user accounts. You can also do this from the command line by using the useradd command. When you come upon one of these places where a command can do the same job as a program or utility, test your skills by performing the same task, but from the command line.

PART II

An Interface for All Occasions

Hour

HOUR 4

Living in a Graphical Workspace

The easiest way to work with any operating system, and the associated applications and utilities, is to use a graphical user interface. If you have worked with the Microsoft Windows or Apple Macintosh operating systems, you're probably already a pro with the GUI. This chapter shows you how to work within the KDE and GNOME interfaces just as easily as you work with other GUIs. By following along with the lessons presented during this hour, you learn the following:

- How to access your user account and switch between graphical interfaces

- Functions of each desktop element, how to open applications, and where to find extra help on KDE and GNOME

- Tricks for customizing the panel and the icons that reside on the panel

- Ways to resize windows and move them out of your way when they aren't needed

Finding a GUI: An Open and Shut Case

During the Linux-Mandrake installation, we suggested that you choose the option not to start the X Window system when the computer reboots into the Linux operating system. If you followed along with us, what you see after the system is rebooted is a bitmap picture of the Linux penguin (cute little critter), information about the Linux kernel, some information about the computer, and a login prompt that looks something like this:

```
localhost login:
```

Also, if you remember during the installation you were asked for a root password, and an additional username and password for an unprivileged user. You'll want to use the root account only to perform system administration. We'll be sure and point those places out to you as you go along. For these lessons, use your user account. We're going to play musical chairs as we access the user account, take a look at two popular graphical user interfaces, and then exit the system.

Create separate accounts for each person who will be using the computer. You'll learn how to create and manage user accounts in Hour 7, "System Administration Tasks."

Lesson 4.1: Logging In and Starting KDE

NEW TERM Your computer is quietly waiting for you to do something with it. But, it needs for you to *log in* and tell it what to do. When you log in, you are requesting access to the computer by providing a username and password. The Linux operating system checks your login information against information in its database and if it finds a match, presto, you're in! From this point, you have access to your own user account, as well as any programs and files for which you have access permissions.

This first lesson shows you how to access your user account and display the KDE graphical user interface. Try these steps:

1. At the login prompt, type the username that you selected during the installation and press Enter. You'll see the password prompt on the next line.

2. Type your password and press Enter. You won't see any characters entered or the cursor move while you type the password if you chose the default setting of using shadow passwords during the installation. You'll see a prompt that looks something like the following (where author is replaced with your username):

```
[author@localhost author]$
```

This is the handy-dandy command line. Linux geeks live for this command-line experience. For right now, you can use it to get to the default user interface, KDE.

3. Type **startx** and press Enter. You'll see a black and white screen with a black X. This X is the cursor. You'll need to wait a minute longer and KDE will appear on your screen.

Before you move on to the next lesson, there are a few things you need to be acquainted with. The desktop in Figure 4.1 shows KDE and a few of the features you'll need to know about before you go any further.

FIGURE 4.1
The KDE desktop.

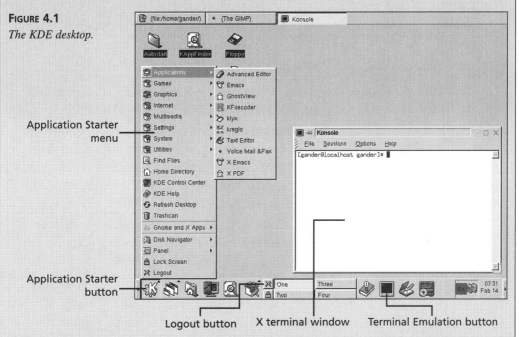

Application Starter menu

Application Starter button

Logout button   X terminal window   Terminal Emulation button

4

- When you click the Application Starter button, the Application Starter menu appears. This menu organizes all the packages installed on the system into submenus. You'll find all kinds of applications and utilities just by browsing through the various menus.

- The Logout button (and the corresponding Logout command on the Application Start menu) is used when you no longer want to work inside a GUI and want to return to the command line.

- The Terminal Emulation button opens an X terminal window when you click it. You can find the Terminal Emulation button by holding the mouse pointer over each button and reading the screen tip that appears. The X terminal window works much like the command line.

Lesson 4.2: Switching Between GUIs

You've seen what KDE looks like. Maybe you'd like to check out GNOME and compare the two. Before you can do this, you need to open the Desktop Switcher tool using one of the methods in Table 4.1.

TABLE 4.1   Where to Find the Desktop Switching Tool

To Open the Tool From Here	Do This
KDE Application Starter button	Click on System, Desktop Switching Tool
Command line or X terminal	Type **switchdesk** and press Enter
GNOME Main Menu button	Click on KDE menus, System, Desktop Switching Tool

Now follow these steps:

1. Click the GNOME option button to reconfigure X Window to use the GNOME user interface.

2. Place a checkmark in the Change only applies to current display checkbox so that you only change the interface for your user account and then click OK. A dialog box will let you know that you need to restart the X Window system so that you can take a look at GNOME.

3. Click OK and the dialog box will disappear.

4. Click the Logout button, or click the Application Starter button and select Logout from the menu. The Session prepared for logout dialog box will appear.

5. Click Logout. You'll be returned to the command line.

6. Type **startx** and press Enter. Again you'll see the black and white background with the X shaped cursor. After a minute, you'll see a status bar for Enlightenment and then GNOME will appear on your screen and will look something like Figure 4.2.

Lesson 4.3: Logging Out of the System

NEW TERM   When you're finished working with the computer and don't want your user account to be available to anyone who may be passing by, you'll need to *log out* of the system. Logging out of the system means that any files that you stored in your user directory will not be available to other users and your desktop settings cannot be changed by anyone but you.

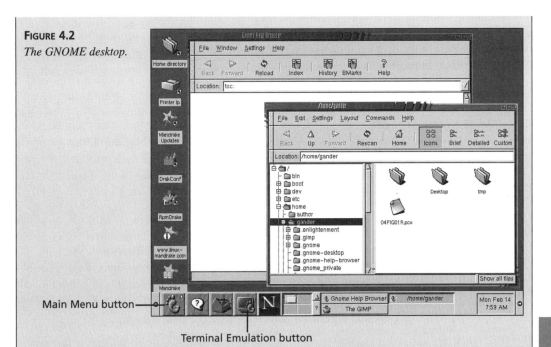

FIGURE 4.2
The GNOME desktop.

Main Menu button ⎯⎯

Terminal Emulation button

To log out of the system, follow these steps:

1. Exit the user interface by selecting Logout from the Application Starter (in KDE) or the Main Menu (in GNOME). A logout dialog box appears on the screen.

2. Click Logout (in GNOME you will also need to click Yes). The X server will shut down and you'll be returned to the command line.

3. Type **logout** and press Enter. The login prompt (with the cute penguin) appears on the screen.

   You can just leave the computer in this state until the next time you want to use it. You just need to log back into your user account. But, if you want to turn off the computer, or if you need to restart it so that you can use another operating system, keep following along.

4. At the login prompt, type **root** and press Enter. The password prompt will appear.

5. Type the root password and press Enter. The command-line prompt for the root account displays.

6. You have two shutdown options. To completely shut down the computer so that you can turn off the power, type **shutdown -h now** and press Enter. To restart the computer, type **shutdown -r now** and press Enter. You'll see Linux shutting down the system and turning off system services.

4

It's up to you to get yourself back to your favorite GUI so that you can work the rest of the lessons in this and the next hour and customize the look of the graphical desktop.

Moving Around the GUI

Since most of you reading this book probably have some experience working with a graphical operating system, such as Microsoft Windows or Apple Macintosh, this next section takes you on a few quick tours of both the KDE and GNOME user interfaces. We try to give you enough information to get you up to speed and point you in a few directions so that you can learn more about KDE and GNOME on your own.

Taking a Look at the Desktop

Both KDE and GNOME are very popular with a wide variety of Linux users. We'll let you decide on the interface that you want to use. We'll show you how both of the Linux interfaces are similar to each other and to Windows and the Mac. You'll also find a few differences along the way. You'll see some of these similarities in Figure 4.3, which shows a KDE desktop, and Figure 4.4, which shows a GNOME desktop.

- KDE contains a taskbar that runs across the top of your screen. Whenever you are working with an application, you'll see an icon for that application on the taskbar. The taskbar also shows icons for applications that are open, but minimized. If you want an application window to appear at the front of all others, or if you want to display a minimized window, click the application's icon on the taskbar.

- On both the KDE and GNOME desktops, you'll see quite a number of desktop icons. These icons open applications, files, folders, and start utilities. Desktop icons can be rearranged, or deleted, and new icons can also be added.

- The panel lives at the bottom of the screen in both KDE and GNOME by default. You'll use the panel when you want to open applications and switch between virtual desktop areas. The panel also tells you the time and it can be hidden to create more desktop space.

- In GNOME, the Main Menu button lists available applications and utilities. In KDE, you'll find the same list by clicking the Application Starter button.

FIGURE 4.3

The KDE desktop is very customizable and provides easy access to a variety of applications and utilities.

Desktop icons   Taskbar   Panel

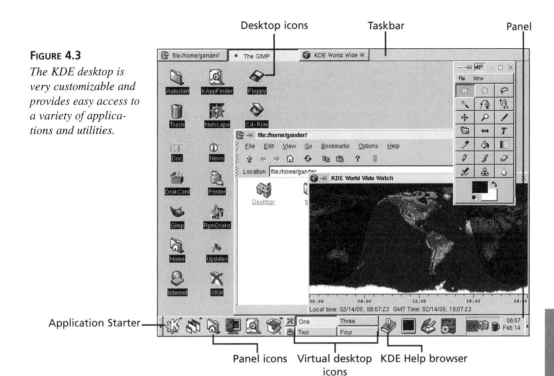

Application Starter

Panel icons   Virtual desktop   KDE Help browser
                     icons

4

FIGURE 4.4

The GNOME desktop looks pretty good, but will look better with some customization.

Desktop icons

Pager

Virtual desktop icons

Panel icons

GNOME Help browser

Main menu

Panel

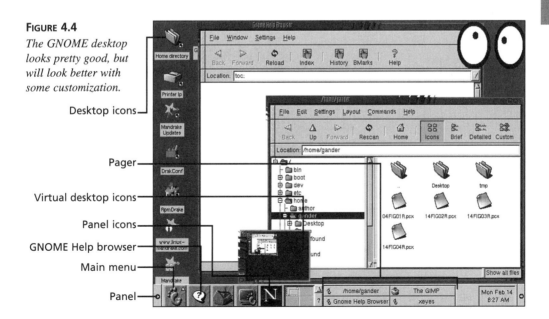

There is also a hidden menu in GNOME. Click the GNOME desktop to display the Enlightenment menu system. You will find that all of the same user menus from GNOME and KDE are displayed and you can start applications from the Enlightenment menu if you want. Right-click the GNOME desktop to display the Enlightenment Settings menu. This menu gives you access to the Enlightenment window manager's configuration dialogs and editor which we talk about later in this chapter.

- Panel icons offer a shortcut method for opening programs that you use frequently. You can customize the panel by adding and deleting icons.
- Both KDE and GNOME have the capability to use multiple desktop areas. The virtual desktop icons provide a means to navigate between desktops.
- The GNOME pager works the same as the KDE taskbar. Any open applications and files are shown as icons on the pager.

Lesson 4.4: Finding Useful Applications and Utilities

Many of the applications and utilities that were installed with Linux-Mandrake are available in the KDE and GNOME menus. Take a few minutes to look through the menus and find out how much fun you're going to have once you get started. This lesson is easy, just look through the list of menus and open a few programs that you'd like to explore:

1. Click the Application Starter button in KDE or the Main Menu button in GNOME to see the list of menus.
2. Move the mouse pointer to a menu item that has an arrow to the right. You'll see a list of applications.
3. Click the application that you'd like to explore. Voilà! You've just opened your first program.

Desperately Seeking Help

When you need an all-purpose reference for the KDE and GNOME interfaces, check out each one's respective Help browser. Each of these Help browsers works differently and contains different information. The next two lessons show you how to access each Help browser and introduce you to the different areas of information that each Help browser contains.

Lesson 4.5: Using the KDE Help Browser

The KDE Help browser not only contains information about the user interface, but it can access help files for many applications and it contains a search function. Here's how to get started with the KDE Help browser:

1. Click the KDE Help browser icon on the panel or select KDE Help from the Application Starter. The KDE Help browser opens. The Help browser looks and works much like a Web browser (see Figure 4.5).

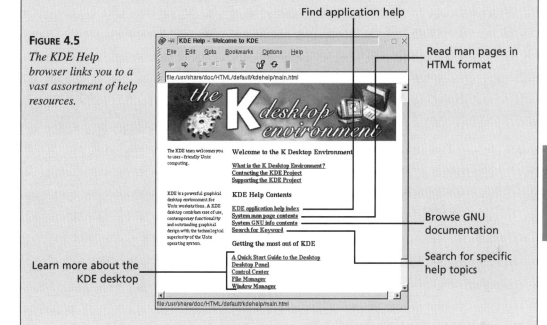

FIGURE 4.5
The KDE Help browser links you to a vast assortment of help resources.

Find application help

Read man pages in HTML format

Browse GNU documentation

Search for specific help topics

Learn more about the KDE desktop

2. Click on a link in the Getting the most out of KDE section at the bottom of the main page if you want to learn more about working with the KDE desktop. You'll be taken to the table of contents page for the selected handbook.

3. Read through the handbook by clicking on the Next link to move from page to page, or use the Back and Forward buttons to flip back and forth between pages.

4. When you are ready to go back to the home page, open the Goto menu and select Contents. Now you're ready to try another help avenue.

5. Click on the KDE Application help index link to display a list of applications and utilities that you'll find in the KDE menus. Again, click on the link for the program to display the help contents.

To work with multiple browsers, consider this trick. When you want to open a link in a separate browser, use the File, New Help Window command to open a duplicate of the displayed page. You can then navigate to new pages while keeping the original page displayed.

Exploring the GNOME Help Browser

The GNOME Help browser also works like your familiar Web browser. But, unlike KDE, it does not contain a search feature or easy access to application help. It does contain these useful features that you may want to take some time to explore:

- The GNOME User's Guide contains information about working with the interface and help files for the CD player and calendar.

- Man Pages takes you to the entire list of man pages organized by category. These are the same man pages you encountered in Chapter 3, "Troubleshooting the Linux-Mandrake Installation," but they are easier to find and read. Again, browse in Web style and use the Back and Forward buttons to maneuver.

- Info pages directs you to the GNU documentation.

- GNOME Documents contains information about a few GNOME utilities, such as the help browser, a few games, and the user's guide.

You'll find help files in many of the applications you may use. Open the Help menu and see what's available.

Exploring the Panel

Even though the KDE and GNOME panels share some of the same capabilities, they don't act the same. KDE provides flexibility for placing the panel and the taskbar anywhere you want on the screen. GNOME contains corner panels and edge panels. By default, each of the panels comes equipped with a number of icons that start some useful applications. It is possible to customize the panel by removing icons, adding new icons, and moving icons around.

Lesson 4.6: Moving the Panel Around the Desktop in KDE

This lesson covers moving the KDE panel and taskbar to a different side of the screen. GNOME does not provide this same flexibility. Follow these steps:

1. Click the Application Starter button, move the mouse pointer to Panel, and click Configure. The Configuration dialog box will open and display the Panel tab.

2. In the Location section, click the option button that corresponds to where you want to move the Panel. For example, if you want the Panel along the right edge of the screen, select the Right option.

3. If you want to move the taskbar, click an option button in the Taskbar section. To get rid of the taskbar, click the Hidden option button.

> To hide the panel when you don't need it, display the Options tab in the KPanel Configuration dialog box and select the Auto Hide options in the Visuals section.

4. When you are finished, click OK to close the dialog box and apply the changes.

Lesson 4.7: Adding Application Launchers to the Panel

When you find an application that you use frequently, you can add an icon for the application to the panel. Next time you need the application, you can just click the panel icon.

To add an application launcher to the KDE panel, follow these steps:

1. Click the Application Starter button and move the mouse pointer to Panel, Add Application. You'll see a list of the menus found on the Application menu.

2. Move the mouse pointer to the menu that contains the application that you want to start from the panel and then click the application. An icon for the application will appear on the panel.

It's just as easy to add a launcher to the GNOME panel:

1. Click the Main Menu button, move the mouse pointer to the menu that contains the application that you want to add to the panel, and right-click the application. A menu will appear.

2. Click Add this launcher to panel. An icon for the application will appear on the panel. Next time you want to start the application, just click the icon.

Lesson 4.8: Creating Screen Notes for Panel Icons

You may find that the screen notes that display when you hold the mouse pointer over a panel icon are not descriptive enough. You can change the screen note to fit your needs. The approach is the same in both KDE and GNOME:

4

1. Right-click the icon and select Properties from the menu that appears to display the kfm dialog box (in KDE) or the Launcher properties dialog box (in GNOME). The Launcher properties dialog box appears, as shown in Figure 4.6.

FIGURE 4.6

Change the text that displays screen notes on the GNOME panel.

Screen note text ⎤

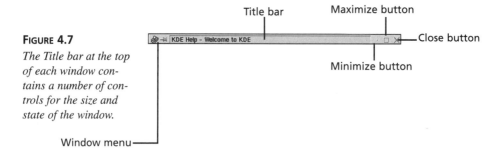

2. Click the Application tab (in KDE) or the Basic tab (in GNOME).

3. Clear the text in the Comment text box and type the text that you want to appear as the screen note.

4. Click OK. The next time you hold the mouse pointer over the icon, you'll see the changed screen note.

Working with Application Windows

When you're working in a GUI, all your applications, utilities, and files appear inside a window. Figure 4.7 shows you a quick tour of the buttons found on a window's title bar. While we're at it, let's also take a refresher course of resizing windows and moving them around.

FIGURE 4.7

The Title bar at the top of each window contains a number of controls for the size and state of the window.

Window menu ⎯⎯

Title bar   Maximize button

KDE Help – Welcome to KDE   ⎯Close button

Minimize button

A Technical Overview of the X Window System

The X Window system is based on the classic client/server model. An X server (a software program that runs on your computer) provides all the access to the graphics hardware on the system. An X client is an application that communicates with the server passing requests for services. The requests are things like "draw a circle," "watch for keyboard input," "pay attention to mouse input," etc. The X server draws a circle, makes a mouse event change, sends input to the screen from the keyboard, and so on.

Because X Window is client/server based, it makes a perfect fit for network-oriented graphics systems running on TCP/IP networks. The Internet is a TCP/IP network as are the web-based intranets in use in many private networks. That makes it possible to have lots of clients sending requests to an X server. This means that not just the local client but those out on the network can be configured to send requests to your X server. Carrying this out further, if you have a TCP/IP connection you can log into a computer on the network, run your X application remotely, and have the server display it on your local system.

X Window makes windows but it does not resize them, move them, paint the borders pretty colors with nice decorations and frames, or add the buttons at the top; that is left to another program called a *window manager*. The window manager doesn't affect the presentation of the window created by the client, it just provides the frame and buttons which move, resize, and close the window. Window managers can do more than that. They may be configured to allow the user to select the focus policy, mouse button bindings, decorations, window orientation on the display, and much more. The window managers provide window management services to a graphical user interface (GUI) like KDE or GNOME.

Only one window manager can be on an X server. The KDE GUI uses kwm as its window manager. GNOME can run under more than one window manager but not as well with others. The Enlightenment window manager works best; ICE is reputed to work well also. KDE can't run under anything but the window manager made for it, kwm, and GNOME can't run under kwm. This is the reason that when you use the Desktop switcher tool you have to logout of X completely, and then restart the X server with a new window manager to change desktops from KDE to GNOME and back again.

4

Adjusting the Window Size

The Window menu is the easiest place to find all the commands that control window size and placement. The icon for the Window menu is different depending on the application. By default, it is located at the upper-left corner of the window. Click the icon to display the list. You can right-click the title bar to display the Window menu.

The thumbtack icon is the Stick/Unstick button. You can use it to hold the window in place on your screen even if you move to a different virtual desktop area.

Click the Minimize button to reduce the window to an icon on the KDE taskbar or the GNOME panel.

Use the Maximize button to fill the entire screen area with the window. Click the Maximize button a second time to return the window to its original (reduced) size.

When the window is smaller than the screen, you can drag any side or corner of the window border. You can make the window any size you like.

Moving Windows Out of Your Way

If you need to quickly move a window, click and hold on the title bar while you drag the window to the desired position.

Here's a cool trick. Double-click the title bar. The working area of the window will disappear and all you'll see will be the title bar. Double-clicking the title bar again will restore the window top its former size.

When you're finished working with a window, click the Close button. But, remember to save your work before you close an application window.

> One way to keep your desktop uncluttered is to shade all the windows so that only the title bar shows. Then, when you want to work with a window, unshade the window by double-clicking the title bar.

Lesson 4.9: Changing the Window Focus Policy

NEW TERM When you want to work with a window, you normally click inside the window to make it active or in focus. There are other methods of making a window active, which are determined by the *focus policy*. The focus policy settings determine which keyboard or mouse actions make a window active.

KDE and GNOME handle the focus policy differently. Let's take a look at KDE first:

1. Open the Control Center by clicking the Control Center icon on the panel or by selecting Application Starter, KDE Control Center.
2. Click the plus sign next to the Windows category to display a list of options.
3. Click Properties to display a selection of window options.
4. In the Focus policy section, choose an option from the drop-down list.
   - If you want to make a window active by clicking inside the window, choose the Click to focus option.
   - If you want to use the mouse to determine which window is active, select Focus follows mouse. All you have to do is place the mouse over the window that you want to be in focus. If your mouse is moved off the window and onto the desktop, the window will stay active. If the mouse moves to another window, that window will become active.

- The Classic focus follows mouse option works much like the Focus follows mouse option (described above). When the mouse is placed over a window, that window is active. The difference is if the mouse is placed over the desktop area, there are no active windows.

5. When you are finished with your changes, click OK.

6. Close the Control Center by clicking File, Exit.

Play around with the new focus settings and see how you like them. You can always go back and try a different focus policy.

To change the focus policy in GNOME, try this:

1. Click the GNOME Configuration Tool icon on the panel, or open the Main Menu and select Settings, GNOME Control Center to display the Control Center.

2. Click the plus sign next to Desktop to expand the list and then click the Window option. You'll see a list of window managers in the right side of the Control Center.

3. Click the Run Configuration Tool for Enlightenment button to start the Enlightenment Configuration Editor.

4. Click the Behavior option. You can change the focus policy from the Advanced Focus tab.

Lesson 4.10: Customizing Window Title Bar Buttons

In the last lesson for this hour, you learn how to move the window icons around the title bar. KDE provides a straightforward method for customizing the placement of these buttons. You won't find this feature in GNOME. Experiment with moving a few window icons:

1. Open the Control Center.

2. Click the plus sign next to Windows to expand the list and then click Buttons to display the options for changing the placement of buttons.

3. Select the position for each type of button. As you click an option button, you'll notice the change made in the sample title bar at the top of the dialog box.

   - If you want a button to be located on the left side of the title bar, click the Left option button.

   - Click the Right option button to move the button to the right side of the title bar.

   - When you don't need a button, click the Off option button.

4. When you are done making your changes, click OK and then close the Control Center.

Summary

During the past hour, you have worked through a number of exercises that built upon your present knowledge of graphical user interfaces and applied it to the KDE and GNOME interfaces. When you started this lesson, you may have already made the decision about which GUI you wanted to use. If you haven't made a GUI choice, work with both interfaces until you find your preference. In this lesson, you learned a few GUI basics and worked with the panel and a few windows. In the next lesson, you build upon these skills by customizing the desktop and learning how to work with multiple desktops.

Q&A

Q I want to rearrange the icons on the panel. How do I do this?

A Right-click the icon that you want to move, and select Move Applet (in GNOME) or Move (in KDE) from the menu. Then move the mouse where you want to store the icon (you'll notice that the icon follows the mouse pointer) and click to place it there. The icon will be safe in its new home. If you want to get rid of an icon, right-click it and select Remove from panel.

Q I like to listen to my CDs while I work at the computer. Is there an easy way to always keep a CD player at hand?

A In GNOME, you can add an applet to the panel. This is a simple CD player that plays, pauses, stops, and skips between tracks. Click the Main menu button. Move the mouse pointer to Panel, Add applet, Multimedia, and select CD Player. A miniature CD player appears on the panel. Just pop in your favorite tunes, press the Play button, and enjoy the music. There's already a CD player icon on the KDE panel.

Q Can I change how windows appear on the screen when they are opened, moved, and resized?

A This function is set in the Control Panel. Go to the Windows, Properties options. If you want the window to fill the height of the screen, place a checkmark in the Vertical maximization only by default checkbox. You can also control how multiple windows appear on the screen in relation to each other by selecting an option from the Placement policy drop-down list.

Workshop

Once again, if you want to test your skills, try the following quiz and exercises.

Quiz

1. What tool enables you to easily move back and forth between using a KDE desktop and using a GNOME desktop?

2. You find that you are frequently searching through the application menus looking for the same program. What can you do to make it easier to find and start the application?

3. You can use the window buttons to minimize, maximize, and close windows. Which button do you use if you want to perform some other function to a window?

4. Name the different ways you can get a window out of your way and create more desktop space.

5. Explain window focus policy and the different ways you can make a window active.

Exercises

1. It's not always easy to remember where you may have found a certain help topic. As you're browsing through the KDE or GNOME Help browsers, set bookmarks for the help files you may need again. The process is different for each browser. Use the Add Bookmarks command in the Bookmarks menu of the KDE Help browser. In GNOME, use File, Add Bookmark.

2. Customize the Application Starter menus. In KDE, click the Application Starter button, move the mouse pointer to Panel, and click Edit Menus. The Menu Editor is where you can move applications and menus around on the menu. When you first open the Menu Editor, the KMenuedit Handbook opens in a separate window.

4

HOUR 5

Changing Your View of the Desktop

The previous hour was spent exploring both the KDE and GNOME desktop environments. You learned where to find some fun and useful applications. You may have spent some time customizing the panel so that you can more easily find favorite applications. Then, to wrap things up, there was a tour of the workings of windows.

This hour builds on this knowledge by showing you how you can arrange all those windows onto multiple desktops. Then, you can have some fun and spruce up your desktop with colors, window dressings, and wallpapers. We cover both KDE and GNOME again during this hour. At the end of the hour, you'll be

- Organizing windows using virtual desktops
- Sprucing up the desktop with background colors and wallpapers
- Using screensavers to lock others out of your user account
- Changing the appearance of window borders and other elements with color schemes and themes

Commuting in a Virtual World

One of Linux's strong suits is that it is a true multitasking operating system. The cool thing about this is that you can have a multitude of applications open on your desktop and not notice much degradation in your computer's performance. In the previous hour, you learned how to work with multiple windows and arrange them on the desktop. You'll now learn to more efficiently manage open applications by working with multiple desktop areas.

NEW TERM   These multiple desktop areas, or *virtual desktops*, give you the feeling you are working with multiple computer screens. When using virtual desktops, you can play games on one desktop area and then quickly move to another desktop area that contains a spreadsheet and calculator with which you're putting together an important report for the boss.

You'll find the navigation controls for these virtual desktop areas on the panel. On the KDE panel, you'll find four buttons that are labeled One, Two, Three, and Four. In GNOME, you'll see a box divided into four rectangular areas.

Working with Multiple Desktop Areas

Figures 5.1 and 5.2 show the navigation controls for the KDE and GNOME desktop areas. One difference you'll notice is that the KDE desktop areas have names (One, Two, Three, Four) and the GNOME desktop areas only contain the outline of any windows that are open on that desktop. Most likely, you are working in the first desktop area, which is the top left virtual desktop button. If you want to look at another desktop, just click another desktop button.

By default, there are four desktop areas that you can use. The virtual desktop icon for the desktop area you are viewing will be highlighted. To move to a different desktop, click one of the other virtual desktop icons.

The GNOME pager contains a Tasklist button. When you click this button, a list of open application windows appears. Just click the Tasklist icon for the window you want displayed when you can't remember on which desktop area the window is stored.

Virtual desktop #1   Click here to see desktop #3

FIGURE 5.1

The virtual desktop buttons on the KDE panel.

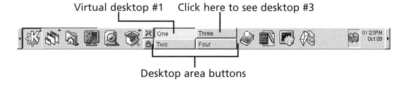

Desktop area buttons

Virtual desktop #1   Tasklist button   Pager settings button

FIGURE 5.2

The pager controls navigation between virtual desktops in GNOME.

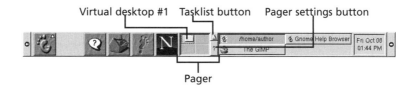

Pager

Lesson 5.1: Relocating Windows

KDE has another method of moving and organizing windows into and out of different desktop areas. Try these steps:

1. Click the application window's Menu button and move the mouse pointer to the To desktop option. A list of the desktop areas will appear as seen in Figure 5.3.

FIGURE 5.3

Use the Window Menu in KDE to move windows around desktop areas.

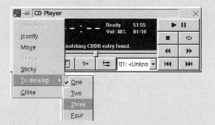

2. Click the desktop where you want the window to be relocated. The window will disappear from the current desktop area and will be moved to the selected desktop area.

3. When you want to work with the window you moved, click the corresponding virtual desktop icon. You'll see a different desktop area and the relocated window will be ready and waiting for you.

Can't remember where you stored a window? Click either the application icon on the KDE taskbar, the GNOME panel, or the GNOME tasklist.

Customizing the Virtual Desktop

After working with the four virtual desktop areas, you may find that you can get by with fewer desktop areas, or you may find that you need more.

5

The path you follow to get to the tools to change virtual desktops in KDE and GNOME is different. You'll also find that the tools look different. The method for changing the number of desktop areas in GNOME is quick. Just right-click on the desktop to open the Enlightenment Settings menu and click. The dialog box contains two sliders (one horizontal and one vertical, as shown in Figure 5.4). When you move the sliders, the number of desktops will change.

FIGURE 5.4

In GNOME, you can change the number of virtual desktops and the array they are displayed in as Panel icons.

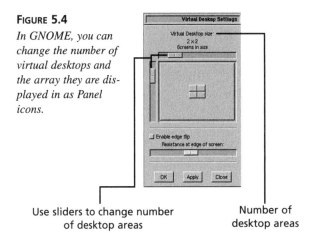

Use sliders to change number of desktop areas

Number of desktop areas

Lesson 5.2: Changing the Number of Desktop Areas in KDE

To make it easier for you to navigate your virtual world, KDE gives you the flexibility of renaming the desktop area icons. In addition, you can also change the number of desktop areas with which you can operate. Follow these steps:

1. Click the Application Starter button and move the mouse pointer to Panel, Configure to open the KPanel Configuration dialog box.

2. Click the Desktops tab. From this tab you can change the number of desktop areas, the size of the icon on the panel, and the title of the desktop area (see Figure 5.5).

3. To change the title given to an icon, select the text in the text box and type new text.

4. To change the number of desktop areas, click and drag the Visible slider to the right to create more desktop areas, or drag to the left to reduce the number of desktop areas.

Use descriptive text for the desktop area titles. Desktop area names should reflect the type of applications you use or type of work you perform in each desktop area.

FIGURE 5.5

Not only can you change the number of desktop areas in KDE, you can also give desktop areas descriptive names.

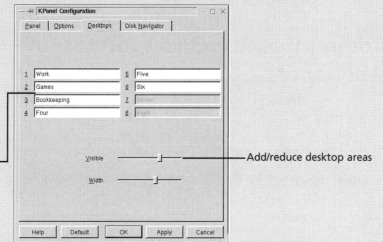

Use descriptive desktop area titles

Add/reduce desktop areas

5. To change the size of the desktop area icon on the panel, drag the Width slider.

6. When you've made all the changes, click OK.

Using Sticky Windows

NEW TERM Windows don't necessarily need to appear on a single desktop area. If there is one window that you want to be able to work on no matter which desktop area you might be in, make the window *sticky*. You may want to have a calendar available on every desktop area you visit. Sticky windows move with you as you hop from desktop area to desktop area. So, no matter which desktop area is displayed, your calendar will always be there to remind you of important dates.

Lesson 5.3: Sticking Windows to the Desktop Area

To create sticky windows, follow these steps:

1. Click the Window menu for the window that you want to appear on all the desktop areas and select Sticky (in KDE) or Stick/Unstick (in GNOME). In KDE, you'll notice that the Sticky icon (the pushpin located next to the Window menu icon) changes.

2. Click any of the virtual desktop icons. The window that you made sticky will appear on each window.

3. If you don't want the window to appear on each desktop area, click the Sticky icon or go back to the Window menu in GNOME. The window will now only appear in the original window in which it was opened.

Adding Desktop Backgrounds and Wallpapers

One way to make your desktop attractive is to use a color, a combination of colors, or an image as the desktop background. Both KDE and GNOME provide the same background options and are handled almost the same way. We'll use the KDE interface in the following lessons to show you how you can make your desktop more colorful.

There are several ways in which you can change the desktop background. To get to the place where these changes are made, try one of the methods in Table 5.1.

TABLE 5.1 Changing Background Settings in KDE

To Change Settings From Here	Do This
KDE and GNOME panel	Click the Control Center icon and select Desktop, Background
KDE and GNOME Main Menu	Move the mouse pointer to Settings Desktop, Background
KDE desktop	Right-click and select Display properties

The background display settings (shown in Figure 5.6) list three options for designing a cool desktop background. The easiest is a solid color background. For a bit more color, try a two-color background that you can blend in an assortment of gradients. There's also an assortment of scanned photographic images stashed around the filing system that you can try.

The Plain Vanilla Desktop

The steps for creating a solid color background are straightforward. Select the One Color option, and then click the color bar below the option. From the Select Color dialog box that appears, choose a color. Click OK to get yourself out of the dialog boxes. If you want a desktop with some splash, try the next two lessons.

So you want to customize individual desktop areas in KDE? If you want to apply the same background to all desktop areas, place a checkmark in the Common Background checkbox. If you want to apply the background only to a single desktop area, click the desktop name.

Choose a single
desktop area   Preview screen

FIGURE 5.6
*The Display Settings
dialog box makes
desktop décor a snap.*

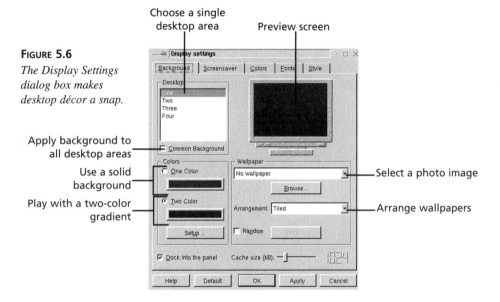

Apply background to
all desktop areas

Use a solid
background

Play with a two-color
gradient

Select a photo image

Arrange wallpapers

The Two-Tone Touch

NEW TERM A *gradient* is a combination of two colors, usually one light color and one darker color. Each color is shaded from light to dark as it blends in with the other color, which is also shaded from dark to light.

Lesson 5.4: Creating a Gradient Background

Creating a gradient starts by selecting two colors and then by applying one of the gradient options:

1. Create the first color by selecting the One Color option button and then clicking the color bar. The color you select will display in the color bar.

2. Select the second color for the gradient by selecting the Two Color option and clicking the color bar. After you've selected the color, you'll notice the change in the preview screen.

5

3. Click the Setup button to display the Two color backgrounds dialog box.

4. Select a blend option or you can use a two-color pattern. When you have made your selection, click OK to return to the display settings.

   - When you want a horizontal gradient, use the Blend colors from top to bottom option.

   - To use a vertical gradient, select Blend colors from right to left.

   - If you'd rather use a pattern, click the Use pattern option button and select a pattern style from the list. You'll see a preview of your selection in the Preview window.

5. To see how the changes look on the desktop, click Apply. When you've achieved the perfect desktop, close the Display settings dialog box.

Selecting a Desktop Wallpaper

Selecting a desktop wallpaper is almost as easy as using the one color background. In the Wallpaper section of the Desktop Display settings dialog box, use the drop-down list to select the image you'd like to appear on the desktop. When you make the selection, the wallpaper will appear in the preview monitor. If you don't like the selection, pick another.

You can further change how the wallpaper appears on the screen by selecting an option from the Arrangement drop-down list. Try a few of these arrangements, which work well with most background images:

- To display several copies of the image in a checkerboard pattern, use the Tiled option.

- If you'd like to see two copies of the images face to face (that is, one normal, the other reversed), try the Mirrored option.

- The Centered option places the image in the center of the screen with background color around the edges. If you use Centered, choose either a single color or a gradient to display in the desktop area not covered by the picture. And, try colors that match the image. If you want to see less background color, use the Centered Maxpect option.

- Cool variations of the Centered option are the Centered Brick and Centered Warp options. You get the image in the middle of the screen and a pattern in the background. You can change the pattern colors using the One Color and Two Color option buttons.

- Symmetrical Tiled and Symmetrical Mirrored work the same as Tiled and Mirrored, but you may find that the Symmetrical options retain the original aspect ratio of the image better.

- The Scaled option fills the entire desktop with the image, but the image may be distorted.

Like surprises? Click the Random checkbox and you'll see the background change every 600 seconds. You can customize the random generator by clicking the Setup button.

Changing the Décor with Screensavers

The original idea for screensavers was to protect a computer monitor from burn-in. Burn-in was caused when an image appeared on the screen for too long and traces of it became permanent. Not a pretty sight. Screensavers were designed so that the image on the monitor was constantly changing, thereby preventing burn-in.

That was the past. Today, most monitors turn themselves off when the computer isn't in use. So, screensavers have become office art. But, you'll only see this artwork if you haven't been working for a while. And when you're tired of watching the screen jump, spin, and cavort, just move the mouse or press any key on the keyboard and reality strikes again.

There are a variety of places where you can hunt for screensavers. Use Table 5.2 to get to find the selection of screensavers.

TABLE 5.2 Searching for Screensavers

Start Your Search Here	And Follow This Path
KDE or GNOME panel	Click the Control Center icon and select Desktop, Screensaver
KDE or GNOME Main Menu	Move the mouse pointer to Settings, Desktop, Screensaver
KDE desktop	Right-click and select Display properties, and then click the Screensaver tab

Lesson 5.5: Password-Protecting the Screensaver

One advantage of using a screensaver is that you can leave your user account open yet still keep unauthorized persons from seeing what's on your desktop. You'll do this with a password.

1. Scroll through the Screen Saver list and click the one you'd like to use. You'll see the screensaver in the preview monitor (see Figure 5.7).

FIGURE 5.7
*GNOME contains
many more screen-
savers than KDE.*

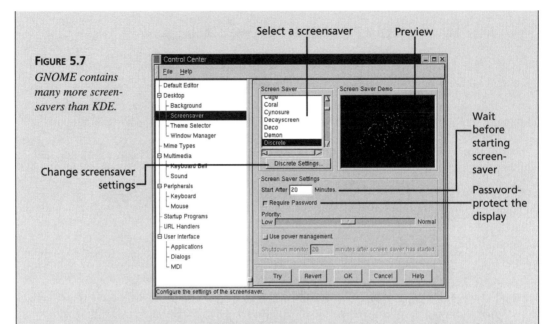

2. You may choose to use the default settings, or you can change settings such as colors and speed by clicking the Setup button (in KDE) or the Settings button (in GNOME). When you have changed the settings, close the dialog box.

3. Change the entry in the Settings text box to the number of minutes you want the computer to sit idle before the screensaver starts.

4. Select the Require password option. When the screensaver is active, any mouse or keyboard movement will bring up a dialog box containing the current username and asking for the user password.

As an alternative to screensavers, consider shutting down the monitor instead. GNOME can use power-management features to power down the monitor after a specified amount of time.

5. Click OK when you have finished setting up the screensaver. You may also want to close the Control Center if it's open.

Adding New Color to Windows

If you just want to change the color of the window borders that display on the KDE desktop, all you need to do is go back to the Control Center and select the Desktop,

Colors option. There are several color schemes from which to choose. As you click on color schemes, you'll see the change in the preview window. If a color isn't quite what you had in mind, you can always change the color of individual window elements.

Lesson 5.6: Trying the KDE Themes

There are almost 70 pre-designed desktop themes available through the KDE theme manager. These themes are not installed on your computer. They are packaged in archive files and will be installed after you select a theme and decide which theme elements to install. There are some pretty bizarre themes, but they're all creative. Follow these steps:

1. Open the KDE Control Center and select the Desktop, Theme Manager option. You'll see the Manager for Desktop Themes as shown in Figure 5.8.

FIGURE 5.8

Themes can bring a funky or a conservative look to the desktop.

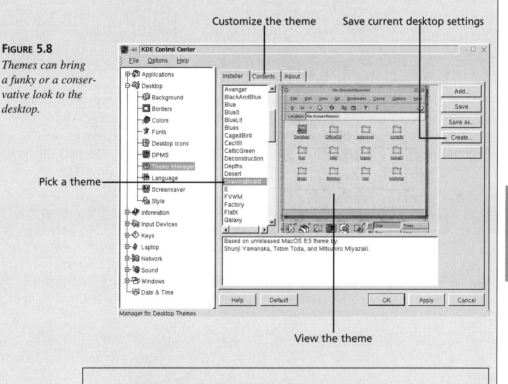

5

 Save your current desktop setup before you experiment with themes. To do so, click the Create button to display the kthememgr dialog box. Type a title for your desktop setup in the Name text box and type a few words to describe the desktop settings in the Description text box.

2. Browse through the list of themes. There are quite a few to choose from. When you click a theme, you'll see a sample in the preview window. Notice that colors, window border, and icons all have their own look.

3. If you want to use the theme just the way it is, click OK and close the KDE Control Center. If you have to have it your way, continue to do a little customizing.

4. Click the Contents tab. Here's where you can select which screen elements to use for the theme.

5. Place a checkmark next to the theme elements you want to use on the desktop. Not all of the elements listed are available. The availability of an element is indicated to the right of the element. The theme manager will only install those items that you select, and only if they are available.

6. Click Apply. The theme manager will unpackage and install the theme. Enjoy the new look! Close the Control Center when you're done.

Customizing Desktop Icons

Now that you've made all these changes to your desktop, there may be one item that seems left out, the desktop icons. You may notice that the icon text is encased in a box and it may not look very good with the desktop background. You may also think that the icons are too close together. KDE contains settings so that you can make your desktop more appealing. To get started, open the Application Starter and move the mouse pointer to Settings, Desktop, Desktop icons.

The desktop icons settings (see Figure 5.9) allow you to customize how icons appear on the desktop. If you find that the desktop icons are too close together, you can change the horizontal and vertical grid spacing. By increasing the horizontal spacing, you increase the amount of space between columns of icons. By increasing the vertical spacing, the amount of space between rows of icons will be larger. To alter the amount of space between icons, click the + (plus) button to increase spacing, and the – (minus) button to decrease spacing.

You can also change the appearance of icon text. Work the next lesson, try a few different icon looks, and see what a difference an icon can make in the desktop.

FIGURE 5.9

Improve the look of your desktop by using a transparent text background.

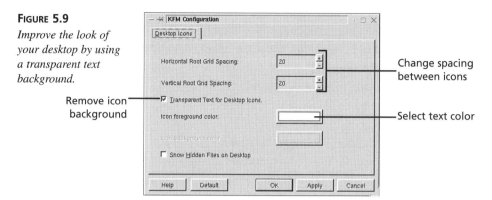

Change spacing between icons

Remove icon background

Select text color

Lesson 5.7: Using a Transparent Background for Icon Text

If the icon text (appearing below each desktop icon in KDE) is contained inside a color box, you can change it so that the background disappears. What you'll see behind the text is the desktop background. Try these steps:

1. Place a checkmark in the Transparent Text for Desktop Icons.

2. Click the Icon foreground color color bar. This displays the Select Color dialog box where you can choose the color you want to use for the text that appears below the desktop icon.

 Or, you can use a different color for the text background. If you'd rather do this, don't mark the Transparent Text for Desktop Icons checkbox and click the Icon background color color bar to change the color.

5

3. Click OK when you are ready to apply the new icon settings.

Summary

During the past hour, you found that working in a virtual desktop environment can not only help you keep your desktop clutter-free, but also can help keep applications out of your way and out of sight when you don't need them. You also had some fun making your desktop fit your personality. You may have experimented with colors, images, schemes, and themes. There's a lot more to working with and customizing the desktop than we covered during these past two hours. Explore the KDE and GNOME documentation, or you might want to check out their Web sites at http://www.kde.org and http://www.gnome.org.

Q&A

Q **Is there anything I can do to change the appearance of the pager on the GNOME panel?**

A Click the GNOME Pager Settings button. It's the small question mark below the tasklist. You can make the pager smaller, move it on the panel, or make it disappear altogether.

Q **I tried to use a wallpaper in GNOME, but I had to browse the filesystem. Is there another way to find wallpapers and change the desktop background quickly?**

A Try this one. Right-click on the desktop and move the mouse pointer to Enlightenment Menu, Desktop, System Backgrounds. You have several categories from which to choose. When you display a category, a thumbnail image of all the images in the category will appear. What? You can't see all the images? Some image lists are longer than your screen. Move the mouse pointer over the images. As you get to the bottom of the screen, the list will scroll and you'll see more images. Just move the mouse pointer to the top of the screen and the list will move in the opposite direction.

Q **What do I do if I don't want to use the same screensaver all the time?**

A If you're using GNOME, you're in luck. Use the Random Screensaver choice. Every time you turn around, you'll see a new assortment of lines, boxes, and other objects moving around your screen. In KDE, you can use the X screensaver choice.

Q **I'm using GNOME and I've changed the window borders to a color I like, but I don't like the way the elements such as options buttons and text appear inside the window. Do I have any recourse?**

A Yes, you do. Open the GNOME Control Center and select Desktop, Theme Selector. There are 11 themes from which to choose. When you click one of the available themes, a preview will appear at the bottom of the Control Center. If you want to try the different window elements, you can play with them in the preview area. If you like the way Microsoft Windows displays elements, select the Redmond95 theme.

Workshop

Time for another pop quiz and after the quiz, we'll hand out some extra credit assignments. We covered a large area of the desktop and it's time to see how well you followed along. Don't worry, we won't be grading papers today.

Quiz

1. Where do you find the navigation controls for the virtual desktops and how do you move from desktop area to desktop area?

2. When does it make sense to use sticky windows?

3. What options do you have when you want to change the desktop background?

Exercises

1. You've probably used some of the background wallpaper images that were installed with Linux-Mandrake. You can create your own wallpaper and download wallpaper from the Internet. If you want to create your own wallpaper, you can use a graphics program such as The Gimp, which we cover in Hour 19, "The Gimp." After you've collected a few wallpaper images, see if you can get them to display on the desktop. You can also download themes from http://www.themes.org.

2. During the last part of the hour, you changed the look of a number of items on your desktop. If you're using GNOME, you may want to consider customizing the panel so that it is color-coordinated with the desktop background. You can change the background color of the icons on the GNOME panel. To get started, right-click on the panel and select Global properties to display the Global panel configuration dialog box. From here, you're on your own. But remember, you can always click the Help button at the bottom of the dialog box.

5

PART III

Understanding the Filesystem

Hour

Hour 6

The Marvelous, Mystical Filesystem Tour

The Linux filesystem is the place where you keep Linux. It contains all of the utility files, application files, device files, system files, data files, and every other kind of file you might need. We'll begin this magical tour with a close up look at the Linux file. Linux sees everything as a file, so it's important to know just what a Linux file is, and how Linux sees it in the filesystem.

Next we'll look at the directory structure where the files are kept. The Linux filesystem is organized like a tree—much like the filesystems of DOS and UNIX—where the first directory is the trunk and all of the other directories are branches of the tree. We'll start by using the Linux command line to work with the filesystem and then we'll introduce you to some excellent graphical file managers. During the next hour, you learn how to get around the Linux filesystem by

- Using the command line to view directories and move between directories
- Creating subdirectories from the command line
- Working with the Midnight Commander and KFM file managers

Exploring the Directory Structure

NEW TERM   A Linux *file* is a unique collection of information with a unique identification. This identification (filename) is made up of the file's name and a location (directory).

Linux can store many files in a single directory. It can store directories inside other directories. It can even store files with the same name, but not in the same directory.

Linux files may contain many kinds of information. As you begin to explore Linux, you will learn a lot more about the different types of files and their various purposes. There are three types of files with which you need to be familiar:

- *User data files* contain information that you create and usually are comprised of simple data made up of text and numbers. The simpler files (.txt files) may be read with a text editor. The more complex files, those created by graphic or spreadsheet programs, require an interpreter program to read them.

- *System data files* keep track of users' logins, passwords, permissions, and other things. As a regular user, you won't be involved with these files. If you are the system administrator, however, you may be required to edit these files to maintain the system.

- *Executable files* are the instructions that tell your computer what to do. These files are usually called programs. When you tell the computer to do something, you are telling it to execute the instructions in one of these files.

Before messing around in the filesystem, it is safe to say that it helps a lot if you know what you are doing. But failing that, at least you can understand the system a little better in the beginning by learning about the filesystem that was set up when you installed Linux-Mandrake. You will find useful features in some of the directories; others should be left to the Linux experts.

- The / (root) directory is the base of the Linux filesystem. It contains all of the files and subdirectories in the Linux filesystem. Never store files in this directory.

- The /bin directory is where the basic Linux commands and programs are kept.

- The /boot directory is where boot configuration files and commands are kept.

- The /dev directory is where the device files are stored for the hardware components on your computer.

- The /etc directory contains the system configuration files and initialization scripts.

- The /home directory contains the user accounts for all of the users on the system except for the super-user who has the /root directory (see below). Each user has a home directory in which to store personal files. You cannot access another user's files from your user account.
- The /lib directory contains the libraries for C and other programming languages.
- The /lost+found directory is where to look for a file if Linux has lost it.
- The /root directory is the home directory for the superuser or system administrator.
- The /sbin directory contains tools for the system administrator to use.
- The /tmp directory is a directory where all users can store files temporarily; but if the system is rebooted, all the files stored here will be lost.
- The /usr directory contains files that are not a part of the Linux operating system, like the X Window system files and the Linux game collection.

Of Directories and Subdirectories

NEW TERM   The Linux, DOS, and UNIX filesystems are all similar in that they are organized in a tree directory structure. The directory at the bottom of the tree, the one that is the parent of all of the other directories, is called the *root directory* and is represented by a forward slash . Everything else grows out of it, branching like a tree, with all of the directories and subdirectories forming the limbs and branches.

Directory names are like filenames and they can use the same characters, numbers, and symbols. The way that you can tell the difference between a filename and a directory name—the slash (/) character is used to separate directories and files. If there is nothing in front of the slash, the slash signifies the root directory.

Directories contained within other directories are called *subdirectories*. The relationship between the two directories is expressed as a parent/child relationship. Your user home directory is one of these branches—it starts at / (root), and all users have a subdirectory within the home directory. For example, in the path

/home/Joe

/home is obviously a subdirectory. Since the slash (/) character has nothing preceding it, this indicates the root directory, and so /home is shown as a subdirectory of the root directory. You know this because of the slash character usage.

During this hour, you'll explore the filesystem along with our imaginary user, Joe. Joe's home directory is located at /home/Joe. As you look at Joe's filing system, you may notice that he's a bit ahead of you. He needed to set up a few examples. Joe has created a directory structure in which to store his project files. Joe started with a subdirectory called books.

He also needed a subdirectory for each project; Joe's current project is called Linux. Then he needed a place to store different elements of the project, so he has a chapters subdirectory. Finally, there is a file in the directory. All this results in the following filename:

```
/home/Joe/books/Linux/chapters/Hour6
```

 Long filenames are a pretty common occurrence in Linux, but they can make a mess out of typing things on the command line. Filenames can be as long as 256 characters and they can contain letters (both upper- and lowercase) and numbers. You can also use special characters like the dot (.), dash (-), and underscore (_) characters. Filenames cannot contain reserved metacharacters like the asterisk (*) or question mark (?).

NEW TERM To make Linux a little easier to deal with, there are two versions of Linux filenames. The one explained previously would be tiring to type in again and again. It is called an *absolute filename*. Absolute filenames always begin with the slash (/) character, which indicates the root directory, and then slashes are used to specify the exact path through the directories to the file's location. Absolute filenames work from anywhere in the filesystem.

The second type of filename refers to a file's location in respect to the working directory's location. It is called a *relative filename*. Relative filenames refer to files that are in the subdirectories of the working directory (your present location).

As an example, if Joe were working in the /home/Joe/books/Linux directory, he could get the file with the relative file specification (which just names the directories between his current working directory and the file) like this:

```
chapters/Hour6
```

Since the filename does not begin with a slash, the system will begin searching for the file from the working directory (/home/Joe/books/Linux). This is a bit shorter at least. Relative filenames work only if you stay in the same working directory. If Joe's working directory changed to /home/Joe/books, the relative path to the file would change to /Linux/chapters/Hour6.

Here are some short-cut conventions that you can use for directories that are easy to use and remember:

- One dot (.) specifies your current directory.
- Two dots (..) specify the parent directory of your current directory.
- All filenames that include (.) or (..) are relative filenames.

As an example, on a terminal in your home directory, type

```
cd ..
```

and press Return. You are taken to the parent directory of your home directory, the Linux /home directory. To confirm this, type

```
pwd
```

and press return.

You may also use directory short-cuts for other commands like the copy command cp. To copy a file into your working directory, type

```
cp ./<filename>
```

and press Return. The file will be copied into your working directory. Of course it then follows that using the two dots preface (../) puts a copy of the file in the parent directory of your working directory.

If you are working on a file that you would like to save to your home directory using the copy command, just type

```
cp ~/<filename>
```

and press Return. The file copies to your home directory where you may get to it easily whenever you wish.

Getting Into the Home Directory

Linux has a subdirectory called /home. In this directory, users are assigned a directory and they may create their own subdirectories in which to store files, as well as delete and modify these files. There are no system files or files belonging to other users stored in an individual user's home directory.

When you installed Linux-Mandrake on your computer, you created a user account for a non-privileged user. The user in this example is named Joe, yours is probably different. Linux created a home directory for user Joe at

```
/home/Joe
```

When you log in to Linux, you will be in your home directory.

6

Understanding Linux File Commands

In the introduction, you learned that you would be using the command line to move around in the filesystem. Now, before all of you Windows and Macintosh people start to skip ahead to firmer ground, you should know that this is easy. It only requires you to know a few commands, one of which doesn't even have any options!

Determining Your Location with the pwd Command

NEW TERM In the old days of text-only terminals, commands were typed into a teletype, which then displayed the computer's response. The pwd command told the computer to print the working directory name. The *working directory* is the default directory where the Linux commands perform their actions. In other words, pwd tells the computer to print the name of the current directory.

Lesson 6.1: Looking Around Your Home Directory

Let's retrace the steps of the early computer pioneers and try out a few simple commands on the command line. Before you begin, open an X terminal window. You'll find icons for terminals on both the KDE and GNOME panels. You'll also find terminals in the Utilities menu.

1. When you open an X terminal window, you'll see a prompt that looks something like this:

   `[Joe@localhost Joe]$`

   and the cursor should be located right next to the prompt. Type **pwd** and press Enter. The response will appear on the following line and will look something like this:

   `/home/Joe`

   You'll also notice that a prompt appears on the next line, waiting for another command.

2. Type **ls** and press Enter. The ls command returns a list showing the contents of the directory in which you are working. The list of files and directories may look something like this:

   `Desktop  books  practice  tmp`

   The response to the ls command shows the contents of the /home/Joe directory. How do you know if the four objects returned by the ls command are files or directories? You don't. The ls command can be used with a modifier to display more information about the contents.

3. To find out the modifier options, you have to ask the shell. Type **ls -help** and press Enter. The whole list of command modifiers and their uses appears on the screen. Use the scrollbar on the terminal window to read through the list of modifier options. Lots of options, aren't there?

4. To display more information about the directory contents, you'll need to modify the ls command to use the long list format. Type **ls -l** and press Enter. This command returns information in the following format:

```
total 3
drwxr-xr-x   5  Joe  Joe  1024 Nov 9 08:18 Desktop
drwx------   3  Joe  Joe  1024 Nov 9 14:37 books
-rw-rw-r--   1  Joe  Joe     0 Nov 9 14:40 practice
drwxr-xr-x   2  Joe  Joe  1024 Nov 9 08:15 tmp
```

Now, all of this may seem like garble to you so let's straighten it out some. The listing above is made up of eight columns. Just remember that the first line in the display tells you the number of subdirectories in the directory. Each line that follows lists each item.

The first character in the first column indicates whether the item is a directory (d) or a file (-). In this example, the first, second, and fourth items are directories and the third item is a file.

The next nine characters in the first column are in groups of three characters each and they reflect the file's access permissions. The first group of three is the owner's permissions, the second group is the group permissions, and the last group of three characters is the permissions for all other users. In the way they are shown here the permissions are Read (r or -), Write (w or -), and eXecute (x or -). The dash indicates that the permission is denied. You'll learn more about file permissions more in Hour 7, "System Administration Tasks."

The second column indicates the number of links there are to the file. For a directory, this number is the total of all the files in the directory plus two.

The third column is the name of the group that owns the file.

The fourth column is the name of the user who owns the file.

The fifth column is the size of the file in bytes.

The sixth column is the file's mdate or date of last modification.

The seventh column is the time when the last modification occurred in hours and minutes.

The eighth column is the name of the file.

6

> You learn about the directory information displayed here in more depth during Hour 7.

Changing Courses with the `cd` Command

The `cd` command is used to change the directory in which you are working. Think of this as being physically moved from one place in the filesystem to another. When you want to change your current working directory to one of its subdirectories, you use the relative filename. For example, if Joe wanted to change from his home directory to the books subdirectory, he would type

```
cd books
```

at the command line and press Enter. His command prompt would change to show the new working directory, as follows:

```
[Joe@localhost books]$
```

If Joe were to use the `pwd` command, he would find that he is now working in the /home/Joe/books directory.

All this will work as long as the subdirectory or file you want is in the directory structure below your working directory. If you specify a file that is in another directory, Linux won't be able to find it unless you use its absolute filename and specify the whole directory path.

> When working with long filenames, you may not be able to get the whole filename on one command line. The Linux command-line editor sees line wraps as end-of-line characters and will not finish reading the part of the command that continues on the second line. The solution—use the slash (/) character at the end of each line that continues to a second line.

Lesson 6.2: Moving Around the Filesystem

You now have three commands in your arsenal that you can use to fight through the filesystem maze. Let's use these commands to go to the /usr directory. This directory contains some useful documentation about many of the programs you'll find with the Linux-Mandrake distribution. Once again, you'll need to open an X terminal window for this lesson:

1. To go from your present position in your home directory to the /usr directory, type **cd /usr** and press Enter. The prompt will change to look something like the following:

   `[Joe@localhost usr]$`

2. Type **ls -l** and press Enter. The command line will list the contents of the /usr directory.

> There's no place like home. If you are lost and want to go home, all you have to do is type **cd** by itself on a command line and press Enter. You will be whisked back to your home directory. Or, use pwd to display your location in the filesystem.

3. Type **cd** and press Enter. You are returned to your home directory and the prompt will change to show the directory you are in and look like this:

   `[Joe@localhost Joe]$`

4. Type **cd /** and press Enter. You will be moved to the root directory and the prompt will change to

   `[Joe@localhost /]$`

5. To see a list of the contents of the root directory you can use the ls -l command again. The ls -l command will return a list of what is contained in the root directory.

6. Type cd and press Enter again. You'll be returned to your home directory. If you don't believe us, just type pwd and press Enter.

Managing Directories from the Command Line

6

If you remember your old DOS commands, you'll find some similarities when creating, deleting, and moving directories within the Linux filesystem. For now, we suggest that you only work with directories within your home directory. After you learn more about Linux, you can create directories in other places.

Creating Directories

Creating directories in Linux is pretty straightforward. The command is the same as the DOS command, mkdir. When you use this command, be sure that you are located in the working directory in which you want to create the new directory.

The Syntax for the `mkdir` Command

The following code shows the syntax for the `mkdir` command. You'll use this command when you want to create a subdirectory within any directory:

```
mkdir newdirectory
```

where *newdirectory* is the name you want to give to the new directory.

Deleting Directories

It's quite simple to delete a directory. But, before you try to delete a directory, you'll need to delete the contents of the directory. You can use the `rm` command to delete files.

> Linux can use wildcards to do things with the `rm` command. This can be very dangerous. For instance, the following command will remove everything in the current directory:
>
> ```
> [Joe@localhost Joe]$ rm *
> ```
>
> And if you make a mistake, you will find that your files are lost forever.

Before you use the `rm` command, make sure you are in the directory that contains the subdirectory or file that you want to delete. If you want to remove a file in any directory other than the working directory, use the absolute filename.

The Syntax for the `rmdir` Command

The following code shows the syntax for the `rmdir` command. You'll use this command when you want to remove any directories from your user home directory.

```
rmdir directory
```

where *directory* is the name of the directory you want to delete.

If the directory is not empty, you'll see a message that says

```
rmdir <directory> Directory not empty
```

This is an interesting message because it is about as close as Linux gets to a safety feature or warning message. No files will be removed and the directory will be left in place; you need to manually delete the files first.

Getting Started with Graphical File Managers

There are two graphical file managers that you can find easily. If you are using the KDE graphical interface, the default file manager is KFM. For GNOME, you'll work with the GNU Midnight Commander. The file manager is one of the windows that opens automatically when you log into the graphical interface. If the file manager does not appear on your desktop, you'll find an icon on the KDE and GNOME panels; or in the main menu, it's either the Home Directory or File Manager selection. There may also be an icon on the desktop that will open the file manager.

The KFM and Midnight Commander file managers are graphical user interfaces for the Linux filesystem. Unlike the command line, which you used earlier, file managers allow you to see what you are doing in the filesystem. You'll find similarities between these file managers and file managers for other operating systems. KFM and Midnight Commander can perform all of your filing tasks.

Since both KFM and Midnight Commander basically work in the same manner, we'll show you some file manager basics using Midnight Commander (see Figure 6.1). As we go along, we'll show you how the two file managers do things a little differently.

FIGURE 6.1

When you first open the file manager, your home directory is displayed.

Expand directory
Collapse directory
Tree view
Directory view
Change pane size

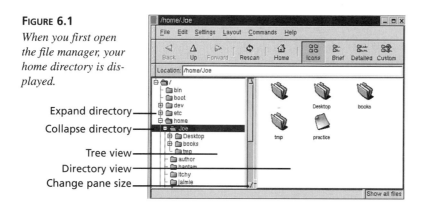

6

All the commands you can perform with the file manager are contained in the menus. The most commonly used commands can be found on the toolbar. If you hold the mouse pointer over a toolbar button, a screen tip appears that tells you the command that the button executes.

The left pane shows the tree view of all of the directories located in the Linux filesystem. If you don't see the directory tree in the KFM file manager, select View, Show Tree from the menu. The right pane shows the directory view and it displays the files and directories contained in the directory that is highlighted on the tree view in the left pane.

> To change the size of the tree view and directory view panes, click and drag the slider at the bottom of the line between the two panes.

Lesson 6.3: Viewing the File List

The file manager graphical interface makes it easier to move around the filesystem and view the directories. Because there are really no files set up in your home directory (user account), we are going to move to the safest place for you to poke around, the /usr directory.

1. In the Midnight Commander tree view, click the /usr directory. In KFM, click the arrow next to Root (to display the list of directories), and then click the /usr directory. The contents of the directory will appear in the directory view as folder and file icons.

2. Click the plus sign in Midnight Commander or the arrow in KFM to the left of the /usr directory icon in the tree view. This expands the tree view and displays the subdirectories in the /usr directory.

3. The Linux How-Tos are a good source of help. You'll find them in /usr/doc/HOWTO. Select this directory in the tree view and display the contents of the HOWTO directory in the directory pane, as shown in Figure 6.2. These How-To's are plain text files that provide help for working with the operating system, applications and utilities, and hardware components. You may find something of interest here, so take a moment and scroll through the inventory. These files can be opened in any text editor.

Changing the Look of the Directory View

When you first open the file manager, the directory view displays directories and files as icons. There are other display options. You can display files and directories as text or as text with a description. The Midnight Commander has four icons on the toolbar that change the directory view. You can also change the view from the Settings menu. In KFM, you need to select a view from the View menu:

FIGURE 6.2

*Expand directories to
see subdirectories in
the tree view; select
directories to see the
contents in the direc-
tory view.*

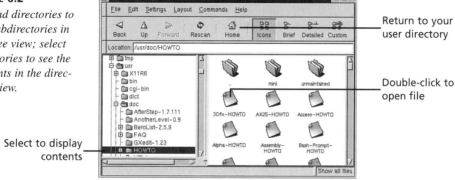

Return to your
user directory

Double-click to
open file

Select to display
contents

- The Icon view is useful if you are looking for a quick way to determine file types. This view shows a picture icon that represents a file type with the name of the file underneath.

- The Brief or Short view is a simple list of the files and subdirectories stored in the directory.

- The Detailed or Long view gives you the file's size and its *make* or creation date and time.

- Text View provides a simple text list of the files with some information about file ownership and permissions.

 KFM can display a miniature graphic of the contents of some files (use View, Show Thumbnails). This is nice for previewing graphic files and other file formats that KFM recognizes.

Selecting Files

In order to do any work on files, such as renaming or copying them, you must first select the appropriate files in the file manager. The conventions for selecting files are pretty basic and familiar. There is even a way to have the file manager do the selecting for you by telling it the types of files you want.

Selecting files with the mouse is relatively simple. You may want to use a view other than the Icon view to select files with the mouse.

6

- To select a single file, click it.
- To select contiguous files, click the first filename or icon and then hold the Shift key and click the last file in the block you want to select.
- To select files that are not next to each other, hold down the CTRL key and click the filenames or icons you want to select.

Lesson 6.4: Using Filters to Select Files

You can use the file manager to make file selections for you if you don't want to search through the whole directory looking for them. You can either search for a specific file or for a group of files that have a common element. Common elements can be a file extension or a combination of letters. To set the criteria for sorting the files

1. In Midnight Commander, select Edit, Select Files. In KDE, go to Edit, Select. The Select File dialog box will open.
2. Type in the criteria you want to select. (Figure 6.3 shows the Midnight Commander being used.) It can be a file extension such as .pcx, in which case you would type `*.pcx`. Or, you might want to select files that begin with emacs, so you would type `emacs*`.

FIGURE 6.3
You'll need to type enough information in order to make a close match.

3. Click OK. The file manager will search through the filesystem. All of the files that match the criteria will be selected in the file manager window.

Managing Files and Directories

As you begin working with the applications that were packaged with Linux-Mandrake, you'll need space to save your work. These files can be saved in your user account. To make your filing system more organized, you can create directories and move files between directories.

Creating Directories

You could save all of your files in your home directory but, after a while, things would get crowded and difficult to manage. If you are trying to keep track of your work, like spreadsheet files, graphics, or word processor files, you can create a folder (subdirectory) for files by type of file, or perhaps you might want client folders for all your projects for clients.

To create a new subdirectory, select the directory in the tree view under which you want to create the subdirectory. In Midnight Commander, select File, New, Directory from the menu. In KFM, select File, New, Folder. This brings up a dialog box. All you need to do is type a name for the directory.

> If you don't see the new directory in the tree view or directory view, click the Rescan or Reload button.

Lesson 6.5: Moving a File to a Different Directory

If you were using any of the Linux applications and created any files, these files were automatically stored in your home directory. Now that you have created one or more new directories for your files, you can move some of them out of your home directory and into those subdirectories of your home directory which you created.

1. Make sure that the subdirectory into which you want to move the file is displayed in the tree view.

> More than one file manager window can be displayed at a time to make it easier to drag files from one window to another. To open another Midnight Commander file manager window, select File, Open New Window. In KFM, it's File, New Window.

2. In the directory view, click and hold the file you want to move. Then, drag the cursor to the directory where you want to move the file. In Midnight Commander, when you release the file it is moved to the selected directory. KFM will display a menu and you will need to tell KFM whether you want to move or copy the file to the new directory.

Renaming Files and Directories

From time to time, you will want to rename files or directories to facilitate working with them. This can be easily done. Right-click the file that you want to rename and select Properties from the menu. In the Properties dialog box, type a new name for the file or

6

directory in the File Name text box (see Figure 6.4). When you've done this, click OK and you'll see the file with the new name in the file manager.

FIGURE **6.4**

Both files and directo-
ries can be renamed
from the Properties
dialog box.

Edit File Name text
box

practice Properties   ×

Statistics | Options | Permissions |

Full Name: /home/Joe/practice
File Name: practice

File Type: text/plain
File Size: 0 bytes

File Created on: Tue, Nov 09 1999, 02:40:50 PM
Last Modified on: Tue, Nov 09 1999, 02:40:50 PM
Last Accessed on: Tue, Nov 09 1999, 10:02:14 PM

        OK   Cancel

Deleting Files and Directories

You will need to delete files and directories from time to time. The process is a simple operation but you must make sure that the directories that you want to delete are empty. Linux won't delete directories that have anything in them. To delete a file or directory, right-click the file or directory and select Delete from the menu that appears. The file or directory will magically disappear from the file manager.

Remember that anything you delete in Linux is gone immediately. You cannot get it back, so be careful about what you delete. If you are using KFM,
you may want to move the file to the trash instead.

Summary

It's been another long hour, but you know more about how the Linux filesystem is organized and how you can navigate through the maze of directories, subdirectories, and
files. You were introduced to the command line and a few commands to help you get
around and find out where you are. We also showed you the GNU Midnight Commander
and KFM file managers. You'll find these file managers to be easy ways to manage your
filing system.

Q&A

Q Help! I've forgotten where I stored a file. What's the easiest way to locate the file?

A There is a Find File utility that you'll find helpful. From Midnight Commander, select Commands, Find File. Type the name of the file into the Find File dialog box. If you can't remember the entire filename, use wildcards. A list of directories will be displayed. Select the file you want and click the Change to this directory button.

Q I like to display files and directories in the file manager as text, but I'd like to make the text larger. Can I do this?

A It's easy to change the font size in KFM. Select Options, Configure File Manager to open the configuration dialog box. The Font tab controls the size and typeface of the text that is displayed in the directory view. You can change the text color from the Color tab.

Q I threw some files in the KDE trash and I want them back. What do I do?

A Open the Trash and copy the files back into your home directory.

Workshop

The filing system is one of the more important aspects of Linux. You'll need to be familiar with the filesystem so that you can efficiently store your files. Before you graduate to more file-management tasks, test your basic filing skills.

Quiz

1. What command tells you where you are currently working in the filesystem?

2. Which command gives you a list of the contents of your working directory as well as detailed information about each item in the directory?

3. What does a Linux filename consist of and how long can it be?

Exercises

1. Create a directory structure under your home directory in which to save your files. You may want subdirectories for correspondence, financial records, and scanned photographs. You may want to further divide subdirectories; for example, the correspondence directory may have subdirectories for each of your pen pals or clients.

2. In your quest to find out which user interface you prefer, GNOME or KDE, play around with the default file manager for each—Midnight Commander for GNOME, and KFM for KDE. If you haven't decided on a GUI, the difference in file managers will help you decide.

6

HOUR 7

System Administration Tasks

Even if you are running Linux on a single computer, you can still think of this single computer as a one-machine network. When several people have access to the same computer, you can create user accounts so that each person can set up the desktop to fit individual preferences, and have a private place to store personal files.

You can also create areas where two or more users can share files. These directories can have permissions so that multiple users can work with and make changes to the file or, with different permissions set, may have only the ability to read the file. All this is done using the user and group accounts, and must be performed by the root account, better known as the superuser or system administrator. It's a tough job, but you'll have the help of Linuxconf to maintain your list of users and groups.

After you've set up user and group accounts, you'll need to create directories in which users can share files. From there, users can assign ownership and permissions to files that are used by the group. In addition to maintaining user and group accounts, you'll want to maintain the health of your computer. Over the following hour, you learn what it's like to be a system administrator by performing these tasks:

- Create accounts for users and assign users to groups
- Share files with users in a workgroup
- Gather information about the computer system
- Use the Time Machine to change the computer clock

Configuring Accounts with Linuxconf

One of the utilities that you will see again and again through the course of this book is Linuxconf. Linuxconf is a graphical system-configuration tool. With Linuxconf, you can set up networking (either a small computer network or a dial-up connection), work with user and group accounts for file sharing, and perform other regular system-maintenance functions like setting the date and time, and perform many other tasks. Now, recall that you can perform all these tasks from the command line. That's just what Linuxconf does for you, but with one exception—it's much easier to see what you are doing.

In order to work with Linuxconf, you must either be logged into the root account, or you must have superuser access from your user account.

> When you are logged in as root or superuser, you must work carefully. The root account has permission to change anything within the Linux filesystem. So, you don't want to delete any important files.

Starting Linuxconf

If you are in the root account, it's easy to start Linuxconf. GNOME users who are logged into the root account will find Linuxconf in the System menu. Both GNOME and KDE users can click the DrakConf icon on the desktop and select Linuxconf from the graphical interface. If you do so from a user account, you will be prompted for the superuser password. If you still can't find Linuxconf, open an X terminal window, type `linuxconf`, and press Enter.

If you would rather use Linuxconf from your user account, you'll need superuser access. This means that you must know the root password.

If you click the Linuxconf icon on the KDE desktop when you are logged in to your user account, a panel will ask you to enter the root password. Once you have done so, Linuxconf will open.

In order to start Linuxconf as the superuser, open an X terminal window, and at the command prompt, type **su** and press Enter. You'll be asked for a password. Type the root password and press Enter. Now, type **linuxconf** at the command line and press Enter.

When Linuxconf opens, the Config tab should appear. To work with user and group accounts, click Users accounts. Doing so opens the User account configurator shown in Figure 7.1.

FIGURE 7.1

Give each user an individual account and use groups for file sharing between users.

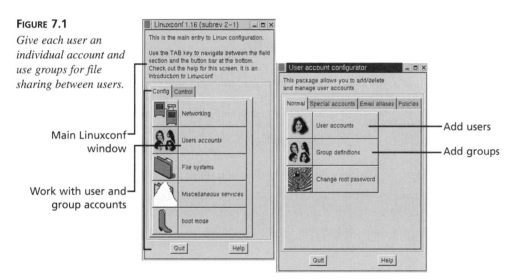

Main Linuxconf window

Work with user and group accounts

Add users

Add groups

Closing Linuxconf

When you are finished using Linuxconf, you'll need to click the Quit button at the bottom of each of the open windows. After you've pressed all these buttons, the Status of the system panel will tell you that the state of the system is not in sync with your new changes. All you need to do is tell Linuxconf to make the changes by clicking the Activate the changes button.

7

Working with User Accounts

Each person who will be using the computer needs to be assigned a *user account*. This user account consists of a username (which can be some form of their name or a made-up name) and a password. Each user then receives a personal home directory on the system for personal file storage. This also allows users to set up the desktop as they wish within their user accounts, and they don't have to use the settings of other users—or change other users' settings.

NEW TERM What do you do if users want to share files? The users need to be organized into *workgroups* whereby each workgroup has a common job task or common need to share specific information. You manage these workgroups by creating group accounts and then assigning users to the appropriate group. After user and group accounts are set up, directories and files can be created and usage permissions can be set.

Adding Users to the System

Your first task is to create an account for each user who does not already have an account on the system. For each user account, you need the full name of the user, a login name, and a password. Use a login name that will be easy for your user to remember and choose a password that will be hard to decipher. Passwords should be a combination of upper- and lowercase letters, numbers, and characters. There are a few characters that you cannot use—?, *, /, and \. This list also includes shell command separators like ;,@, @@,|,||, dash and emdash.

One way to make passwords easy to remember is to take a word that the users will remember and change it. For example, you can take the word "chicken" and change it to "ch1CK&" to make it harder to break the code, and then add something extra (like "ch1CK&32") to add to the complexity.

Lesson 7.1: Creating an Account for a New User

Before you start adding users to the system, make a list of the people to whom you want to give access. Then, assign usernames and passwords. Your users will need this information to log on the system. If you are keeping a notebook for the computer system, make a note of these users and their account information (but not the passwords). Remember to keep your notebook in a safe and secure place.

1. Click on User accounts on the Normal tab of the User account configurator window. This opens the Users accounts window shown in Figure 7.2.

FIGURE 7.2

The Users accounts window lists all the user accounts that have been created on the system.

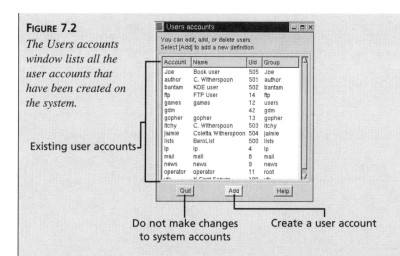

Existing user accounts

Do not make changes to system accounts

Create a user account

2. Click the Add button at the bottom of the Users accounts panel to display the User account creation window shown in Figure 7.3. The Base info tab should be selected. This is where you keep information about how each user logs in.

FIGURE 7.3

At a minimum you need the user's full name, a login name, and a password.

Account name

User's real name

Leave blank to use default directory name

Create account and then assign a password

3. Make sure that the The account is enabled option is selected.

4. Type the Login name and the Full name (first and last name) of your new user.

Linuxconf will create a user directory automatically. If you want the user's home directory to have a name other than the username, type the directory path in the Home directory (opt) text box.

7

5. Click the Accept button. The Changing password panel will appear.

6. Type the user's password and click Accept. The panel will reappear for you to type the password a second time to confirm your choice. A notification panel then confirms that the password for the user has been changed.

> Choose your passwords carefully. If you type a password that Linux doesn't think is suitable, an error message will appear telling you why this is a bad password choice. You may type another password or you may elect to keep the one you chose and ignore Linux' advice.

7. Click OK. The Users accounts panel will show your new user in the listing. The user account created during this lesson is highlighted in Figure 7.4.

FIGURE 7.4

Once you apply the changes, the new users will have access to their own accounts.

New user added—
to system

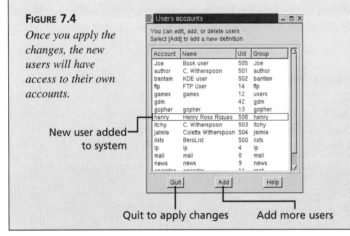

Quit to apply changes   Add more users

Updating User Accounts

There are times when it is necessary to make changes to user accounts, perhaps to change the password or the username. Updating the account information is as easy as creating a new account.

If you've closed Linuxconf, you'll need to start the program, open the User account configurator (by clicking the Users accounts button on the Linuxconf main window), and then click the User accounts button to display the list of users shown in Figure 7.4.

The next part is simple. Click the user account that you want to update; the User Information window for the user you selected will appear. Make your changes here and click the Accept button to apply the changes.

At some point, perhaps during extended leaves, you may want to place a user account on restriction. When you want to temporarily deny access to the computer, deselect the The account is enabled option for that account. The user's account and files will stay in place, but the user will be unable to log in.

Lesson 7.2: Changing a User's Password

It is always a good idea to change user passwords on a regular basis. This makes it harder for outsiders to get into your system. You'll also need to change passwords if a user forgets a password or if they think someone else may have discovered their little secret. Follow these steps to change a user password:

1. Click on the appropriate user account in the Users accounts window. The User information window for that user will appear as shown in Figure 7.5.

2. If you need to make any changes to the user information, select the text that you want to change and type the new text.

FIGURE 7.5

To maintain security, update passwords regularly and keep passwords a secret.

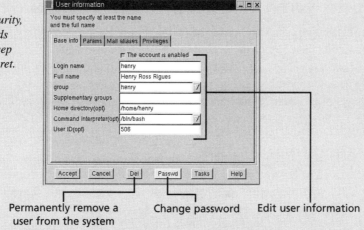

Permanently remove a user from the system   Change password   Edit user information

3. Click the Passwd button to display the Changing password window.

4. Type the new password and click Accept. Then, type it again to confirm it, and click Accept again. The new password will be exchanged for the old one. Also, the User information window will close and you will be returned to the Users accounts window.

5. Click the Quit button and make sure you activate the changes when you close Linuxconf.

7

Removing a User Account

When users are no longer using the system, their user accounts can be closed. If the files created by the deleted user are needed by anyone else on the system they can be saved and used by others. If they are not needed, you can delete the files to create more space for other users.

To delete a user, select the user account from the Users accounts window to display the User Information window. Then click the Del button. You will be asked how you want to use the account's data. The three choices that you have are

- Archive the account's data. This method compresses the files left behind in the user's home directory into a single file. This file is placed in the /home directory with all the other user's home directories—in a directory called /oldaccounts.

- Delete the account's data. Selecting this will remove all the contents of the user's home directory.

- Leave the account's data in place. This option will remove the user from the user list but retain the user's home directory and its contents in place.

Working with Group Accounts

When several users have a need to share the same files, you'll want to place these users into a single group. You can create many groups on the system and assign any combination of users to each group. The important thing to remember is that all members of the group need to share the same group of files. When users are assigned to a group and a group is given permission to access specific files and directories, users can begin sharing files by visiting the directory in which the files are stored.

Creating New Groups

The first step before you can enable file access between users is to form a group. It isn't necessary for every user on the system to belong to a group; only those people who need to have access to a group's files need to belong to that specific group.

Lesson 7.3: Assigning Users to a Group

Before you create a group, make sure that each person in the group is assigned a user account and make a note of each user's username. You'll then need to open Linuxconf and display the User account configurator window.

1. Click the Group definitions button to open the User groups window. You can see in Figure 7.6 that several groups have been created already. Each user is assigned an individual group, and there are system groups that are used to control the operating system. Don't make any changes to these system groups.

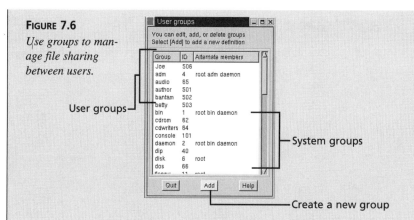

FIGURE 7.6

Use groups to manage file sharing between users.

User groups

System groups

Create a new group

2. Click the Add button to display the Group specification window shown in Figure 7.7.

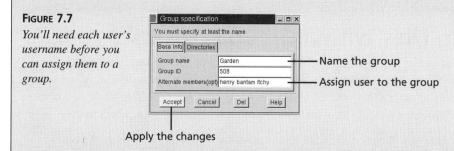

FIGURE 7.7

You'll need each user's username before you can assign them to a group.

Name the group

Assign user to the group

Apply the changes

3. Type a name for the new group in the Group name text box.

4. Click in the Alternate members(opt) text box and type the username for the first user you want to add. Then press the spacebar and type the second username. Continue until you have all the members you want in the group.

5. Click the directories tab and, in the Home base directory text box, type the pathname for the directory in which the group will store their files. Don't worry if the directory does not exist; Linuxconf will create the directory for you with the appropriate permissions.

6. Click the Accept button. The Group specification window disappears and the members that you added appear next to the group name in the User groups window, as seen in Figure 7.8.

7

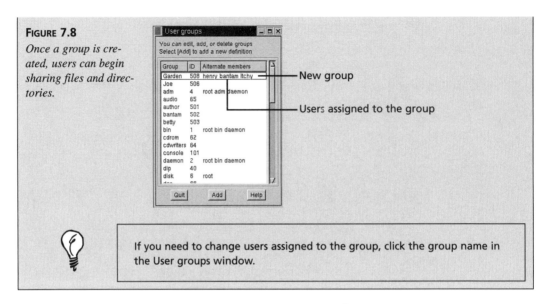

FIGURE 7.8

Once a group is created, users can begin sharing files and directories.

New group

Users assigned to the group

If you need to change users assigned to the group, click the group name in the User groups window.

Sharing Files with a Group of Users

A very effective way to organize people working on a project and enable them to share their work is to form a workgroup with all the members of the project. This permits the workgroup to share access to files created by the group members. The group member who created the file can control the access permitted other group members to that file.

It is the assignment or denial of file access permissions that is the heart of the Linux (UNIX) security system. There are three kinds of access permissions—read, write, and execute. These are assigned to three kinds of users—Owner, Group member, and Miscellaneous (others). By controlling the access to files, you control the whole thing. The user who creates a file establishes who has access to the file to read it, to write to it, or to execute it if it is an execution file.

Lesson 7.4: Setting Group Access Permission for a Directory

If you (as root or superuser) create a special directory in which members of a group store their files, you need to give the group permission to access the directory. Follow these steps to do so:

1. Open the file manager and display the appropriate directory in the right pane, as shown in Figure 7.9.

FIGURE 7.9

*The system administra-
tor will need to give
group members access
to any directories used
by the group.*

Directory for
workgroup

Edit properties to
change directory
permissions

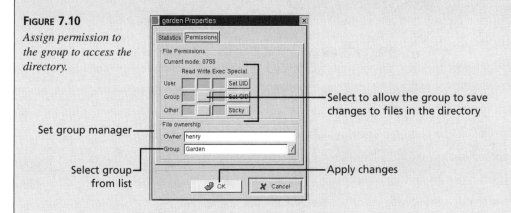

2. Right-click the directory and select Properties from the menu that appears. This
   opens the Properties dialog box for the directory (see Figure 7.10).

FIGURE 7.10

*Assign permission to
the group to access the
directory.*

Set group manager

Select group
from list

Select to allow the group to save
changes to files in the directory

Apply changes

3. Clear the text in the Owner text box and type the member of the group who will
   manage the directory structure and files for the group. Only the owner of the directory will be able to write files to the directory.

4. Click the Group list box down arrow and select the group who will be using the
   directory. Group members will have access to the directory but cannot place new
   files in the directory.

5. If the owner of the directory wants to give the group members the ability to make
   changes to files in the group directory and save those files back to the directory,
   select the Group Write button.

6. Click OK. The members of the group can now begin to work with their group's
   files in the group's directory.

7

Setting File Permissions

After the group's directory has been set up and permissions for the group owner and members have been applied, it's time for the owner to move files that the group will need into the group's directory. Once the files have been moved, the owner will need to decide how the other group members can work with the files.

As mentioned earlier in the hour, setting file permissions is the way that you maintain security for your files and still allow other users access to them when it is needed. Recall that you used the `ls -l` command on the command line to get a long listing of the contents of a directory. Part of that information is a string of characters and dashes, which indicates the file access permissions of the files.

To set file permissions, right-click the file and select Properties from the menu that appears. This opens the Properties dialog box for the file. Click the Permissions tab to display the Access permission options for the file (as shown in Figure 7.10). You can allow the following types of file access:

- The Read option gives read-only access to the user (aka the owner) and the group.
- The Write option gives those selected users and groups the ability to make changes to the file.

> You can set permissions on more than one file at once. To do so, highlight all the files that need the same permissions before you right-click and select Properties.

You'll then need to set the group who will have access to the files by displaying the Group drop-down list and selecting the group who needs to have access to the files.

Gathering System Information

Finding out something about your system is an integral part of getting anything new to fit in smoothly. Information is available about the Linux-Mandrake distribution you are running plus information about the system release version and the Linux kernel. You can do this from your user account.

If you are using the GNOME user interface, you can find this information in the main menu under Utilities, System Info. The System Information window displays information about the Linux distribution you are running, its kernel number, and some information about the current usage of your computer. To find out how much of your hard disk is being used, how much memory is being used, and information about the CPU, click the Detailed Information button.

KDE users can find out much of the same information by starting at the main menu and selecting Settings, Information. This displays a menu of the different items that you can track. You can also open the KDE Control Center and select the Information category.

Updating the Time

Daylight savings time changes occur twice annually in temperate time zones everywhere (excluding Hawaii, Puerto Rico, the Virgin Islands, most of Arizona, and parts of Indiana). Now we would tackle daylight savings time, that major obstacle to maintaining a good attendance record and remembering when your TV shows are on, but Linux handles this automatically. While this is handy, it does not take care of problems like moving from one time zone to another or resetting the clock to the right time if it has lost a few minutes.

To change the time or date from the KDE interface, open the main menu and select Settings, Date & Time. Click those items you want to change—such as the hour, minute, or date—then click the up or down arrow to change the display to what you want.

Summary

During the past hour, you learned something of what it would be like to be the system administrator for a computer network. This is just a small part of the responsibilities of a system administrator. When several users share a computer, directories, and files, the administrator needs to make sure that everyone has a proper account, that groups are set up, and that everyone has access to the files that they have permission to use.

Q&A

Q I keep hearing about log files in Linux. I know that they show changes that were made to the computer's configuration. How can I view changes that were made to the system by Linuxconf?

A Open Linuxconf and click the Control tab in the main window. Then click on Logs to open the system logs window. This window has two options—Boot messages and Linuxconf logs. Click Linuxconf logs. A list of configuration changes will appear in another window and you can click any change to see the commands that were executed.

7

Q Are there any other utilities that I can use to see what's going on with my computer?

A It depends on which user interface you are using. A quick way to see how much hard disk space is being used is with KDiskFree, which is in the KDE main menu under System. There's also the K File System Control (found in Utilities in the KDE main menu), which also shows how your hard disk is being occupied. KDE also has a User Manager, but this is available only if you are logged into the root account.

If you are using GNOME, try GNOME DiskFree. You'll find it in the Utilities menu of the GNOME main menu. This utility shows you how much space is free on the hard drive. Also in the Utilities menu is a utility to change the password you use to log into your user account. And, the GNOME System Monitor is in the Utilities menu; look at it if you want some specific details about what your computer is doing.

Q Is it possible to use Linuxconf to change the time for my computer?

A Yes. Open Linuxconf and click the Control tab in the main window. Then select Date & Time. You'll need to type the correct date and time in the text boxes of the Workstation date & time window.

Since you need to be logged into root to use Linuxconf, you may also find the Time Machine a handy tool. You'll find it in the GNOME main menu by selecting System, Time Tool.

Workshop

Managing users and groups is a simple method of sharing files. After you've tested your knowledge of system administration, try out your new skills on your own system.

Quiz

1. What method do you use to share files with other users on the system?
2. How do you give members of a group the capability to make changes to a file?
3. Where can you find out how much space is being used on your computer's hard drive?
4. When do you need to change the time on your computer's clock?

Exercises

1. You may want to learn more about how file permissions work. One way to do this is to read the man pages about some of the file commands. Look up the `chmod` command, which changes access permissions. There's also the `chown` command, which changes the ownership of files and directories. You may also want to look up the Linux Security HOWTO (`/usr/doc/HOWTO/Security-HOWTO`) to learn how to keep your computer system secure. It covers physical security, users and groups, file permissions, passwords, and backup and restore procedures.

2. Get out your system administrator's notebook and record the users that you've created. Next, decide how users will share files. You may want to create a directory where the family managers share household budget information. Another directory can be accessed by members who are creating a Web site together. You'll also want to make note of any groups that you formed and the directory structure used to share files.

7

HOUR 8

Backing Up the Filesystem

Making backups is one of the most important maintenance jobs required of the system administrator, or of anyone who owns a computer. Whether you have a single computer or many networked computers, you need to maintain a good backup system to ensure that your data is protected from loss or corruption. It is therefore important for you to spend some time organizing your data and establishing a good backup system.

When planning a backup strategy, it is important that you know what you should back up, what media you can back it up on, and what tools you can use to control your backups. Today, you learn about the following:

- Which important files need to be backed up
- How to use backup and archive commands
- How to use backup media

Deciding How and What to Back Up

There is hardly any doubt that, as you learn to fly with Linux-Mandrake, some of your experimental maneuvers may result in unexpected "customizations" to your Linux system. Sometimes these changes can't be restored easily and you may not even be able to restore things the way you would like them by simply reinstalling the system from scratch. But, since your CD-ROM or original floppies can serve as an excellent backup, it might not be necessary to back up your whole system.

> The Upgrading Your Linux Distribution mini-HOWTO (found in the /usr/doc/HOWTO/mini directory or at www.linuxdoc.org/HOWTO/mini/Upgrade.html) provides a solid plan for backing up your Linux system.

Important Files to Back Up

The files that you generally make changes to are the system configuration files found in /etc. Other configuration files for programs you have installed should also be backed up. You should also archive some directories—the /usr/lib and /usr/X11R6/lib/X11 directories (the latter because it contains your X Window configuration files).

If you built or upgraded your own kernel, you should also back up your kernel source files, found in /usr/src/linux.

> As you probably remember, we have been nagging you all along to keep a notebook that documents the changes made to your Linux system and problems you've encountered along with the solutions. Well, here is yet another time where keeping track of what you do, and writing down what you back up, can be a big help if something unfortunate happens to your system.

You should back up the home directories for each user. These directories are found in /home except for root, which is found in /root.

If you configured your Linux system to receive e-mail, you may want to back up the incoming mail files for your users. They are found in /var/spool/mail.

Using the find Command

find is certainly one of the more useful commands for any filesystem administrator. Using find with the proper arguments can help you locate files across the whole system by filenames, file permissions, or by their last modification times. This command can also execute programs for the files that it finds. find can also produce a list of the files it finds and then that list can be used by tar to archive the files (and the list).

Locating Files with the find Command

▼ SYNTAX

When you need to find certain files in the Linux filesystem, use the find command. The syntax for the find command is

```
find path expression
```

The path argument indicates the place in the filesystem where you want to start looking (such as in /, the root directory) or the specific path to a directory to be searched.

The expression arguments specify the options that find should use to perform the specific tasks that you want. The expression begins with a -, (,), ,, or an !. All the arguments after it are interpreted as the remainder of the expression. If you don't give find a path, it will use the current directory. If you don't give find an expression, it will use -print as the expression.

For example

```
find / -mtime –7 \! –type c –print > /tmp/backuplist.weekly
```

The above command will accomplish the following task:

- The path argument (in this case /) begins the search with the root directory.
- The -mtime –7 expression argument looks for files modified in the last 7 days.
- The /! -type d expression argument excludes files of type d. (You need the / character to tell the shell that the ! is not a shell command but a negation for the find command.)
- The -print > /tmp/backuplist.weekly expression argument prints the list of filenames in the /tmp directory as backuplist.weekly.

▲

There is not time or room in this hour to go through all the uses of find. You can get information about how to use GNU find from its man page. It takes some practice to use it to its best advantage, but it's well worth the time and effort.

Using the Backup Tools

There are several good tools included in your Linux-Mandrake distribution for backing up or archiving your files and directories. This section covers the Linux command utilities.

Working with `tar`, `gzip`, and `cpio`

Once you have selected the files and directories you want to back up, you can use the `tar` command to back them up directly to your backup media. `tar` works with whatever media you have, but it does not compress files. The `tar` command also makes a multivolume archive for use with small capacity media such as floppy disks or tapes.

The `tar` command has 49 options (at last count) that enable you to copy and restore from archives in various ways. *Tar* is an acronym for *tape archive* and it was developed to make backups to tape media. Its strengths include its capability to back up whole directory structures and restore them intact. Its drawbacks include a lack of *fault tolerance*. This makes it susceptible to problems with bad blocks on storage media, something that occurs frequently on floppy disks and tapes. Even though `tar` was originally developed for tape backups, it works admirably on other media as well.

Using `tar` to Create an Archive

Once you have compiled a list of files (using the `find` command), you can then tell `tar` to archive those files. The syntax for the `tar` command is

```
tar functionoptions files
```

Where `functionoptions` is a single letter indicating the operation to perform (function) plus one or more single letters (options to the function). There is no space between the function and options letters in the command. And `files` is the list of files which `tar` will place in an archive.

In the following example:

```
tar -cv -T /tmp/backuplist.weekly -f /dev/cdrw
```

`tar` performs the following tasks:

- The `-cv` argument creates an archive (function c) and prints lots of information while packing or unpacking the archive (option v).
- The `-T /tmp/backuplist.weekly` argument backs up the files listed in the backuplist.weekly file.
- The `-f` argument tells `find` to use the backuplist.weekly file as the archive name.
- The `/dev/cdrw` argument stores the archive in the /dev/cdrw directory.

There are many different ways that organizations and individuals back up their data. Therefore, rather than waste time going through the list of options, it is better if you look at the man page for `tar`.

Once you have your archive tar'd, you can compress it with the gzip utility. The resultant .tgz file will be much smaller. However, there are the same fault-tolerance problems with gzip as there are with tar. Most compression programs, including gzip/gunzip, depend on having the data stored across an uninterrupted smooth array with no missing or bad blocks in order to be able to restore that data properly.

Test your backup media to ensure that it doesn't contain any bad blocks or sectors. By taking the time to do this, you won't find yourself unable to get gunzip to work and then be unable to use tar to open the archive.

There is another archiving utility included in your Linux distribution that helps you avoid some of the problems associated with tar—cpio. The cpio utility provides a solution to one of the problems with tar. The problem stems from the way that tar stores backups. The tar archive is stored as a single file, which means that if the archive file is corrupted in any way, tar has no way to access any of the files contained inside.

The cpio utility archives files together like tar does, but it uses a simpler method to store them and can recover from data corruption. It can copy the files in and out of both cpio archives and tar archives. But cpio still doesn't really recover well from damaged gzipped files, though.

Working with the Dump Utility

There is a utility on the Linux-Mandrake installation CD called dump. The dump utility examines the files on your Linux filesystem and determines which ones need to be backed up. It then copies these files to the given media (tape). If the dump is too large for the media, the dump is broken into volumes. The dump utility can be used to back up entire filesystems or incrementally to back up all files that have changed since the last incremental backup. If you want to use dump, check the man pages for its command syntax.

Working with Floppy Disk Drives

Certainly the easiest way to back up a small number of files is to copy them onto floppy disks—either by simply copying them or using the tar and gzip utilities. For people with only one Linux computer, this might be an adequate backup plan and even suitable for a long time. Of course, your ability to utilize the 3.5-inch floppy drive as a backup device depends on how much data you need to back up. A full backup for a large system can require as much as 2GB of storage, which is way too many floppies for sure. There are other options for that sized job; we discuss those in the section "Creating Backups on CD Read/Write Media," later in this hour.

Although the 3.5-inch floppy disks won't store a large amount of data they still can do a fair job if your general backup plan is to save the install media for your installed applications, and then just concern yourself with backing up your working files every few days. You do have several options for using floppy disk drives as backup devices. You can format them as DOS floppies and then read the files stored on them in Linux. Or you can install a Linux filesystem (an ext2 filesystem) on the floppy disk and just copy data there. The following section discusses using the 3.5-inch floppy drive as a DOS drive and storing Linux files on it.

DOS Floppies

During the initial setup, Linux-Mandrake mounts and configures your floppy drive to automatically determine the filesystem type. In other words, when you mount a DOS disk in the floppy drive, it will recognize the vfat filesystem and mount the drive as a DOS drive. The same process takes place when you mount a disk with an ext2 filesystem. Linux checks the filesystem type and mounts the floppy as a Linux drive. No matter which filesystem is mounted, you can read files from it and save files to it. This is a big improvement over having to mount each floppy filesystem by hand.

Another big advantage to this is that it enables you to download Linux RPMs and applications to whichever computer is convenient. Unlike many applications for Windows and Macintosh, which sometimes require many megabytes of space, Linux applications tend to be much smaller and sleeker. In fact, quite a number of them, even many of the complex ones, are small enough to download to a single 1.44MB floppy disk. You can just take the floppy disk straight to your Linux machine and install the application.

Ext2 Filesystem Floppies

Ext2 is the Linux native filesystem type. If you format a floppy disk with Linux, it will place an ext2 filesystem on the floppy that you can mount and use as an extension to the Linux system on the hard drive. By using an ext2 filesystem on your floppy disks, you can use the Linux filesystem management tools to keep track of your data and you may be able to restore or recover damaged data.

Cross-Platform Filing

When you installed Linux-Mandrake, you did so on a partition of a Windows machine hard drive and by installing Linux/Windows connectivity. This allows you to use the Linux file managers to access the Windows drive. You may also store Linux files on this Windows drive.

Lesson 8.1: Moving Files to a DOS Partition

To copy or move files from a Linux partition to a DOS/Windows partition requires a simple drag and drop. Follow these steps:

1. Open a KDE file manager, select Expand Tree from the View menu, and then navigate to the Linux directory where the file you want to move or copy is stored.

2. Make sure that your Windows partition is mounted. Open a second KDE file manager and navigate to the Windows directory where you want the file to be moved or copied.

3. Click the file you want to move in the first file manager, drag it to the right pane of the second file manager, and then release the button.

4. Select Move or Copy from the pop-up menu. The file is moved or copied.

 You can transfer a file from a Windows partition to a Linux partition in the same manner.

Using DOS Files in Linux-Mandrake

There are some types of DOS files that Linux can read (like .txt files for example), and there are viewers for most graphics formats, except for some like Microsoft's Windows Metafile (.wmf) format. There is also a collection of tools developed before Linux containing support for non-native filesystems called *Mtools*. The Mtools package contains a collection of commands that allow you to manipulate Windows directories and files from Linux. The Mtools package is installed during the Linux-Mandrake installation if you selected DOS/Windows connectivity. To find more information about the Mtools commands and their actions, see the man pages for the following commands:

```
mattrib
mcd
mcopy
mdel
mdir
mformat
mlabel
mmd
mrd
mread
mren
mtype
mwrite
```

There are several Linux applications that can deal effectively with files in Windows formats. Emacs, Maxwell, and WordPerfect can read .doc files and export Rich Text Format (RTF) files. There are also office productivity suite applications such as StarOffice and ApplixWare that can convert files with varying amounts of accuracy, but you may have to edit the translated files by hand to get exactly what you want.

Using Zip Drives to Store Files

Iomega Zip and Jaz drives have been around for some time and they come in different sizes. The Zip drives are available in 100MB and 250MB sizes and the Jaz drive can store up to 2GB of data. The disks can be formatted with a Windows vfat 32 filesystem or with an ext2 Linux native filesystem and used as another hard drive.

Creating Backups on CD Read/Write Media

As we mentioned earlier in the hour, there are systems that will require large media storage for complete backups. When you're backing up a networked system with many users and various backup requirements, you will not be pleased with the need to maintain stacks of disks or tapes (which still must be carefully stored away from corrupting influences). The solution, which is probably the best at the moment, is to use a CD-R or CD-R/W drive to create backups on compact disks. This will give you a less corruptible non-magnetic storage media with a 100 year life span should you need it for the long term.

Summary

One of the most important maintenance tasks that you can adopt is performing regular backups. Backups are important in case files are lost, deleted, or corrupted due to user error or acts of nature (such as power outages). By keeping these files on a separate storage medium, you ensure that you can keep Linux in good working order.

Q&A

Q I have an Iomega Zip drive connected to my computer. Are there any resources to help me set up my Zip drive to work on my Linux system?

A You should read the Zip Drive mini HOWTO at www.linuxdoc.org/HOWTO/mini/Zip-Drive.html. You may want to look into the latest Zip parallel port drivers at www.torque.net/~campbell. Check out the jaZip program that works on both Iomega Zip and Jaz drives. You'll find jaZip at www.scripps.edu/~jsmith/jazip.

Q I have a CD-R/W attached to my computer. Where can I find information about how to use it with Linux?

A The first place you should start is the CD-Writing HOWTO at
metalab.unc.edu/linux/HOWTO/CD-Writing-HOWTO.html. This HOWTO gives you all the information you need to set up your CD-R/W and what programs you need in order to burn your own CDs.

Q In addition to keeping my filesystem backed up, is there anything else I can do to protect my Linux system?

A You may want to consider hooking up your Linux system to an uninterruptible power supply (UPS). If the power goes out unexpectedly, Linux will not shut down properly and you may have problems getting the system to boot after the power returns. By attaching a UPS to your system, you can set up Linux so that when the power goes out and the UPS starts its alarm, Linux will shut itself down properly. To learn more about how to do this, read the UPS-HOWTO
(www.linuxdoc.org/HOWTO/).

Workshop

Keeping your Linux system safe means that you must constantly back up important files. Understanding what you've learned over the past hour means that you must test your knowledge.

Quiz

1. What are the most important files in the filesystem that should be backed up?
2. Which backup tools can be used to back up and archive important files?
3. What type of media can be used to store backups?

Exercises

1. Here's another opportunity to add a section to the notebook you've been using to keep track of your Linux system. Create a backup plan for your Linux system. Decide which files need to be backed up and how often. Then choose a medium (floppy, tape, or CD) on which to store your backups. Then, find a secure place to store the backup media.

2. Get on the Internet and see whether you can find other applications that will help you back up files and create compressed archives (such as the .zip files you may be accustomed to in the Windows operating system).

HOUR 9

Managing Applications

A few hours ago, in Hour 4, "Living in a Graphical Workspace," you learned how to browse through the KDE and GNOME menus to find some of the applications that are available on your Linux computer. After looking through all those menus and the lists of applications, you may have thought to yourself, "There couldn't possibly be any more applications included with this Linux distribution." Well, think again.

The GNOME and KDE menus contain only a few of the hundreds of application packages found on the Linux-Mandrake CD-ROM. There are a large number of applications that are installed, but are not included in the menus. And there may be applications that were not installed. All of this depends on which components you selected during the Linux-Mandrake installation. During this hour, you learn how to search your system and the CD-ROM to find more applications.

After you are more confident with Linux, you may want to do some exploring on your own and find application packages for Linux on the Internet. You'll be amazed at how much is out there. And all of it is free, except for your download time.

There are two tools that will help you find installed applications and install more applications—KPackage and Gnome-RPM. At the end of this hour, you will know how to use these tools to do the following:

- Find applications that are not found in the GNOME and KDE menus
- Make sure that applications are loaded correctly, and remove unwanted applications
- Install application packages from a CD-ROM
- Download and install packages off the Internet

Finding a Few Good Programs

Applications are where it's at when it comes to computers. The appeal of computers is the ease with which software programs can perform everything from composing short letters to creating complex Web graphics. The joy of Linux is the availability of an enormous collection of software applications. Some of these applications are on the Linux-Mandrake CD; others can be found on the Internet.

NEW TERM Once you find these programs, it's a simple matter of convincing a *package manager* to install the program for you. Package managers simplify the installation and upgrading of the Linux software packages. Not only do package managers load new applications on your Linux system, they help you keep those applications current and running as they are intended.

Through the magical powers of the package-management system, you can even repair installed applications by searching for damaged files and replacing them. The package manager ensures that file dependencies are maintained whenever packages are installed and uninstalled. Package managers even inform you of additional packages that need to be installed in order to make the selected package work properly.

Before you decide to start adding and subtracting applications from your Linux system, you should first take a look through the package managers and see what is already installed on the system. KDE and GNOME each have their own package-management utility. Let's see how they can be put to work for you.

 Clicking the RpmDrake icon on your desktop will open the Mandrake front-end for the Kpackage utility described below with an added feature that will let you display the packages on your Linux CD that are not loaded on the system.

Getting Started with Gnome-RPM

Linux-Mandrake is built on the Red Hat Linux distribution and uses the Red Hat Package Management System (RPMS) to manage applications. Gnome-RPM is the GNOME graphical front-end for Red Hat's package management system, a tool that makes manipulating applications and comparing installed programs with their source code (and other such complicated technical things) into simple tasks.

All the good simple tasks like installing, upgrading, and uninstalling packages have to be done by the root account. But users can query packages and verify them to determine their status.

To find Gnome-RPM, select System, GnoRPM from the main menu. You can also type **gnorpm** in an X terminal window.

Take a moment to examine the Gnome-RPM window shown in Figure 9.1. The directory tree that appears on the left lists the categories of packages that are installed. The right panel displays the list of packages contained in each category. To expand the directory list, just click the plus sign next to a directory name.

FIGURE 9.1

Gnome-RPM lists all the packages that are installed with the Linux operating system.

Click to expand list

Display packages in a category

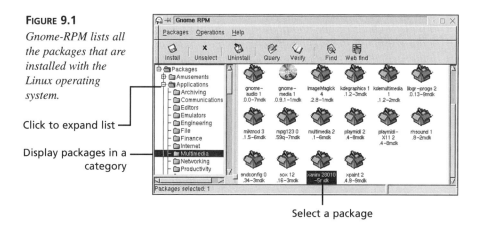

Select a package

Lesson 9.1: Finding Installed Applications with Gnome-RPM

Gnome-RPM can tell you quite a bit of information about the applications you installed with Linux-Mandrake. For this exercise, you do not need to be logged into the root account. Any user on the system can view information about installed applications. Here's how to learn more about what you can do with your Linux system:

1. Select a package from one of the categories and click the Query button to display the package information for the application. An example is shown in Figure 9.2.

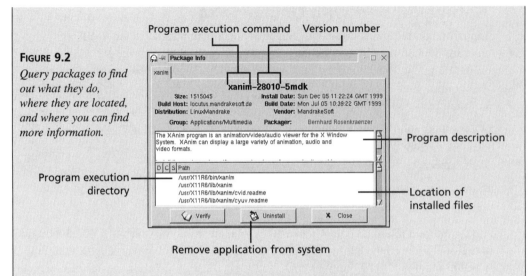

FIGURE 9.2

Query packages to find out what they do, where they are located, and where you can find more information.

2. If you can't find this program in the KDE or GNOME menus, open an X terminal window and type the program execution command found at the top of the Package Info window. The program will either open, or a message containing more information about how to run the program will appear in the X terminal window.

3. Whenever you suspect that a program is not working correctly, click the Verify button. Gnome-RPM will verify that this application is properly installed and look at the program files for problems. After it compares what you have installed with the source, it will inform you of any problems.

> If you want to learn more about an application, look for the documentation files for the package. (You'll see the letter D in the first column of the list.) Make a note of the directory path and filename for the documentation file and open the file in a text editor or browser window.

4. When you are finished reading the package information, click the Close button.

Browsing Through KPackage

KPackage is the KDE package manager, and although it does most of the same things as Gnome-RPM, it does them a little differently. There are several ways to get to KPackage. You may find an RPM icon on the KDE desktop; if not, try the KDE Application Starter menu under Utilities. You can also type **kpackage** in an X terminal window. The KPackage package manager interface is shown in Figure 9.3.

Expand package tree   Package information

FIGURE 9.3
*KPackage displays
package information in
the right pane.*

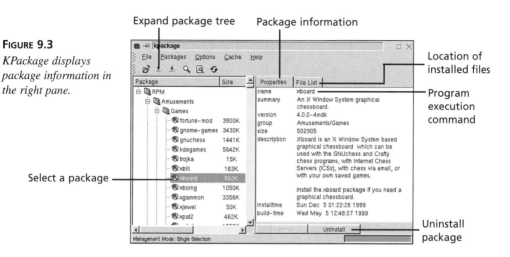

Location of
installed files

Program
execution
command

Select a package ———

9

Uninstall
package

To see the entire list of installed packages, click the Expand Package Tree button on the
KPackage toolbar. When you select a package from the category list (on the left side of
the window), the detail is shown on the right.

When you display information about a package, the Install/Uninstall button
is activated. If you request information about a package that is installed, the
button will read Uninstall; if the package that you request information
about is not installed, the button will read Install.

Lesson 9.2: Uninstalling Applications with KPackage

You may decide that some of the applications listed in the package managers are just
taking up space on your system and you'd like to have the space for other applications
that you may want to install later. Before you can uninstall programs from the Linux system, you need to be logged into the root account.

In both KPackage and Gnome-RPM, you'll find the button that uninstalls a package at
the bottom of the information window. Here's what you need to do to remove any packages that you no longer want installed on your system:

1. Select the package that you want to uninstall and display the package information
   window.

2. Click the Uninstall button to display a verification dialog box like the one shown
   in Figure 9.4.

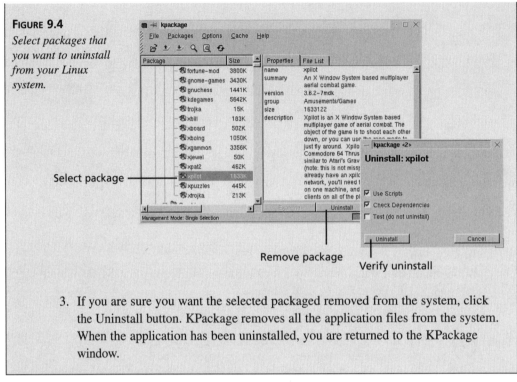

FIGURE 9.4

Select packages that you want to uninstall from your Linux system.

Select package ⎯

Remove package

Verify uninstall

3. If you are sure you want the selected packaged removed from the system, click the Uninstall button. KPackage removes all the application files from the system. When the application has been uninstalled, you are returned to the KPackage window.

Installing Applications

Now that you've had a chance to look around your Linux system and see all the installed software, it's time to load more software. To install software packages on your Linux machine, you need the aid of a package manager. The package-management system enables you to maintain your Linux system and its applications by providing an easy path to upgrades and new applications.

Obviously, the first place you should look for more software is on the Linux-Mandrake CD-ROM. Unless you elected to install every component during the initial installation, there's still plenty of software on the CD for you to try.

In addition to the software on the Linux-Mandrake CD, you can also install packages from other Linux distributions. For example, if you have a Red Hat or Slackware distribution, pop that CD into your CD drive and see what's available.

And since Linux was conceived and developed over the Internet, every application that works with the Linux operating system is available on the Web. All you need to do is find the package you want, download it, and install it.

Finding Applications on the Linux-Mandrake CD-ROM

The first place you should look for more software is on the Linux-Mandrake CD. Not only is it easy to find and load these applications, but you also can be relatively sure that these packages will install correctly with Linux-Mandrake.

> No matter which Linux distribution CD you may use, you'll find all the available packages in the RPMS subdirectory of the CD-ROM.

9

Lesson 9.3: Using Gnome-RPM to Install Packages

It's time to get out the Linux-Mandrake CD once again and take a look at which packages you did not install when you loaded the Linux operating system on your computer. To install application packages from the CD, log into the root account and follow these steps:

1. Place the Linux-Mandrake CD-ROM in the CD-ROM drive and mount the CD-ROM.

2. Open Gnome-RPM and click the Install button on the toolbar. The Install window opens and displays a category list that contains the RPMS packages on the Linux Mandrake CD that are not installed on your computer.

3. Click the Expand Tree button. The list of categories expands to show all of the packages in that category (as shown in Figure 9.5).

FIGURE 9.5

Find more applications to install on the Linux-Mandrake CD-ROM.

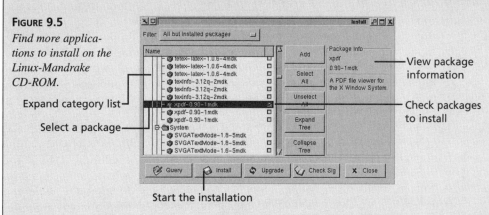

4. Click the name of a package to read a description of the package.

5. Place a checkmark in the box next to the packages you want to install.

6. Click the Install button. A status dialog box appears while the package is being installed. When the installation is complete, you are returned to the Install window.

> If any other packages are required in order to make the selected packages work correctly, a Dependency Problems dialog box will appear. To install these dependencies, click the No button, select the required packages, and try the installation again.

7. When you are finished installing applications, click the Close button to return to Gnome-RPM.

Downloading Packages from the Internet

Of course there are many applications that are not included in the Linux-Mandrake distribution. Many are available from the Linux sites on the Internet. It is Linux after all, so any distribution site is fair game. It pays also to make regular visits to the sites of the different distributions to see what's available and changed there.

Linux is growing so rapidly that new things are appearing almost daily. It is a good idea to regularly look around the Internet at the various Linux sites and mirrors. The mirrors often have tools in their pub directories that are not available on all sites. In this way, you can keep your applications upgraded as well as acquire new ones.

Lesson 9.4: Using KPackage to Install Applications

Downloading and installing Linux software from the Internet is easier than you may think. If you consider yourself a Web traveler, give your downloading skills a try. Here's how to install Linux software that you find on the Internet:

> Before you begin this lesson, you need an Internet connection. Turn to Hour 11, "Getting on the Internet," if you need to create a dial-up connection. You also need to be logged into the root account.

1. Open your favorite Web browser and navigate to rufus.w3.org. Here you'll find more applications than you could possibly need. When you find one you like, download it to your computer. You can store it in a subdirectory of the /root directory.

2. Open the KFM file manager and navigate to the directory in which you stored the RPM file that you downloaded.

3. Click the package that you downloaded. KPackage opens with the Install Package panel showing in the left pane and the Properties sheet and File list for the package you have selected in the right pane (see Figure 9.6).

FIGURE 9.6
KDE knows when you want to load a package.

Download package

Package information

Install package

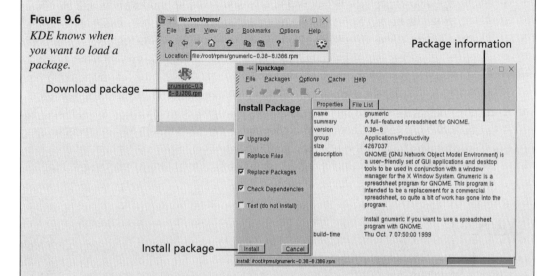

The Install Package dialog box presents you with several options:

- When you want to install a new or upgraded package or reinstall an installed package, use the Upgrade option. The Upgrade process ensures that all vestiges of the old package (if there was one) are removed and that the original settings are applied. The Uninstall function doesn't always do a good job of cleaning up dependencies between applications and modules.

- To replace files in an installed application, select the Replace Files option. The KPackage utility repairs damaged applications by replacing damaged or missing files.

- Use the Replace Packages option to replace a package. Use this option along with the Upgrade option.

- When you want to check all the dependencies that occur from installing a package, select the Check Dependencies option.

> - When you select the Test (do not install) option, KPackage looks at the filesystem to determine whether the installation of a package will succeed. Use this method to determine whether a bothersome application is installed properly.
>
> 4. Click Install after you have made your selections. KPackage will begin the installation. After the package is installed, you will be returned to the KPackage panel with nothing showing in the right pane.

Summary

During the past hour, you learned that there might be more Linux applications available on your computer than you first thought. After looking through the Linux-Mandrake CD (and maybe some of the other Linux distributions), you probably found even more applications that may be useful to you. And if all this isn't enough, you can get on the Internet and download Linux applications to your heart's content (and the size of your hard drive).

Q&A

Q Is it possible to install or uninstall more than one package at a time with KPackage and Gnome-RPM?

A If you are using Gnome-RPM, each time you click a package, it is selected. Notice at the bottom of the Gnome-RPM window that the status line tells you how many packages are selected. If you click the Uninstall button, all the selected packages will be removed from your system. If you want to deselect all the selected packages, click the Unselect button.

KPackage has two management modes that control whether you can select a single package at a time, or whether you can select multiple packages. To switch from being able to select one package at a time to being able to select multiple packages, click Packages, Multiple Selection Mode.

Q Is there any easy way to find packages on the Internet that I can download and install on my Linux machine?

A Gnome-RPM has a snazzy Web find utility. If you are connected to the Internet, click the Web Find button. Gnome-RPM will contact the `rufus.w3.org` Web site and download the list of Linux packages available. You'll need a while to browse through the list; it's a long one. When you find an interesting package, click it to display the package information. If you want the package, you can either install it directly or download the RPM file first and install it later.

Q Where can I learn more about how the Red Hat Package Management System works?

A Try the RPM-HOWTO found at www.linuxdoc.org/HOWTO. There's also an RPM+ Slackware mini-howto.

Workshop

Here we are at the end of another hour and it's time to see how well you understand all this package verification, installation, and uninstallation stuff. Since the reason most people need an operating system is to run applications, you should make sure you understand what you've learned over the past hour.

Quiz

1. What is a package manager and which package managers are available in the Linux-Mandrake distribution?

2. How do you find software programs that are installed on your Linux computer but do not show up in the KDE or GNOME menus?

3. Where can you find packages that can be installed on your Linux computer?

Exercises

1. Use Gnome-RPM to create a desktop shortcut for any applications to which you'd like to have quick access. Select the application and click Packages, Create desktop entry. You'll be asked to select an icon for the desktop shortcut and a location for the shortcut. Save the shortcut in the /home/username/.gnome-desktop directory.

2. Keep track of updates on some of your favorite Linux programs. When a new version comes out, you may want to upgrade it. Use the Web Find utility in Gnome-RPM to keep up to date with your software.

HOUR 10

Networking the Small Office/Home Office

Linux is a good choice for networking in general. This is evidenced by all the networks in existence today running on some member (like Linux) of the UNIX family of operating systems.

Linux is a particularly good choice for a small office network. Because Linux is smaller and friendlier than its big UNIX cousins, it is a little less intimidating to work with. And, Linux can help you as you create and manage your Linux Web-based Intranet.

Setting up a network and tailoring it to meet your present needs, planning for its future growth, and using it to further your business goals all require careful planning. The speed and efficiency of Linux can be harnessed and made to work well for you in almost any network environment, as long as you have a good plan.

> The focus of this hour is on network planning and the information is mostly directed toward the job of planning for a network large enough to require some measure of network administration. Some of you may find this to be beyond your present needs, and it also may seem a little daunting. The information contained in this hour will become more useful and comprehensible to you as your network knowledge and requirements grow.
>
> If you are planning a small office network or a home network with several workstations and would like to get the ball rolling, the guidelines in this hour will help you get started with a good plan.

In this hour, you assess your needs and assets and plan a successful network installation by learning about the following:

- When to start planning for a network and putting a network plan in place
- Keeping good documentation and equipment records
- Setting up an Intranet
- Keeping your network in good working order

When Is the Right Time to Build a Network?

NEW TERM   The right time to build a *network* is as soon as the need for one arises. The purpose of a network is to serve people. A network should serve people in ways that make them more productive. It should help them by removing bottlenecks and obstacles from their working processes and by speeding communication and reducing wasted effort in group projects. It can also help promote optimum allocation and use of resources by providing some structure to planning for the organization's growth.

The time to build a network is as soon as you have two or more computers to network together. That may seem a little oversimplified. But, if you begin early and plan your network to maximize what you have, as your organization grows you can add more components to your network and it can grow with you.

The Importance of Planning

Good network planning is essential to ensuring that your needs and goals are met, that your equipment acquisitions are guided, and that network growth maintains purpose and direction.

The successful implementation of a network is always the direct result of careful planning. Planning processes address specific needs and necessary changes, as well as define the resources needed to meet the hardware/software requirements and the networking goals of the organization.

NEW TERM The relationship between *network planning* and network implementation must be carefully considered. To be effective, network planning must relate to a desired and identifiable change that is to be implemented, and its focus must remain on instituting that change in an orderly fashion.

Planning focuses on three factors: people, processes, and organizations. Any healthy, robust enterprise seeks to develop and grow. If workgroups are organized carefully and can share resources, communication, and the enhanced working environment provided by networking, your users will be more productive, work processes will flow easier, and the whole process will reflect positively on your organization's bottom line.

Network planning will stand or fall based on the network's ability to meet user needs and the future requirements for growth and expansion of the organization. Future user demand may well be a difficult thing to assess, but the organization's overall plans for growth are frequently documented in projections for production goals, manpower needs, and budgets.

Consider How the Network Will Be Used

Determining how the network will be used and by whom is an integral part of deciding where to place peripherals (such as printers and scanners), network components, and workstations. Of course, if your organization is small and you only have two computers, this can be an easy job. However, if you have only one scanner, one modem, one CD writer, but six printers, two parallel port Zip drives, and the second computer isn't in the same room…well you can see the potential problems.

If you have a large group of people to consider, and more machines and peripherals, you will certainly see the potential for mayhem increase geometrically. Maintaining control of the placement of users and equipment is central to the optimum utilization of the network. Your prime consideration for placing equipment and assigning users is to understand who will be working with whom and who needs to share what.

Placement of Workstations and Peripherals

When selecting locations for workstations and equipment, some important factors need to be considered. The environment effects the location for equipment the most because of user considerations. It might be great theoretically to lock the workstation in a closet to keep it away from the dust and traffic, but the users will probably not like working there.

The desires and needs of the users will be a much more important consideration when deciding where to place the workstation than the difficulty in cabling it into the network. Workstations must be ergonomically situated to provide the users with the best working environment and facilitate interaction with other members of the workgroup.

The placement of the workstations and workgroup members influences the location of the server and peripherals. Providing easy access to the printer or other peripherals to as many of the workgroup members as possible is important, and if this is planned well, you may be able to reduce expenses for network cabling or additional components.

There are also some environmental concerns to consider when placing equipment. Just like the old mainframes which had to be kept in *clean* rooms with temperature control and air filtration and the like, microcomputers must be secured from many of the same hazards—if only to a different degree.

Keep Dust Away from the Equipment

Dust is one of the most serious enemies of electronic equipment. Clogged cooling fan motors cause equipment to overheat. Built-up dust deposits on component surfaces can cause shortouts. A thin layer of dust on disk surfaces will transfer to the read-write heads in the drive and destroy them over time.

Don't Overheat the Network Components

Excessive heat can freeze up disk drives and damage the media. Overheated cooling fan motors fail and the result will be other components overheating and failing. Excessive heat can cause other problems too: processor errors, memory chip errors, and a shortened life span for network equipment.

Avoid Power Supply Problems

Most electronic equipment is sensitive to fluctuations in the power supply. The network server in particular must have a good source of *clean* power (no drops or spikes). You need to ensure that the network server is not connected to a power supply that is subject to fluctuations or additional loads, or connected to the same circuit as other office equipment.

NEW TERM Even if your power supply seems to be perfect, consider installing an *Uninterruptible Power Supply* (UPS) device. These devices provide a battery back-up power supply that usually lasts about 15 minutes and provides time to shut down the computer and other applications in an orderly manner.

Unlike Windows systems, which can just restart themselves (more or less) when the power comes back, members of the UNIX family of operating systems (including Linux) can be damaged by having the power shut off abruptly. The system needs to be able to shut down in an orderly fashion to avoid damage to important files.

Make Network Peripherals Accessible

Network printers must be placed in an area that provides easy access for users. If printers will be connected to the server, you should remember that parallel cables should not exceed 25 feet. If the printer cannot be located that close to the server, another solution must be found.

10

Even if the printer can be located within the 25-foot cable length, the overall performance of the network may be reduced because of the server's need to allocate resources to the network printing function.

The best solution is to attach the printer directly to the Local Area Network (LAN), which provides flexibility about its location. There is a box made by Intel called a *netport* that will allow you to connect a printer anywhere on the network.

A second choice is to connect the printer to a workstation that serves as the print server. The drawback to this solution is that the workstation's capacity to do other work is reduced, and it may not be available to use as a workstation while it is printing a big network print job. Other components of the network must be accessible to users and for maintenance tasks as well.

Select Network Hardware, Interface Cards, and Cabling

Networks run on a system of cables, hubs, routers, servers, and other peripherals. Depending on which network layout you choose, you may reduce your need for network hardware. The distance between components will determine what number of switches, routers, and additional network components are required. Placing your workstations and peripherals in close proximity will reduce the network hardware requirements.

Networks are normally connected by one of four types of cable:

- *Coaxial cable* contains a central conductor surrounded by an insulating layer that is covered by a mesh layer conductor. It is relatively immune to electromagnetic interference and good for noisy installations where signal interference from other cables or equipment usage may exist.

- *Unshielded twisted-pair (UTP) cable* is probably the most popular choice for small networks because it can be used for every situation except for those requiring fiber-optic cabling. Telephone cable in many buildings is UTP and there is almost always extra capacity that can be used for networking.

> UTP cable comes in different grade categories, which are designated by numbers. The grade for network use is UTP category 5.

- *Shielded twisted-pair cable* resembles coaxial cable in the way that it is constructed. The difference is that shielded twisted-pair cables have a central core of paired cables. Then a braided insulating conductor is wrapped around it, like the coaxial cable. It, too, is noise resistant but can carry a signal farther than UTP.

- *Optical fiber* is the most efficient transmission carrier; it is also the most expensive. The fiber cables can carry both broadband transmissions (radio wave transmission of multiple distinct signals like cable TV and radio channels) as well as baseband (single signal transmission). They can carry transmissions farther (100km and up) at very high speeds, and with near immunity to environmental hazards and electromagnetic interference.

> The test equipment for fiber optic networks is very expensive and you need technically trained people to install it. It is unlikely that a small network would need this type of cabling.

Selecting the hardware you will use for networking requires you to decide on a network *topology* (layout) that best suits your needs. The price of network hardware has dropped dramatically recently and you can purchase high-speed auto switching hubs and network interface cards at a fraction of the cost of just a few years ago. The prices for network hardware components fluctuate over time and locale so you need to look around.

> If you don't have a large network or a large budget, you can still connect
> two computers with two Ethernet cards and a cable. Two 10Mbit 10base2
> NICs (Ethernet cards) are cheap, and you can use thinnet cables (a type of
> coax) and BNC connectors (they resemble silver Ts) to hook everything up.
> You don't need a hub.
>
> You can set up TCP/IP networking between the two machines that you use
> with both Linux and the Windows operating system. The directions to do so
> are available at www.mandrakeuser.org/connect/cmlan.html.

NEW TERM   You need a *network interface card* (NIC) for each computer and each
peripheral directly attached to the network. The connector on the peripheral
has to be the same as the one connecting it to the network at the attachment point.

Document Everything About the Network

It is absolutely essential that network planning be documented. Allocating your resources
and planning for new acquisitions will require a detailed inventory. The best time to collect this information is while you are preparing the equipment to connect to the network.

Draw a map of the network that shows the location of the workstations, server, cabling,
and how peripherals are attached. This will help you plan for access and avoid potential
problems like high-traffic areas or having to run network cabling in areas where there
might be interference from power lines or equipment.

In addition to the information about the physical layout of the network, you need to collect detailed information about each of the components you are going to install on it.

Keeping Equipment Records

It is necessary to keep good records with detailed information about all the equipment
that you have on the network. Conduct the most detailed inventory you can of existing
hardware. This will facilitate any changes you need to make to workstations or peripherals in the future, help you to allocate workstation resources, and give you important
guidelines for making decisions about purchasing additional equipment.

In order to configure the network properly, the documentation for the equipment on the
network must contain specific bits of information. We created a number of forms for our
business that we use as guidelines for collecting the information for each piece of equipment attached to the network. We share a few of these forms with you as we look at the
different network components that require detailed documentation.

You may have to look inside the equipment to collect some of the information needed for the equipment inventory sheets. This is also an excellent opportunity to get out the canned air and clean things up.

Determining Workstation Configuration

You need to collect information about each computer on the network. The Workstation Information Worksheet shown in Figure 10.1 lists the major points that you should document about each component of the network.

FIGURE 10.1

Document the user, location, and internal components of each workstation attached to the network.

Workstation Information Worksheet

Name of Primary User _____
Location of the Workstation _____
Network Server _____
Other Servers _____

Basic Information

Type of Processor _____
Operating System _____
Type of Monitor _____
Mouse _____
MB of RAM Installed _____
BIOS Manufacturer _____

Disk Drives

Hard Disk Drive   Type of drive _____
Type of controller _____
Drive capacity _____
Floppy Disk Drives   Drive A _____
Drive B _____
Other _____
Additional Drives   Type _____

Modem

Manufacturer _____
BAUD rate _____
COM port _____

Network Card

Configuration _____
Node Address _____

Sound Card

Manufacturer _____
Configuration _____

Other Information

Collecting Printer Information

You need to collect information about all the printers and their optional equipment (like envelope adapters or other attachments) that are attached to the network or to individual workstations. You need this information to configure software applications for users and to set up the network print system. Figure 10.2 shows an example worksheet that can help you collect this information.

FIGURE **10.2**

Collect printer information so that printers can be configured on the network correctly.

10

Printer Information Worksheet

Name of Printer _____
Location of the Printer _____

Basic Information

Type of Printer _____
Manufacturer _____
Model Number _____
Serial Number _____
Emulation Mode _____
Printer RAM _____

Connection Port

Parallel _____
Serial _____
Port Connected to _____

System Connected to

LAN Connection ID _____
Protocol _____
Queue Name _____

Other Information

Putting Together a Network Diagram

You need more than a simple diagram of where the cables will run. You must note the location of all the network components, hubs, routers, repeaters, modems, printers, servers, workstations, UPSs, and even any segments you may patch into the cable. This information can be invaluable when a component fails and no one can remember which closet the last network administrator put it in.

The information included or referenced in the network diagram must be thorough. The model numbers and installation dates of components and cables help you keep track of how old the network segment is and what kind of maintenance needs to be programmed for it.

Building an Intranet

The goal of computer networking is to connect computers and all their supporting hardware components together in such a way as to maximize the utility and availability of resources to the users. You want to be able to make the best use of the expensive components in your network and facilitate sharing devices and information between your users.

Linux-Mandrake can set up a TCP/IP network (like the Internet) to run as your private network or intranet. You will have to configure the networking topology and install the Web server software that came with the distribution and then configure the workstations and peripherals to set up the network. TCP/IP gives you a private intranet that can still connect to the Internet and provides your network users with access to their personal accounts.

Hooking Computers Together

Cabling is the basis for connecting all networks except for a small number of wireless networks that use radio waves. If you have never installed a network before and your network is going to be large and complex, you should consider contacting a cabling company or an industry-certified consultant to help you plan the network and assist you in properly installing the cables and connectors.

Laying Cables

If you are going to install the cable yourself, these tips can help you plan the best cable installation:

- If possible, run cables down corridors or hallways. You won't have to contend with climbing over desks and users to check for cabling problems.
- Avoid locating workstations or peripherals at the outside edge of the cable-length specifications. If necessary, you may have to install a direct line to a workstation from the server, but try to avoid stray cables.
- Always have more cable than you need. Doing so avoids two potential hassles. One, you can avoid those situations where you have to locate the network connector on the ceiling or half way up a wall because you don't have enough slack. Two, in the case of UTP, you can plan for expansion, and also be prepared to switch to an unused cable in a pinch, rather than waste time chasing down cabling problems when you can't afford network down time.

Installing Network Interface Cards

It may be necessary to configure the interface card with some basic information, outlined as follows:

- *Base Input/Output Address*. Personal computers use a hexadecimal number system to identify cards in the system and unique addresses are required for each card.

Common assignments for these Base I/O addresses fall in the range from 200hex to 300hex.

- *Base Memory Address.* Some network interface cards use some of the computer's main memory to speed communications with the CPU. Cards other than NICs use the same system (usually referred to as *shared memory*). VGA cards often use A000h or C000h, and some types of SCSI controllers use the addresses around B200h. Depending on how your workstations are configured to boot up and gain access to the network, you may need a memory area in this region. Commonly shared memory addresses are in the range between A000h and E000h.

- *Interrupt Request (IRQ).* Many network cards use an interrupt to notify the CPU of data ready and waiting for processing. The IBM Token Ring system allows shared interrupts, but IBM isn't usually the most economical route to take. For all other topologies, the interrupt address for each card must be unique. COM ports, printer ports, disk controllers, and other devices use most of the IRQs, but IRQ2, IRQ3, IRQ5, IRQ9, IRQ10, and IRQ11 are often available on many PCs.

The PC Device Settings Worksheet shown in Figure 10.3 lists the information you should document about IRQs, Base I/O addresses, and Base Memory Addresses for each workstation attached to the network.

10

FIGURE 10.3
Make note of the settings of each device installed on each workstation in the network.

PC Device Settings Worksheet

Name of Primary User _____
Location of the Workstation _____

Hardware Device	IRQ	Base I/O Address	Base Memory Address
COM 1			
COM 2			
LPT 1			
LPT 2			
Floppy Disk Drive Controller			
Hard Disk Drive Controller			
Mouse			
Modem			
Network Interface Card			
Sound Card			
Video			

Setting Up a Web Server

NEW TERM   *Web servers* are what the Internet is all about; they are also what intranets are all about. Linux distributions all come with Web server software included in the distribution. It is this server software that you will configure to be the Web server for your intranet.

Documentation and directions for the server can be found in the application package for the Web server. To access this information, you can use Gnome-RPM or KPackage to query the Web server package. For more information about using package managers, turn to Hour 9, "Managing Applications."

Sharing Peripherals

A major consideration for the design of your network is the need your users have to share the peripherals attached to the network. The placement of peripherals is influenced by the way that your physical space is laid out. It also is influenced by the desires and needs of the users.

The way that the system of sharing is organized and the way that the network components interact play a most important role in the overall management of users and network assets. You mustn't forget the human factor; it will influence where the color printer goes, for example, as well as other modified placements of peripherals.

Accessing a Modem and Internet from the Network

Yes, everyone on the network can share the modem for Internet access. The connection with the ISP is made through the network server by the root account. The connection can then be configured for each user on the network.

There are situations where this is not possible. Some or all of the users may have accounts with a different ISP, or perhaps some of them are still using AOL. The information about setting up an Internet account is found in Hour 11, "Getting on the Internet."

Sharing Printers

Printers once were the only real reason for having a network. It is the one peripheral that can vary the most from device to device. That variation by itself can make configuring them a long process.

Until very recently, printers were one of the most expensive components attached to the network, and the ones that are used most. As with any expensive piece of equipment, maximum utilization is a goal.

Since printers vary so much, there is a real need to make sure that their configuration information is readily available. For information about configuring printers, refer to Hour 15, "Printing and Faxing Documents."

Using Scanners on a Network

Scanners, like printers, need to be located close to the users. If they are used as a replacement for a copy machine, they need to be located next to the printer for ease of use.

The type of scanner you need is a function of your requirements, your budget, and which scanner is the one best supported by Linux.

> The SANE drivers available for Linux installations work well with a number of scanners. To find out more information about SANE, point your Web browser to `www.mostang.com/sane`.

10

Tips for Administering the Network

NEW TERM The *network administrator* is the person upon whom all the responsibility for maintaining and operating the network falls. This administrator needs to be able to predict the future, recognize the present needs of the organization, and administer day-to-day network operations.

The network administrator's job begins with planning the network and includes just about everything having to do with the installation, maintenance, growth, and management of the network. The network administrator has a long list of tasks that must be done to administer the network properly.

Establish Routines

Set up daily and weekly maintenance routines. They will help you organize your time so that you don't spend it all doing network maintenance. The following tasks should be done on a schedule:

- Adding new users
- Cleaning up the hard drives
- Installing upgrades
- Doing backups and archiving
- Restoring damaged or lost files and data

- Monitoring network traffic flow
- Collecting data for accounting and optimization
- Generating reports for management

Establish Security Procedures

It is probably safe to say that maintaining the availability of your network's resources is vital to your company's operations. Your users must be able to access resources they need (and perhaps be channeled away from those they don't need) and users who aren't supposed to have access to things should be prohibited from doing so. Here are some tips for practicing good configuration-management security:

- Load the file server with only authorized distribution software.
- Make only authorized changes to the network configuration.
- Maintain a copy of the current network configuration worksheets.
- Periodically review device configurations.
- Maintain a backup of the server software.
- Test software before introducing it into the network.

Maintain the Network

Maintaining a network can be a lot of work. A big part of the job is to manage the daily operations of the network and these include

- Establishing network documentation
- Providing support for the network user
- Developing training programs
- Managing network configuration
- Experimenting with new technologies

Plan for the Future

In addition to all the other jobs, the network administrator must keep abreast of new technology and applications and be able to respond to the user's ever-increasing demands for network services. It will be necessary for you, as the network administrator, to focus your attention toward

- Increasing network performance
- Assessing new hardware and software products
- Expanding network services
- Connecting to other networks

Summary

In this hour, you were introduced to the planning process that you need to go through before you build a network. It is essential that you plan your network, and its growth, before you start hooking computers and peripherals together. This advance planning will help you avoid problems such as incompatible equipment and running out of room to add more workstations to an existing network.

Q&A

Q Do I really need a network? I just have one workstation in my home office and a laptop that I carry around when I call on my clients.

A A network can be very useful in this situation. What would happen if you forget to upload important client files from your workstation to your laptop? If you had a network, you could dial up your workstation from your laptop (while in your client's office) and download the needed files.

Q Is it really that important that I keep track of every piece of computer equipment I own and want to attach to a network?

A It is difficult to overemphasize the importance of maintaining detailed documentation of your network. By keeping track of the network and its attachments, you have an invaluable assistant for maintaining the network once it is installed. Documentation also provides an indispensable tool for planning changes and growth. Also, having the network fully documented (from the planning stage all the way through to its powering up) greatly helps any other users who might act as the network administrator.

10

Workshop

Building a network is not an easy task. There's a lot to consider before you begin the task of hooking computers, printers, scanners, and other devices together. So, before you begin to plan the network, review what you've learned over the past hour and then decide if you are ready to purchase a few hundred feet of cable and tackle the network beast.

Quiz

1. What is the first task you should perform before you start building a network?
2. Why is it important to design your network on paper before you begin the actual creation of the network?
3. Why is the job of network administrator so important?

Exercises

1. Throughout this book, we've talked to you about keeping a notebook next to your computer so that you can keep track of your Linux installation, any changes you've made to the system, and user and group information. Now it's time to add a new section for network planning to your notebook. Reproduce the forms you've seen in this hour and start collecting the information you'll need when you attach the workstations and peripherals to your new network.

2. Take a break and do some shopping. Before you start buying NICs, hubs, and cables, see what is available and at what prices. Remember, your network needs to be within your budget. Before you buy anything, make sure that the equipment is compatible with Linux and the rest of your hardware and software.

PART IV

Putting Linux-Mandrake to Work

Hour

HOUR 11

Getting on the Internet

Checking the email and reading the morning headlines on the Internet is becoming a part of the morning ritual for more people every day. What draws so many people to this information medium? The Internet is bursting with new ideas, entertainment, job opportunities, music, pictures, news, sports, and the weather. We won't bore you with a long commentary on the Internet because we know you want to get connected and start surfing. At the beginning of this hour, we give you two options for creating your Internet connection.

If several users are sharing the same machine and all users need access to the same Internet account, use Linuxconf to create a universal connection that all users can share. If a single person will be using a connection, try the Kppp dialer that is part of the K desktop environment. And, since you're probably familiar with many Internet applications (such as browsers, email, and FTP), we show you some of the best that Linux-Mandrake has to offer, but we won't get into too much detail on how to use them.

We supply just enough to get you on your way. If you're a Web addict like us, loosen your muscles, grab your surfboard, and take a ride during the next hour and learn how to

- Use Linuxconf to create a PPP connection
- Set up Kppp to connect to the Internet
- Configure Netscape Communicator for email and newsgroups
- Download files with GNOME FTP
- Have live conversations with your friends on XChat

What You Need Before You Begin

When you set up an account with an Internet service provider, the ISP provided you with a list of information—username, password, access phone numbers, server names, and IP addresses. You'll need this information when you create the connection on your computer that will be used to connect to the ISP's servers. You have all of the software you need on the distribution CD in the back of the book. You also need a serial modem and a serial communications port with which to dial out.

NEW TERM   We'll deal with setting up a *PPP (Point-to-Point Protocol)* connection. This is the most common type of Internet connection. This protocol is supported by most ISPs and provides a measure of security for the person making the connection and the person receiving the connection.

One point that you may have noticed when you read the Linux-Mandrake compatibility list is that very few modems are supported. You'll find almost no internal modems on the list, and you certainly won't find any Winmodems. Your best bet for a modem is an external (serial) modem that works with any operating system.

If you want to check your system and see where your modem is located, open an X terminal window and type **dmesg**. You'll find lines in the output that look like the following:

```
ttyS00 at 0x03f8 (irq = 4) is a 16550A
```

The ttyS00 designation is the first serial port on the computer. You'll need this information when you configure the connection a little later.

> Linux and DOS use different numbering systems for naming communication ports. The DOS equivalent of COM1 is tty0 and COM2 is tty1. Serial ports in Linux are named cua0, cua1, and so on.

Now that you've collected the information from your ISP and you have a modem connected to your computer, it's time to decide how you want to use the connection and who will be using the connection.

Setting Up a PPP Connection

Setting up a PPP connection allows you to connect to the Internet through a modem and a telephone line. The tools you use to create that connection are a matter of preference. This section outlines two scenarios for creating the PPP connection. The first is Linuxconf, which was used in Hour 7, "System Administration Tasks," to perform system administration tasks such as managing user accounts and granting file access permissions. If you found Linuxconf easy to work with earlier, you'll find it just as friendly when creating an Internet connection. Linuxconf also allows all of the user accounts that may be set up in the system to use the same Internet connection. If you use this method, you may want to find out if your ISP will set up multiple mailboxes for a single account. That way, each user has an individual email address at the ISP, but all users connect using the same PPP connection.

The other method is to use the Kppp dialer that is part of KDE. The Kppp dialer can be set up from a user account; you don't need to be in the root account. Each user on the system will set up a separate Internet connection. Unlike Linuxconf, users do not share a PPP connection. Also, if you prefer the DUN-look of Microsoft Windows, you'll find the Kppp interface very familiar. The plus side to using Kppp is the additional tools that help you keep track of your surf time.

Using Linuxconf

Linuxconf is an easy-to-follow, graphical tool for configuring almost anything you want in your Linux system. Its goal is to assemble all Linux configuration tasks under one interface. That's a big job, and it performs the task admirably. One of the configuration tasks that Linuxconf can help you with is building a connection to your ISP so that you can idle away your hours on the Web. Before you begin, collect the information you received from your ISP to create the connection. Then, fire up Linuxconf. In order to use Linuxconf to configure a PPP connection, you need to be logged in as the root user. You'll find the many ways to locate Linuxconf in either KDE or GNOME by using Table 11.1.

If you forgot to log into the root account, open an X terminal window in GNOME and, at the prompt, type **su** and press Enter. You'll be asked for a password. KDE opens a dialog box that asks you for the root password when you attempt to open Linuxconf. If you can supply the root password, you'll be logged in as a superuser with root privileges.

TABLE 11.1 Opening Linuxconf

From This Starting Point	Open Linuxconf By
KDE Desktop	Clicking the DrakConf icon and selecting Linuxconf
GNOME Main Menu	Navigating to System, LinuxConf
X terminal window	Typing **linuxconf** and pressing Enter

The main Linuxconf window contains two tabs—the Config tab and the Control tab. On the Config tab, click Networking to display the Network Configurator (the Client tasks tab should be displayed), shown in Figure 11.1.

Find Internet access configuration   Supply IP address   Create PPP connection

FIGURE 11.1

Linuxconf performs a number of system administration and configuration tasks.

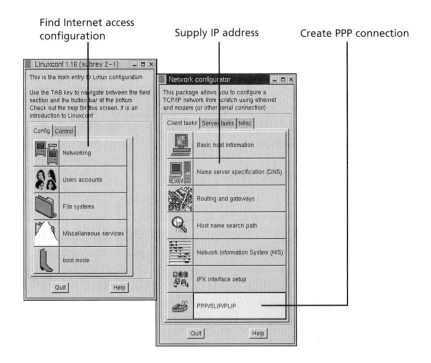

Setting up a PPP connection using the Network Configurator is a two-step process. You'll first need to tell Linuxconf how you connect to the Internet; that is, phone number, username and password, and modem. This is found by clicking the PPP/SLIP/PLIP button. Then, you'll need to supply the name server information supplied by your Internet service provider by clicking the Name server specification (DNS) button. Just follow the instructions in each of the windows, or skate along with the steps in the next lesson.

Lesson 11.1: Setting Up an Internet Connection with Linuxconf

Before you begin this lesson, make sure you have all the information supplied by your ISP, your modem is connected to the computer, and the power is turned on. Then, follow these steps:

1. Click the PPP/SLIP/PLIP button at the bottom of the Client tasks tab on the Network configurator window. This opens the PPP/SLIP/PLIP Configurations dialog box.

2. Click the Add button to open the Type of Interface dialog box.

3. Select the PPP option and click Accept. The PPP interface panel for the connection you are creating will appear (see Figure 11.2).

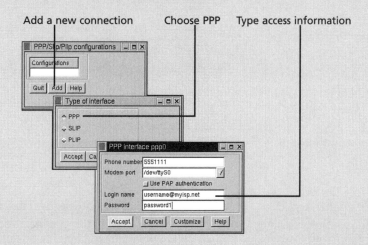

FIGURE 11.2
Type the access information required by your ISP.

4. Type the telephone number you use to connect to your ISP in the Phone number text box.

> When entering a phone number, just type the numbers. Don't use any spaces, dashes, or parentheses. If you need to dial a number to get an outside line, put that number in front of the ISP's telephone number.

5. Select your modem port from the Modem port list box.

6. Select the Use PAP authentication option unless your ISP requires something different.

7. Fill in your login name (usually your email address) and the password you use to log in to your account.

8. Click the Accept button. The ppp0 connection you just configured will appear in the PPP/SLIP/PLIP Configurations dialog panel.

9. Click the ppp0 listing in the PPP/SLIP/PLIP Configurations panel to display the PPP interface dialog box for ppp0, as shown in Figure 11.3.

FIGURE 11.3
Configure modem hardware for your Internet connection.

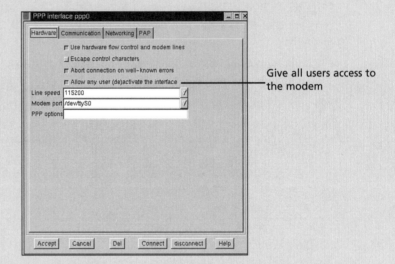

Give all users access to the modem

10. On the Hardware tab, make sure that Use hardware flow control and modem lines is selected along with the Abort connection on well-known errors option.

11. Make sure that the Allow any user to (de)activate the interface option is selected. This way, all users can connect to the Internet through their own user accounts.

> Test the connection. When you click the Connect button, Linuxconf will attempt to detect the modem and then dial up the ISP.

12. Click the Accept button. The PPP Interface panel will close and you will be left with the PPP/SLIP/PLIP Configurations dialog box.

13. Click the Quit button to close the dialog box. Now you are ready to configure the server connection.

14. On the Network Configurator panel, click Name server specification (DNS). The Resolver Configuration panel will appear, as shown in Figure 11.4.

15. On the line for nameserver 1, type the primary DNS number that your ISP gave you. Type the secondary DNS number, if you have one, on the line for nameserver 2.

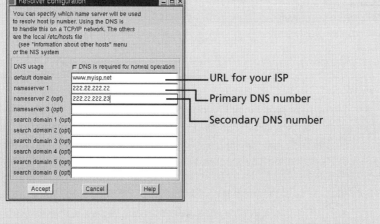

FIGURE 11.4
Enter the IP addresses used by your ISP.

URL for your ISP
Primary DNS number
Secondary DNS number

16. Click Accept. The Resolver configuration panel will disappear.

17. You have now finished with the Network Configurator and Linuxconf. Click Quit at the bottom of each of the windows. The windows will disappear and you are ready to give your connection a try.

Connecting to the Internet with UserNet

Once the root user has created the PPP connection in Linuxconf, each user on the system can use the connection. If you want a quick, no-nonsense method to dial up your ISP, try UserNet. UserNet contains no frills, no fancy timers, nothing. But it sure does make the connection in a hurry and it is so simple. Use Table 11.2 to open UserNet.

TABLE 11.2 Making the Connection to UserNet

To Connect From Here	Try This Path
X terminal window	Type **usernet** and press Enter
AnotherLevel menus	Click on Networking, Usernet

Don't close that terminal. The UserNet interface closes if you close the X terminal window. Instead, minimize the terminal window to get it out of the way. Don't close it until you log off the Internet and close the UserNet window.

UserNet displays all the PPP connections that are configured on your machine and available to the account you are using. The example shown in Figure 11.5 displays a single PPP connection. Other connections would be shown as ppp1, ppp2, and so on, and would be displayed below ppp0.

FIGURE 11.5

When you don't need to worry about keeping track of your Internet time, try UserNet.

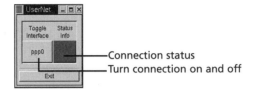

Connection status
Turn connection on and off

To the right of each PPP connection button, you'll see a Status button. When you first open UserNet, the Status button should be red. This means that you are not connected to the Internet, and you cannot pass Go until you click the Toggle interface button for the PPP connection you want to use.

 Turn on the modem. If you are using an external modem, make sure it is turned on and ready before you try to connect.

When you activate the connection, the Status button will turn yellow while the modem is dialing. When the modem has made the connection with your ISP's server, the Status button will turn green. All systems go. When you want to disconnect, click the Toggle interface button for the PPP connection. The Status button will turn red.

 Don't click the Status button when you want to disconnect. Your connection won't disconnect properly.

Now that you have a connection to the Internet, you can skip the next section on using Kppp and get right to the fun stuff, like surfing the Web and downloading cool stuff. Or, if you don't like this method, you can delete the PPP connection in Linuxconf and give the Kppp dialer a try.

Using Kppp

After working with Linuxconf and UserNet, you may find that you want a different approach to configuring an Internet connection. Or, you may not want all user accounts to have access to the same Internet account. Maybe some users don't need Internet access. Then again, maybe you just want a dialer that looks like the dialer found in dear old Windows.

Your alternative is the Kppp dialer. The Kppp dialer is set up individually for each user account. There's no Internet account sharing going on here and you needn't be a root user to make the connection. As an added attraction, the Kppp dialer contains tools that measure the time spent online and amount of data transferred for each session. To begin, you'll need to open the Kppp dialer and you'll find directions in Table 11.3.

TABLE 11.3 Locating the Kppp Dialer

From Here	Take This Route
KDE menu	Go to Internet, Kppp
X terminal window	Type **kppp** and press Enter

When the Kppp dialer opens, you'll see a blank connection box. After you assemble the information needed to make the dial-up connection to your ISP, click the Setup button. This displays the Kppp Configuration dialog box. Your first task is to click the Device tab (shown in Figure 11.6) and tell Kppp where to find your modem. You'll need to select the modem port from the Modem Device drop-down list. You may also want to change the connection speed. If you want to make sure the dialer detects the modem, click the Modem tab and query the modem.

After you have configured the modem, it's time to tell Kppp how to call up your ISP. Click the Accounts tab and then click the New button to open the New Account dialog box—featured in Figure 11.7 displaying the Dial tab.

11

Set up modem   Test access to modem

FIGURE 11.6

Make sure you have selected the right modem device by querying the modem.

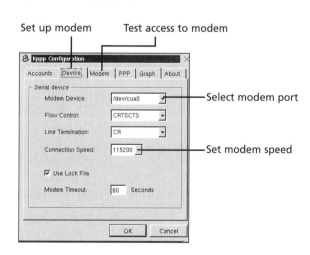

Select modem port

Set modem speed

FIGURE **11.7**

Supply an access phone number and IP addresses for your ISP.

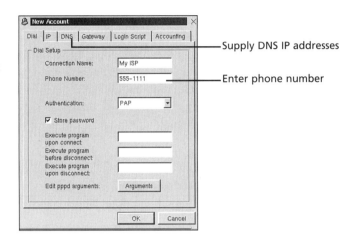

— Supply DNS IP addresses

— Enter phone number

The first thing you'll need to do is name the connection. Use something that will help you remember which Internet account you are using. Then, type the phone number you'll use to access your ISP. Next, click the DNS tab and enter the IP addresses used by your ISP's DNS Server. When you have entered all the information the ISP needs to make the connection, click OK. You'll see the connection name in the Account Setup list on the Kppp Configuration dialog box.

Your dialup connection is almost complete. Click OK on the Kppp Configuration dialog box and you'll see the connection name listed in the Connect to list box of the dialer window (see Figure 11.8). All you need to do is type the username and password needed by your ISP, and then click the Connect button.

FIGURE **11.8**

Type the username and password needed to connect to your ISP and then you'll be ready to hit the Web.

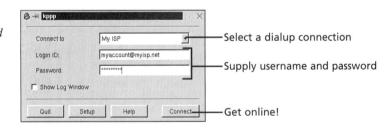

— Select a dialup connection

— Supply username and password

— Get online!

Power on. If you are using an external modem, make sure it is turned on.

Way to go! You're connected! You have your connection established using either UserNet or Kppp as the dialer, and all you need now is some Internet software to surf Web sites and read your email. You may also need a good FTP client. We'll explore gFTP. If you enjoy chatting with others on the Web in real time, check out XChat.

Working on the Web with Netscape Communicator

There are many Web browsers, email utilities, and newsgroup readers packaged with the Linux-Mandrake distribution, and they work with both KDE and GNOME. The most popular of the bunch is Netscape Communicator. Communicator contains a full line of Internet applications, including a Web browser, email client, newsreader, and Web page designer. With the aid of Communicator and a few other Internet applications (such as FTP and IRC chat, which are covered later in this hour), your Internet activities are pretty much covered.

Before you begin looking around the Communicator suite, use your favorite connection method and dial up your ISP.

Exploring Navigator

We'll start the lineup with the Netscape Navigator Web browser. You'll find an icon for Navigator on the KDE and GNOME panels. You'll also find it in the Internet menu in both KDE and GNOME.

You'll notice that Navigator has the same look in Linux as it does in Windows, and it has the same functionality. If you've found a new site to visit, just type the URL address in the Netsite text box and press Enter. The Web page you requested will begin the download process and sooner or later (depending on the amount of graphics and multimedia attached to the page and on your modem speed), you'll get a view of the entire Web page (like the one in Figure 11.9). If you think you want to visit this page again, add it to the Bookmarks list.

When you need to locate information on the Internet, click the Search button. Navigator can help you use a number of search engines and Web databases.

At the bottom of the Navigator window, there's a toolbar that will launch any of the Communicator applications. In fact, you'll find this toolbar at the bottom of all the Communicator applications. When you're done browsing those Web pages and you want to check the mail, click the Email button to launch Messenger.

11

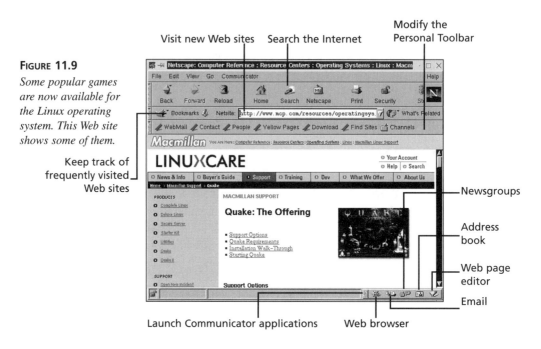

FIGURE **11.9**
*Some popular games
are now available for
the Linux operating
system. This Web site
shows some of them.*

Checking Your Mailbox

The email client used by Communicator is Messenger. Messenger also handles news-groups. With Messenger, you can send and receive email, view attachments in the message area, and create folders in which to sort your mail. You can even send messages that are rich in graphics and HTML formatting. But please conserve the bandwidth.

Keep track of your friends. Use the address book to store email and address information. You can then use the address book to fill in the To field of a new message.

Getting Started with Messenger

When you first open Messenger, you may be told that it cannot access your ISP's mail server. You'll need to set up preferences. So let's get that done and then we'll get on with the program.

Lesson 11.2: Setting Messenger Preferences

Messenger needs to know where to go to check your mail. At the same time, you may want to change a few things about the way Messenger looks. Follow these steps:

1. Click Edit, Preferences to display the Netscape Preferences panel. The Mail & Newsgroups category will be selected.

2. In the main panel of the Mail & Newsgroups category, you can change how Messenger displays messages and how Messenger responds to actions that you perform.

3. Click the Identity option. You'll need to type your name as you want it to appear in the message headers and your email address. This information is displayed to the recipients of your messages.

4. Click the Mail Servers option to display the panel shown in Figure 11.10. Type the name of the outgoing mail server used by your ISP in the Outgoing mail (SMTP) server text box.

Outgoing mail server   Incoming mail server

FIGURE 11.10

Provide Messenger with the names of the servers where it needs to deposit and pick up your mail.

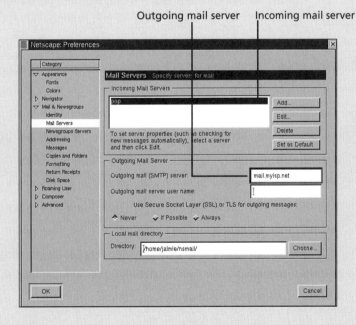

5. To tell Messenger the name of your ISP's incoming mail server, click on POP in the Incoming Mail servers box and then click the Edit Button to display the dialog box seen in Figure 11.11.

Do you lurk the newsgroups? Before you can access the newsgroups, set up a news server from the Newsgroups Servers category.

FIGURE 11.11

Communicator needs to know where to pick up your mail.

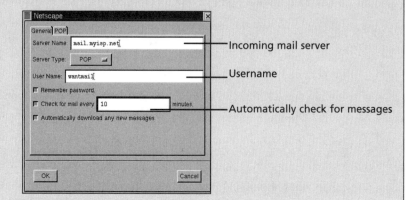

Incoming mail server

Username

Automatically check for messages

6. Type the mail server name your ISP gave you in the Server Name text box.

7. Type the username for your mail account in the User Name text box. Select the Remember Password option if you don't want to have to type your password each time you check for new messages.

8. You may want Messenger to check your mail for you. Let Messenger know how often you want it to check for mail if it is different than every 10 minutes.

9. Click OK to return to the Mail Servers panel. You'll see the incoming mail server listed.

10. Click OK on the Netscape Preferences window to close the panel and apply the new settings. You're ready to get all that mail that's been accumulating in your mailbox.

Checking for New Messages

The first time you click the Get Msg button on the Messenger toolbar, you'll be asked for the password to access your account. After that, you'll see a status dialog box that tells you how many messages are being downloaded and the percentage of download that is complete. When Messenger is done checking your messages, the new messages will appear in the Message List.

Going too fast? You can learn more about the different Communicator programs by looking in the Help menus. Netscape has some very good help documentation.

Creating Web Pages

NEW TERM The best way to share information is through a Web page, or, if you have a lot of information to share, an entire Web site. Netscape Composer is a full-fledged, graphical, what-you-see-is-what-you'll-get-with-the-same-monitor settings (*WYSIWYG+*), HTML editor.

You can insert the usual HTML elements into a Composer page—hyperlinks, images, lines, and tables. Oh yeah, there's the text which is the most important part of any Web page. You can format text in the same way you format text in most word processing programs—font style and size, paragraph alignment and formatting, and colorful text. (Composer even has a rainbow up its sleeve.) And don't forget, use the spell checker before you use Composer to publish your pages to a Web server.

The fastest way to start using Composer is to download a template from the Netscape Web site and edit it so that it contains your text and pictures. And, to tell you the truth, you don't have to use a Netscape template; you can use the information in Lesson 11.3 to copy any Web page you find on the Internet and use it in Composer.

Lesson 11.3: Using Templates to Create Web Pages

Before you attempt this lesson, make sure you are connected to the Internet. Then follow these steps:

1. Click on File, New, Page From Template to display the Netscape Web Page Templates page in Navigator (shown in Figure 11.12). In the middle of the page, you'll see a list of templates.

2. Browse through the list of templates until you find one that closely matches the Web page you'd like to design. To select a template, click the link to display the template in the browser window. If you don't like the template, click the browser's Back button to return to the template list.

3. With the selected template displayed in the browser window, click File, Edit Page. This opens the template in a new Composer window, as shown in Figure 11.13.

11

http://home.netscape.com/browsers/templates/

FIGURE **11.12**

Choose a Web page template that fits your needs and style.

Choose from the available templates

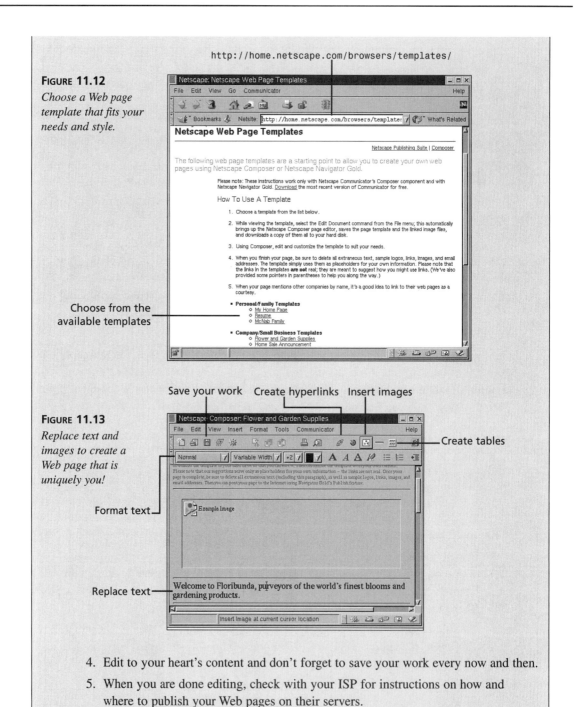

Save your work   Create hyperlinks   Insert images

FIGURE **11.13**

Replace text and images to create a Web page that is uniquely you!

Create tables

Format text

Replace text

4. Edit to your heart's content and don't forget to save your work every now and then.

5. When you are done editing, check with your ISP for instructions on how and where to publish your Web pages on their servers.

Transferring Files with gFTP

Who says Linux applications aren't slick? If you need a utility to transfer files across the Internet, try gFTP. FTP, or File Transfer Protocol, is one of the oldest of the Internet utilities and it is still the best method for file transfer. gFTP can get you access to any FTP site whether you need an anonymous login, or if a password is required. You'll also find one of your favorite browser features—the capability to keep a list of FTP sites that you visit frequently. See Table 11.4 for the directions to gFTP.

TABLE 11.4   Finding gFTP

From This Direction	Follow This Course
GNOME Main Menu	Slide on over to Internet, gftp
X terminal window	Type **gftp** and press Enter

In order to use gFTP for anonymous logins, you'll need to tell the program your email address. Click FTP, Options to open the Options dialog box. In the General tab, type your email address in the first field. You can change any other options to your choosing. Read through the list. Click OK when you're done.

Now it's time to find an FTP site, log in, and look around. The example in Figure 11.14 shows an anonymous login. Type the FTP address in the Host text box and press Enter.

11

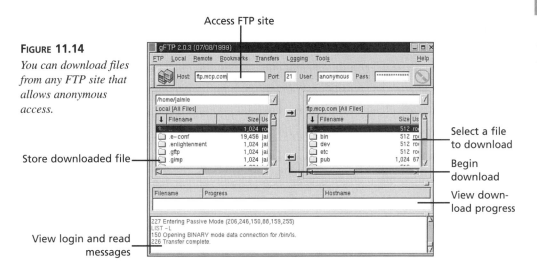

FIGURE 11.14
You can download files from any FTP site that allows anonymous access.

Access FTP site

Store downloaded file

View login and read messages

Select a file to download

Begin download

View download progress

For FTP sites that you visit on a regular basis, you'll want to keep them in the Bookmark list. If you click on the Bookmarks menu, you'll notice a list of FTP sites has been supplied for you. Just click on one of these bookmarks and the FTP site will be accessed and the remote directory window will display all of the folders at that site. You can play with the bookmarks included with gFTP and have plenty to occupy yourself for a while.

To navigate through the remote site, first look for a Readme file in the main directory. Double-click on this file to open a window from which you can read the file. This file contains the most up-to-date advice on how to use the resources contained in the directory. To open folders, double-click on them.

To download files, select the folder in your user directory in which you want to save the file, select the file you want to download, and click the download button (it's the left pointing arrow). Now, sit back, relax, and watch the download progress. And, if something happens to your connection, gFTP will remember where it left off and resume the download. No more lost download time.

Chatting with Your Friends in XChat

Chat, or Internet Relay Chat (IRC), is a popular Internet pastime. Through the offices of various chat servers, it is possible to have real-time conversations with people by typing messages and having the recipient answer you by typing a response. These chat rooms are organized so that groups of people may converse, or private accommodations can be made for private conversations. The Internet Relay Chat program we examine is the XChat program. To launch the XChat program, go to Table 11.5.

TABLE 11.5 Going for a Chat with the Gang

Start Here	And Follow This
GNOME Main Menu	Select, Internet, xchat IRC client
X terminal window	Type **xchat** and press Enter

Two windows will open on your desktop—the XChat: Server List and the terminal window. In the Server List window, you'll need to fill in the information requested in the User info section. You can use an anonymous name if you want. The terminal window is where you will you type your messages and read the responses.

When you're ready to check out a chat room, browse through the list of servers and their available chat rooms in the Server List (see Figure 11.15). To see the chat rooms, click the plus sign next to the server name.

FIGURE 11.15

Select from a number of pre-selected chat servers.

Provide an identity   View list of servers

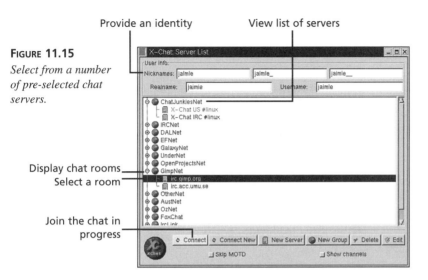

Display chat rooms
Select a room

Join the chat in
progress

After you've looked through the list, click on the chat room you want to enter and then click the Connect button. The Server list window will disappear and the welcome message and details about the server you chose will appear in the XChat window, like the one shown in Figure 11.16.

11

Read conversation thread

FIGURE 11.16

Read the discussion, or be brave and join in.

Type your response

Post your response

Type a nice greeting and someone on the channel will say hello. After that, it's just like talking to someone on the bus.

Summary

In this hour, you configured an Internet connection using a combination of LinuxConf and UserNet, or using the KPPP dialer. You learned how to get around the Internet with the Netscape Communicator suite of Internet applications. You were also introduced to two other tools to enhance your Web experience—XChat and gFTP. There are other Internet tools and utilities that we did not mention here, and we encourage you to try out others.

Q&A

Q My Internet connection doesn't seem to be working like it normally has in the past. I'd like to know if the problem is between my computer and my ISP's servers. What can I do?

A You can use the `ping` command to verify that you are using the correct IP address for your ISP, the time it takes for the ISP's servers to respond to your requests, and if any data is lost in transmission. When you are connected to your ISP, type the following command

```
ping -c 5 myisp.net
```

The `-c 5` option tells the `ping` command to send data packets to your ISP's server for five thousandths of a second. It then reports back to you how long it takes the server to transmit the packet back to your computer. You can change the amount of time if you want. You'll also want to use the domain name of your ISP in place of `myisp.net`. You can also use this command to test the connection between your computer and other servers on the Internet.

Q But, maybe I don't want to use the command line to find out about response times. And, maybe I'd like to know more information about what's happening on the Internet. Do you have any more suggestions?

A Today's your lucky day. KDE contains a set of network utilities. You'll find them in the KDE menu under Internet, Network utilities. From a single interface, you'll find ping, traceroute, host resolution, and finger utilities.

If all you want is a finger utility, there's one of those in KDE also. It's also in the Internet menu, but under User information.

Workshop

Hopefully you had some fun during the past hour playing on the Web. Well, not to burst your bubble, although it seems we do this to you every hour, it's time to test your Web savvy.

Quiz

1. What is the most efficient way to set up an Internet connection that can be used by all user accounts?

2. How do you set up an Internet connection that is used only by the user who set up the connection? That is, it is not available to other users on the system.

3. What are the different Internet activities that you can perform with Netscape Communicator?

4. What is the fastest way to download files off the Internet?

Exercises

1. Plan a Net-get-together with friends and family who may live in other parts of the country, or on the other side of the globe. You can reserve a private room at an IRC server and give everyone a secret pass to get in the door. Party hearty!

2. There's more help than just the man pages and the help files found in the many applications packaged with Linux-Mandrake. You can download help documentation from a number of FTP sites. You may want to learn more about some of the applications covered in this book by visiting any of a number of FTP sites. Only watch out, you may find volumes of information. For example, navigate to `ftp.gimp.org` and download the Gimp Manual. It's 14MB, but loaded with good advice and colorful pictures. Look around and see how much help you can find.

11

Hour 12

Document Processing with KLyX

There are a variety of text editors and word processors installed with Linux-Mandrake. One of the word processors that you may stumble across while browsing through the KDE and GNOME menus, or while looking at the list of packages on the CD-ROM with KPackage or Gnome RPM, is KLyX. KLyX works very well for short documents such as memos and letters. It can also accommodate larger documents and can include such features as page numbers, a table of contents, cross references, pictures, and tables.

You may think that KLyX works just like other word processing programs. Well, KLyX is a little different. To put it simply, KLyX acts more like a professional typesetting system. It takes care of every aspect of producing a document. KLyX uses document classes and templates as the starting point for your letters, reports, and books. Each document class and template contains a list of styles. These styles control how the document looks and keeps track of page, chapter, and section numbering.

In this hour, you use KLyX to create a document that contains text, lists, tables, and graphic images. You also learn how to make your documents look better by

- Creating documents from templates and formatting text
- Using a variety of list styles
- Organizing information with tables
- Inserting graphic images that reinforce the document's message

Creating a New Document

KLyX is one of the applications that you may find listed in the KDE menus. Most likely it will be in the Applications menu. If you can't find it, try typing `klyx` in an X terminal window. And, if that doesn't work, you may need to install KLyX on your system. The first time you use KLyX, you'll see the Question dialog box. KLyX needs to create a directory file in which to store changes that you make to the program's configuration. Click Yes to create the directory and to display KLyX on your screen.

You'll notice that the KLyX window looks very much like other word processing programs. There's an assortment of menus, buttons, and other screen elements. And there's the familiar work area where you enter and format text, tables, and images.

Before you begin using KLyX, take a look at Figure 12.1 and familiarize yourself with the different screen elements.

FIGURE 12.1

KLyX contains features similar to popular word processing programs.

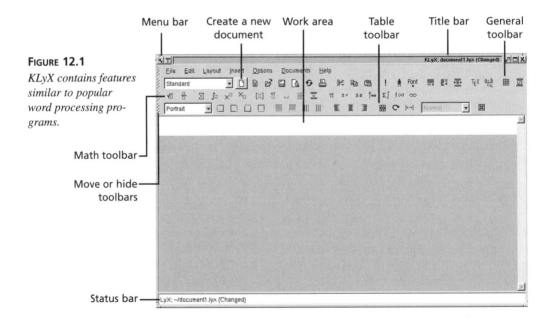

Menu bar   Create a new   Work area   Table   Title bar   General
           document   toolbar   toolbar

Math toolbar

Move or hide toolbars

Status bar

- The Title bar displays the name of the document and contains the window controls that minimize, maximize, and close the window.

- The Menu bar contains all the commands that the program can execute. You may find that the menu commands will work when sometimes a toolbar button won't.

- The General toolbar contains buttons that execute file commands (such as open, save, preview, and print), move text around in a document (cut, copy, and paste), format text and paragraphs, and insert images and tables.

> If you would rather work with just the menus or if you want more room for the work area, you can hide and move the menus and toolbars. Drag the bar at the left of the menu bar or toolbar to move it to another area on the screen. Click the bar to hide the menus and toolbars.
>
> To determine which toolbars appear when you open the KLyX program, select Options, Screen Options, and click the Toolbars tab on the dialog box that opens. If you want a toolbar to appear only when you are using that feature, select the Automatic option.

- The Math toolbar allows you to easily add math equations to a document.

- The Tables toolbar creates and formats tables. Tables can contain any number of rows and columns, and you can change the size of the table as needed. To make tables more attractive or to make information stand out, you can add borders to the table and format the table text.

- The work area is where you type text and insert other items such as tables and images.

- Along the bottom is the *minibuffer*, or status bar, which displays the document on which you are working and the directory path to that document, whether the documented is read-only or can be edited, and if there are any unsaved changes to the document.

12

> If you want to learn more about KLyX, look in the Help menu and read the Introduction, Tutorial, and User's Guide.

Now that you've looked KLyX over, it's time to get started on a document. You may be tempted to just start typing text, but before you begin, consider these different routes that you can take to get started.

- If you just want to begin typing, you can use the default document class and associated styles by clicking on the New button on the General toolbar. This displays the Open dialog box where you select a directory in which you want to store the new file and type a name for the new file.

- The default page layout can be changed if the majority of your documents will look similar. You can change the paper orientation, page margins, default document class, fonts, paragraph spacing, and columns used for each new document you create.

- There are several pre-designed templates that are a good starting point if you create letters, short articles, or book manuscripts. Click the New From Template button. If one of these templates does not exactly suit your needs, modify the template and save it under a different name.

Lesson 12.1: Setting the Default Document Layout

If the majority of the documents you create use the same basic layout, you can change the default page layout features. This means that you don't have to make layout changes each time you start a new document. Once the default document layout is saved, each time you click the New button, your preferred layout is used. To change the default document settings, follow these steps:

1. Click the New button to create a blank page. This displays an Open dialog box. Navigate to the directory in which you want to save the file and type a filename in the Location text box. Then click OK to display a blank document window.

2. Click Layout, Document to display the Document Layout dialog box as shown in Figure 12.2.

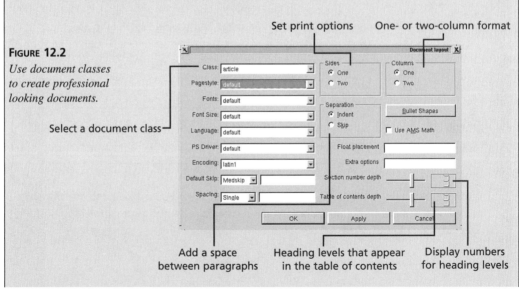

FIGURE 12.2

Use document classes to create professional looking documents.

Set print options   One- or two-column format

Select a document class

Add a space
between paragraphs

Heading levels that appear
in the table of contents

Display numbers
for heading levels

3. Select a document class from the Class drop-down list. You may find these document classes helpful:

   • Article is used for short documents that require section headings. It does not use a header and prints on one side of the page.

   • Book creates large documents that are organized into parts, which are further divided into chapters, and so on. This class automatically adds a header to the document pages and is set up to print on two sides of the paper.

   • Letter is for short documents that require address information or a place for letterhead, recipient information, and a closing. It does not use any section or chapter headings.

   • Report is for documents longer than an article or a letter, but shorter than a book. It uses chapter headings, prints on one side of the page, and does not use a header.

   • Slides can be used to generate slides or overhead transparencies that convey additional information or stress important points during a presentation or speech.

When using the document classes, it might be wise to refrain from changing the other options in the Document Layout dialog box until after you have a chance to see how the default layout looks on the printed page.

4. Documents can be printed on either one side of the paper or on both sides. KLyX will take care of the special formatting required if the document will be printed on both sides of the page (such as in a book). The Two sides option prints pages that leave extra space in the margin to allow for binding the document. This option also uses a different page header format for odd and even numbered pages.

5. Documents can be printed with one line going across the entire page, or in columns. To select the number of columns that appear on the printed page, look in the Columns section. Click the One option button for one continuous row of text. Click the Two option button to display two columns of text across the page.

6. Click OK when you have finished making your changes.

7. Click Layout, Paper to display the Configure Paper Format dialog box shown in Figure 12.3.

12

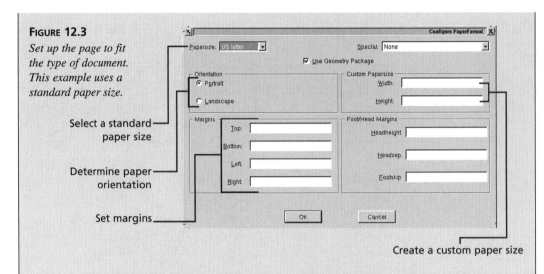

FIGURE 12.3

Set up the page to fit the type of document. This example uses a standard paper size.

Select a standard paper size

Determine paper orientation

Set margins

Create a custom paper size

8. If you will be using a standard paper size, select the size from the Papersize drop-down list.

9. For the selected paper size, decide on a paper orientation:

   • Use the Portrait option if you want the text to run along the short side of the paper. This is how you normally print letters and reports.

   • Use the Landscape option if you want the text to run along the long side of the paper. This works well for long tables and presentations.

10. When you are satisfied with the page setup, click OK.

11. To create the new default page layout, click Layout, Save layout as default. You are asked if you want to save the settings you just changed as the new default. Click Yes. Each time you create a new document, KLyX now uses the document layout settings that you specified.

Entering Text

Now that the page is set up, it's time to start entering text. You'll notice that the cursor is at the upper-left corner of the work area. As you begin typing, the cursor stays one step ahead of the text. If you make a mistake, press the backspace key. The cursor will move backward and the last character you typed will disappear.

To delete an entire word, press Ctrl+Delete or Ctrl+backspace. The text that is deleted is placed onto the clipboard. These key combinations work the same as the Cut button.

KLyX wraps text as you type, so that when you reach the right margin, the cursor automatically moves to the next line. Notice that there is no horizontal scrollbar at the bottom of the KLyX window. KLyX does not exactly display the document on your screen as it will appear when printed. KLyX will take care of the proper text width later. For now, you can read each paragraph without scrolling the window contents back and forth.

To see what the document will look like when printed, click the Preview button or select File, Preview, View DVI.

When you get to the end of a paragraph, press the Enter key. You press Enter only once at the end of each paragraph. Pressing Enter twice does not add any extra space between the paragraphs. Spacing between paragraphs is accomplished with formatting styles. If you want to move around in the document, just click the place where you want the cursor.

You can reverse any changes you make to a document by selecting Edit, Undo. KLyX contains an unlimited number of undos.

Here are a few points you'll want to remember when typing in the KLyX window:

- Press Enter only once at the end of each paragraph. KLyX adds space between paragraphs according to the style that is applied to the paragraph.
- Use only one space at the end of sentences. Because KLyX uses proportional spacing for fonts, the space between words and sentences can vary depending on the number of characters that need to appear on a line. The space between words is always smaller than the space at the end of a sentence.

A good rule of thumb is to save your document and save it often. You don't want to lose any of your hard work, so click the Save button often as you work.

You may find that all your projects don't use the same document class. If you need to create a document that does not use your default document layout settings, you can easily select a different document class (by selecting Layout, Document) and then change the settings for the new document, if needed.

12

Lesson 12.2: Creating a New Document from a Template

KLyX supplies a number of templates that help make the job of document layout a bit easier. Each of these templates is used for a different type of document. If you send a number of letters to clients or friends, you may want to try the letter template. There is a book template for creating longer works that require chapters, sections, cross references, and a table of contents. If you give presentations, try the slides template.

When you create a document from a template, you'll need to specify a directory in which to store the file and a filename before you can select a template. Once the document is created, all you need to do to save your changes is click the Save Changes button.

1. Click File, New from template to display the Open dialog box.
2. Double-click the subdirectory in your home directory in which you want to store the file.
3. Click in the Location text box, type a name for the file, and click OK. The Open dialog box for the templates directory appears, as shown in Figure 12.4.

FIGURE **12.4**
Select a template for the new document.

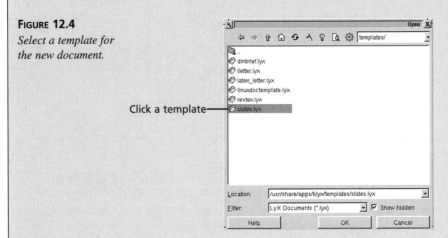

Click a template

4. Select a template. You may find the following templates helpful:

   • To create a standard business letter, use the `latex_letter.lyx` template.
   • There is a template that you can use if you want to volunteer your writing talents and write a user manual or HOWTO for the Linux Documentation Project (named `linuxdoctemplate.lyx`). You'll find that most of the application help files in the Linux-Mandrake distribution (and all Linux distributions) use this template. This template also works well as a starting point for a book layout.

- If you are planning a presentation and want to use slides or overhead transparencies, use the slides.lyx template.

5. Click OK. A new document template with placeholders for documents elements (an example of the slide template is shown in Figure 12.5) appears in the KLyX window.

FIGURE 12.5

Use templates for a quick start to designing documents.

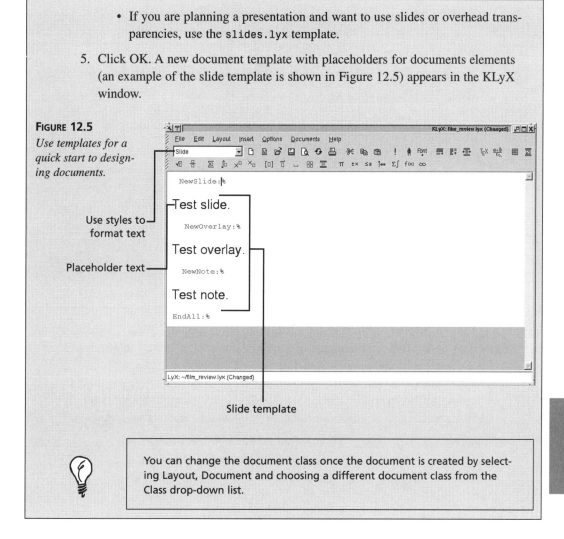

Use styles to format text

Placeholder text

Slide template

> You can change the document class once the document is created by selecting Layout, Document and choosing a different document class from the Class drop-down list.

12

Opening and Closing Documents

You may now have several documents open in the KLyX window. You may want to switch back and forth between documents, or you may want to close a document (and maybe the KLyX program) before you leave the computer. You can always open files again when you return. You can perform these tasks from the menus:

- When several documents are open at one time, switch between documents using the Documents menu. Each open document is listed in the menu; simply click the document you want to view.

- Save the file under a different name with File, Save as. Not only can you make a copy of the file under a different name, but you can also place this new file in a different directory.
- Select File, Close to close the document that appears in the KLyX window.
- Select File, Exit to close KLyX and any open documents.

> When you close KLyX, you are warned if there are any open documents that contain changes that have not been saved.

When you want to open a file that you've saved in your home directory, click the Open button. You'll see the same Open dialog box that you saw in Lesson 12.2. To open a file, display the directory in which the file is located and double-click the filename. The file will open in a separate window. Now you're ready to make some changes to the document you started.

Editing a Document

After you've roughed out the first draft of your document, it's time to go back and do some editing. You'll find places where you need to add some text. That's easy, not the part about writing the text, but how you add it. Just click the place where you want to add the text and begin typing. It's up to you to think of the words. Other text-editing commands require that you first select the text with which you want to work.

Before you can copy a block of text or move it to a different place in the document, it must be selected. To select text, click and hold at the beginning of the text and drag the mouse pointer until you reach the end of the text. You'll notice that the text is highlighted.

You can bypass the mouse by using the arrow keys. Position the cursor at the beginning of the text, and then press and hold the Shift key while using the arrow keys to move the cursor to the end of the text.

Once the text is selected, you can delete the entire block of text, move it to another place in the document, or make a copy of the text and paste the copy elsewhere. Use the Cut, Copy, and Paste toolbar buttons to edit the text.

> If you've added something to the document that you don't like, and don't know how to get rid of it, go back to the last saved copy of the document and try again. Select File, Revert To Saved to undo your changes.

Lesson 12.3: Rearranging the Document

In this lesson, you select existing text in your document and move it to another place in the document. If you're like most people, you do a lot of cutting and pasting when trying to organize your thoughts on paper. Try these steps:

1. Select the text that you want to move.
2. Click the Cut button. The selected text disappears from the screen but is retained on the clipboard.

 You can move a copy of the text and leave the selected text in place by clicking the Copy button.

3. Move the cursor to where you want to paste the text.
4. Click the Paste button. The selected text reappears in the new location. If you want to copy this text to another location, place the cursor at the new location and click the Paste button again. You can do this until other text is pasted to the clipboard.

Formatting the Document

After you've cleaned up the document and made your words sound good, it's time to add some formatting to make your words look good. You have several options for changing how text appears on the page. When you want to change the appearance of a single word or a short line of text, use character formatting. When you want to change the look of an entire paragraph, use paragraph formatting. To give your document a uniform look and be able to control formatting changes, use styles, which are discussed next.

12

Using Styles to Format Paragraphs

NEW TERM Your first step to making the document look good is to change the formatting of an entire paragraph with the Paragraph Environment list found on the toolbar. A *paragraph environment* is often referred to as a *style* in other word processing programs. A paragraph environment is a collection of formatting attributes that can be applied to a paragraph by selecting the paragraph and then selecting the style from the Paragraph Environment list.

Styles come in handy because you can easily change the formatting of paragraphs. Styles are also used to create different levels of text in a document such as headings and table of contents entries. There are a number of styles that are ready for use in KLyX. To apply a paragraph environment to a paragraph, place the cursor in the paragraph, open the Paragraph Environment list, and click a style. Watch how the paragraph looks different on your screen.

Changing the Appearance of Paragraphs

While you're typing along and pounding out those paragraphs, notice how the paragraphs are formatted. The first paragraph on the page is not indented. But each paragraph that follows is indented. Also notice that there is no extra space between the paragraphs. If you would rather not have indented paragraphs, you can change the default format. To change to a paragraph format that places an extra space between paragraphs and does not indent them, click Layout, Document to display the Document Layout dialog box (shown in Figure 12.2) and select the Skip option in the Separation section.

If you need to change other paragraph attributes such as spacing around paragraphs, spacing between lines inside the paragraph, hanging indents, or borders, you need to make these changes from the Paragraph dialog box. To get there, select the paragraph you want to format and then click Layout, Paragraph.

One way to set a paragraph apart from other paragraphs is with the use of *margin notes*. Margin notes are similar to footnotes. These additional tidbits of information appear next to the paragraph, instead at the bottom of the page or at the end of the book.

To create a margin note, place the cursor at the end of the paragraph to which the note is associated, and click the Insert Margin Note button (or Insert, Margin Note from the menu).

Lesson 12.4: Customizing a Single Paragraph

There may be times when you need one paragraph in the document to look different from other paragraphs. You may want to change a left-justified paragraph to a paragraph that is centered on the page. Some paragraphs may require more space above and below the paragraph. Other paragraphs can require a special font to emphasize the paragraph. To make paragraphs stand out even more, draw a border around the entire paragraph, or maybe just a line over the top will do. In this lesson, you change the look of a single paragraph:

1. Select the paragraph that you want to format. You do not need to highlight the entire paragraph, you can just place the cursor in the paragraph.

2. Click Layout, Paragraph to open the Paragraph Environment dialog box shown in Figure 12.6.

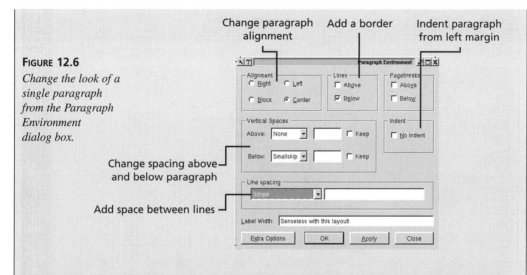

FIGURE 12.6

Change the look of a single paragraph from the Paragraph Environment dialog box.

Change paragraph alignment

Add a border

Indent paragraph from left margin

Change spacing above and below paragraph

Add space between lines

3. Change the paragraph alignment by clicking the appropriate Alignment button.

4. If you want to add space above or below the paragraph, select the spacing from the Above and Below lists boxes in the Vertical Spaces section.

5. To move the first line of the paragraph to the right and away from the left margin, make sure that the No indent checkbox is blank.

6. To change the spacing of the lines within the paragraph, select the appropriate option from the Line Spacing drop-down list.

7. Borders around a paragraph can be used to set off text such as notes or sidebars. You can place a line above the paragraph, a line below the paragraph, or lines both above and below the paragraph. Place a checkmark in the Above and Below checkboxes in the Lines section to add a line above and below the paragraph.

8. When you have finished making your changes, click OK to return to the document. You'll see the result of your changes.

12

Applying Character Formatting

There are several character formatting attributes that you can apply to text. Font size can be changed to show the level of importance of the text. To add emphasis, use bold characters or italics. Underlining can also make text stand out. You can also use two different fonts to show a difference between titles and the body of the text.

To apply character formats to text with the click of the mouse, select the text and then click Layout, Character to open the Character Style dialog box shown in Figure 12.7.

Select font   Normal or bold   Italics

FIGURE 12.7
Make words and phrases stand out by using a font that looks different from the surrounding text.

Noun Style or underline

Color

Font size

The Character Style dialog box provides a quick way to change the look of text. Once you have made your selections, click the Apply button. You'll see the changes made to the text and the Character Style dialog box will remain open. You can format another block of text using the same settings by selecting the text and clicking the Apply button.

> Format text quickly with the Emphasize Style, Noun Style, and Bold Style commands found in the Layout menu.

Creating Lists

When information needs to be ordered, a list can come in quite handy. Lists are great for organizing tasks that need to be done. A list can come in the form of an agenda that is distributed before a meeting. Lists are also found in procedure manuals that outline the steps required to perform a given task. You can create four types of simple lists in KLyX:

- A bulleted list is simply a group of unordered items. KLyX uses the Itemize paragraph environment to format bulleted list items.

- A numbered list consists of items that must be in a particular order, such as steps required to perform a task. The Enumerate style automatically numbers each item in the list. If an item is moved, the numbers in the list are automatically adjusted.

- A definition list contains a series of terms and their corresponding definition and uses the List style. This style puts space between the term and the definition.
- A description list is a series of short paragraphs where the first line of each item is positioned along the left margin and each additional line is indented. This type of list uses the Description style.

Figure 12.8 shows an example of each of the four types of lists.

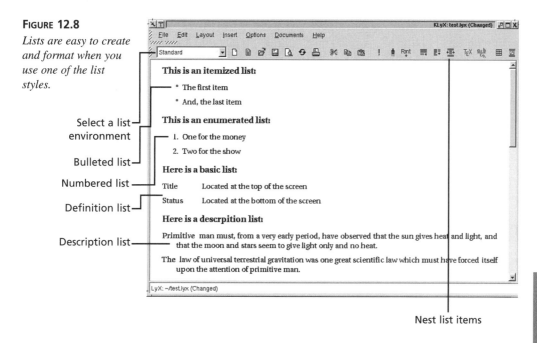

FIGURE 12.8
Lists are easy to create and format when you use one of the list styles.

Select a list environment

Bulleted list

Numbered list

Definition list

Description list

Nest list items

To nest items in the list, select the items to be nested and click the Change Environment Depth button.

Using Headers and Footers

NEW TERM   One way to keep long documents in order is by using *headers* and *footers*. Headers and footers display the same information on each page of the document. Headers appear at the top of the page and footers appear at the bottom. Both are located between the margin and the edge of the page.

12

If you are using one of the document templates, the template may or may not already contain a preformatted header. You can use this default header, or you can change to one of the other header formats provided by KLyX.

To change to a different heading style, open the Layout menu and select Document. The Document Layout dialog box contains several heading styles in the Pagestyle drop-down list (see Figure 12.9).

Lesson 12.5: Numbering Pages

The easiest way to keep a long document in order is to use automatic page numbering in either the header or the footer of a document. In this lesson, you create a header for your document that not only contains a page number, but also other information about the document:

1. Click Layout, Document. The Document Layout dialog box shown in Figure 12.9 appears.

FIGURE 12.9

Using page numbers in headers or footers helps keep printed pages in order.

Select header style

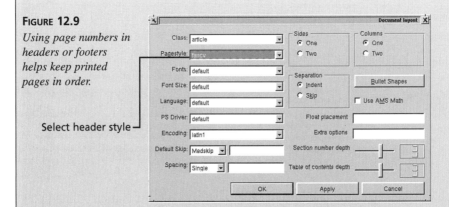

2. From the Pagestyle drop-down list, select an option for how you want the headings and page numbers to display on each page. There are five options:
   - *Default* uses the heading and page number style defined by the document class or template.
   - *Empty* does not use headings or page numbers on the pages of your document.
   - *Plain* contains only page numbers.
   - *Headings* displays page numbers along with either the chapter title and number, or the section title and corresponding number.
   - *Fancy* allows you to create your own headers and footers for a document.

To change the spacing around the header, click Layout, Paper and change the spacing in the Foot/Head Margins section of the dialog box.

3. When you have selected a header style, click OK. You are returned to your document. You'll see those headers when you send the document to the printer.

Design Elements for Your Documents

For some fun and color, you can add graphical images to your documents. KLyX can import any image that you can convert into PostScript (EPS) files (either the .eps or .ps file formats). You can use EPS files in two ways:

- Encapsulated Postscript files appear on a line, separate from any text. The image is treated as a separate paragraph with text appearing only above and below the image. No text will appear to the right or left of the image.

- Inlined EPS files act like just another word in the sentence. You can insert an inlined EPS file anywhere in a paragraph and the text will flow over, under, and around each side of the image.

Turn to Chapter 22, "Graphics Viewers and Utilities," to find a few programs that can convert graphics files into PostScript files. Hint: Try XFig, The Gimp, or Electric Eyes.

12

Along with colorful graphics, you can create tables to organize information and make it stand out from the rest of the text. Another use for tables is during page layout. When you want to arrange text and images, or just columns of text, tables make this task easy.

Looking Good with Graphics

Graphics are a good way to enhance your document's message. Graphics should enhance your text, not be a distraction. A good use of an image is a logo on a letter or a picture of something mentioned in the text.

It's easy to add an image; just select the place in the document where you want to insert the picture and then click the Insert Figure button on the toolbar. This button adds a picture placeholder to the document. Once the picture placeholder is in the document, you can resize it by clicking the image to display the Edit Figure dialog box. Use the Width and Height options to make the image larger or smaller. You can also change the position on the page by changing the paragraph environment.

To change the picture alignment, place the cursor on the same line as the image and click Layout, Paragraph. Change the Alignment options in the Paragraph Environment dialog box.

Lesson 12.6: Adding an Encapsulated Postscript Image

Before you try to add pictures or other graphic images to your document, convert the files to PostScript format. Once this is done, your next step is to create a placeholder for the image and then decide where on the page the image will appear.

To insert an image, follow these steps:

1. Click where you want to insert the image and select Insert, Figure from the menu. You'll be presented with the Insert Figure dialog box.

2. Click OK to select the default option of Encapsulated Postscript and to display a placeholder in the document.

3. Right-click the figure placeholder and select Edit. You'll be presented with the Edit Figure dialog box (shown in Figure 12.10).

FIGURE 12.10

Determine how the picture should appear on the page from the Edit Figure dialog box.

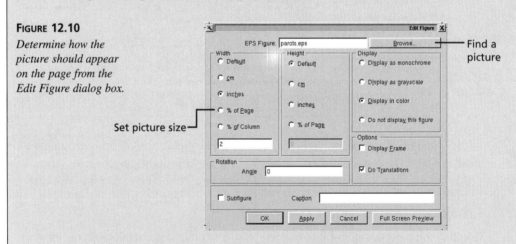

Find a picture

Set picture size

4. Click the Browse button to locate the EPS image file.

5. Set the height and width for the image as it should appear in the printed document. Consider these options:

   • Default inserts the image at its original file size.

   • Use inches or cm (centimeters) to set the size at which the image will appear on the page. Type the height or width in the text box at the bottom of the list of options.

- To retain the image aspect ratio, set the width in inches, cm, or percent of the page. Then, select the Default option button for the height.

6. If you want to add some descriptive text about the picture, type it in the Caption text box.

Hide images on your screen if you want the document to display faster by selecting the "Do not display this figure" option.

Adding Tables to a Document

A *table* is a collection of cells arranged by rows and columns. Each cell in a table can contain text or graphics. The table can be used to organize related information or used as a page layout tool.

To start a table, click the place in the document where you want to insert the table and select Insert, Table. You'll see the Insert Table dialog box. Select the number of rows and columns that you want the table to contain. You don't need to worry about the width of individual cells at this point. KLyX will automatically format the width of the table cells to fit the information you add to each cell. Click OK when you're finished. Your table is in place; now it's time to set it.

Note that the top row of cells is separate from the rest of the table. This row of cells is normally used to display a descriptive label for each column.

12

It's easy to insert text into a table cell. Just click in the cell and begin typing. Adding graphic images is just as easy—click in the cell and insert the image. You can even resize a graphic once it is inside a cell. In fact, just about everything that you can do with text and graphics in your document can be done in a table.

Lesson 12.7: Creating a Table

Try your hand at creating a table to use as a page design and layout tool. Here are the steps you need to go through to create a table:

1. Create the table. Decide on the number of rows and columns that you need. You can add rows and columns later by using the Add Row and Add Column buttons on the Tables toolbar.

Rows are added below the row in which the cursor is placed and columns are added to the right of the cursor.

2. Enter text in each of the cells. While you're at it, format the text as well. You can use many of the character and paragraph formatting styles that you've seen earlier in this chapter.

3. Insert any graphic images that you want to use into the table and resize the images as needed.

4. If you need to change the width of any columns, click in the column that you want to adjust and click the Width of Column button on the Tables toolbar. This button displays a dialog box where you enter the width of the column. The column is resized and the other columns retain their original size.

5. Now it's time to decide whether you want a border around the outside edge of the table. You also can add or remove lines between the cells at this time.

6. To merge two or more cells, select the cells to be merged and click the Multicolumn button on the Tables toolbar.

7. To align the text within a cell, place the cursor in the cell and click either the Align Left, Align Center, or Align Right button on the Tables toolbar.

8. Make adjustments to your table until you have a table that conveys your information and is well organized and designed.

Spell Checking a Document

Just when you think you're finished, there's one last task you need to perform. Before you send the document to the printer, run the spell check utility. To start the spell check, save the file, move the cursor to the beginning of the document, and click Edit, Spellchecker.

KLyX uses the `ispell` program to check each word in the document. It displays unknown words in the Spellchecker dialog box shown in Figure 12.11. The spell check also suggests the correct word and displays it in the Replace text box. If the spell check guessed correctly, click the Replace word button and the next misspelled word will appear in the Unknown text box.

FIGURE **12.11**
*Check your spelling
before you print docu-
ments.*

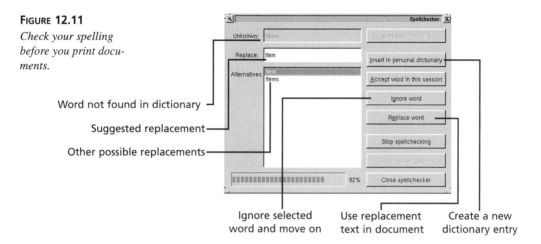

Word not found in dictionary ⎤

Suggested replacement ⎤

Other possible replacements ⎤

Ignore selected
word and move on

Use replacement
text in document

Create a new
dictionary entry

You also have the option to select a different word from a list of possible matches. If you
click a word in the Alternatives list, it will appear in the Replace text box. If you don't
see the correct word in the list, make corrections to the text in the Replace text box.
Again, click Replace word to make the change.

There are other options for dealing with the word that the spell check has selected:

- Sometimes a selected word is correct but not in the dictionary. If you want to leave
  the selected word as is, click Ignore word.

- If you've used the word several times throughout the document and don't want the
  spell check to show you this word again, click Accept word in this session.

- When the correct spelling does not display in the Replace text box or Alternatives
  list, type the correct spelling in the Replace text box and click the Replace word
  button.

- When you will be using a non-dictionary word (such as a name) many times, you
  can add the correct spelling to a personal dictionary. Next time you run a spell
  check, you won't be asked to verify the word. The spell check will do it for you. If
  you typed it incorrectly, the spell check now knows the correct spelling.

Summary

As you've seen, it is possible to create a professional looking document in a short period
of time. KLyX can take care of many of the text-formatting details for you so that you
can concentrate on great text. Over the past hour, you've learned how to make text stand
out on the page, how to arrange text in tables, and how to add graphical images that

enhance your words. As you explore Linux-Mandrake, you'll find other word-processing and text-editing programs. You may find that the skills you acquired during this hour help you find your way through some of the other cool applications found in the distribution.

Q&A

Q I noticed some strange paper and envelope sizes in KLyX. Why?

A The strange sizes you see are European paper sizes. There's also an executive size that has been traditionally used by corporate executives for personal stationery. The paper is of high quality with an engraved letterhead.

Q What is the easiest way to change the type of quotation marks used by KLyX?

A Use the Quotes command in the Layout menu. There are six quote mark styles from which you can choose. Each is a variation of either a curly quote style or a bracket quote style.

Q I have files that were created in Microsoft Word and I'd like to use my files in Linux. Do I have any choices?

A KLyX can import ASCII files. Look under Insert, Insert ASCII File to find your options. You can insert the ASCII file so that each line is a separate paragraph by selecting As Lines. To preserve the original paragraphs, use As Paragraphs. You can also copy text in any X Window program and paste it into KLyX.

Workshop

After you've worked with KLyX for a bit, you'll notice many of the same features used by other word-processing programs. Test your word-processing skills and see how well you have applied them to KLyX.

Quiz

1. How do you move text from one location to another in a document?

2. If you want to place a border around a single cell in a table, how do you do this?

3. Where can you find special symbols that you can insert in your documents and how do you use them?

4. How do you resize graphical images that you've inserted in your document?

Exercises

1. If you use KLyX for correspondence, you might try creating your own letter template. This template can contain letterhead with your address, phone number, and a logo or small graphic. You can also customize other parts of the letter template such as the signature space and the inclusion of carbon copies and enclosures.

2. Try your hand at being a responsible Linux user. The software programs found in the Linux-Mandrake distribution are covered under the GNU General Public License and are supported by individuals. If you find bugs with the program, send a report to the owner. You can usually find out who the owner is by looking at Help, About. Many programs also need programming support and documentation. Find out more at http://www.gnu.org.

12

HOUR 13

Checkbooks Gone Digital

What's the first word that comes to mind when you think of balancing your checkbook? Drudgery? Wouldn't you be happier if someone else kept your bank balance and reconciled the account at the end of each month? Well, you can't always get everything you want. But one way to simplify this chore is to use a financial-management software program.

Bundled in the Linux-Mandrake distribution you'll find the Check Book Balancer (or CBB for short). CBB is an easy-to-use checkbook-management tool that records transactions for your bank accounts, reconciles bank statements with your register, and keeps track of where you spend your money.

The CBB interface contains an area to enter transactions (that is, each check you write and each deposit you make) and an area to view the account register. It looks something like the checkbook register that you carry around in your wallet. At the end of each month, CBB does most of the work of reconciling the account for you. You just let CBB know which transactions appear on the bank statement. As an added bonus, CBB can show you where you spend your hard-earned cash.

During the next hour, you learn how to use CBB to manage your financial affairs. Specifically, you use CBB to

- Create files for each of your checking, savings, and credit card accounts
- Build a category list to keep track of your spending
- Keep your account register up to date
- Reconcile your accounts at the end of each month

Getting Started with CBB

Before you begin using CBB, you should create a separate directory in your user account in which to save your CBB files. In this directory, you'll save account files and category lists. It is best to keep this information separate from files stored in your user directory. Your directory may take the following path:

/home/username/Finances

Once you've created the new directory, it's time to open the CBB and get organized. Use Table 13.1 to find CBB.

TABLE 13.1 Opening CBB

From Here	Try This
AnotherLevel menus	Click Applications, Finance, Check Book Balancer
X terminal window	Type **cbb** and press Enter

The first time you open CBB, a temporary file is created for you. This file is named noname.cbb, and it does not contain any information. You'll see a window that looks something like Figure 13.1.

The first decision you need to make is the date on which you will begin making entries for your accounts. You may want to pick either the first day of the year or the first day of a month, unless your bank uses a different beginning date on your statements. If that's the case, use the bank's beginning date. To tell CBB on which date you will begin entering transactions, click File, Preferences, Set Startdate. In the Set Startdate, type the date on which you want to begin entering transactions, and click OK.

 Save changes to preferences. Whenever you change the preference settings, you'll need to save these changes by selecting File, Preferences, Save Preferences.

FIGURE **13.1**

The CBB window looks like a paper checkbook register.

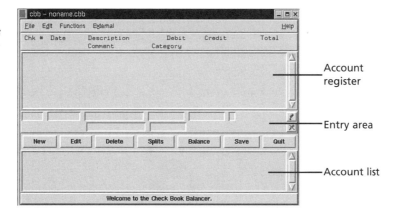

Account register

Entry area

Account list

Creating Account Files

Now it's time to get organized. You'll need to gather information on all the accounts that you will be tracking with CBB. You can keep track of all your checking and savings accounts at each of your banks. You can also keep track of your credit card accounts.

For each account that you want to track, you'll need to create a file for the account and then supply the beginning balance.

Lesson 13.1: Setting Up an Account

Here's how to create a file for an account and how to specify the starting balance. You need to go through this process for each account you want to use in CBB:

1. Click File, Make New Account to open the Make Account dialog box, as shown in Figure 13.2.

Directory path   Filename

FIGURE **13.2**

Make a file for each account that will be used in CBB.

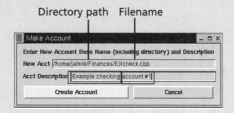

13

2. Type the directory path and filename for the account in the New Acct text box. The filename uses an extension of .cbb.

3. Give the account a title in the Acct Description text box and click Create Account. You'll see an Info/Warning dialog box letting you

know that an empty categories account will be created for you. You learn how to change this category list to fit your spending habits later in the hour.

4. Click OK and you'll be returned to the CBB window where you set the beginning balance for the account.

5. Click in the Date field in the Entry area and type the date of the balance.

6. Click in the Description field and type **Beginning Balance**.

7. Click in the Credit field and type the amount of the beginning balance. The Entry area should look something like the one shown in Figure 13.3.

Date   Description   Beginning balance Accept transaction

FIGURE 13.3

Set the beginning balance for each account.

| | 10/1/99 | Begin Balance | 0.00 | 500.00 | | | ✓ |
| | | | | | | | ✗ |

Clear entry

8. Click the Accept button to add the beginning balance to the register. You'll see a Yes/No dialog box asking if you want to use a category for the entry.

Make a mistake? You can clear the entry fields by clicking the Clear Entry button.

9. Click Yes. You'll see the beginning balance entry in the Account Register.

If you create more than one account, you'll find them in the Account list. To work with a specific account, double-click its entry in the Account list.

Saving Data Before You Exit CBB

As you create accounts, update category lists, and enter transactions into CBB, all your work is stored in memory. You'll want to click the Save button frequently as you enter transactions and perform other tasks.

If you mess up and forget to save the file, CBB automatically creates a backup file and saves data to this file on a periodic basis. If you need to use this backup file, it is named #filename.cbb# and is saved in the same directory in which the original file is saved.

Using Categories to Track Spending Habits

 Categories help CBB track where you spend your money. Each type of item on which you spend money, such as rent or gasoline, is a separate category.

CBB contains a category list, which you can use and edit to suit your needs, or you can create your own category list. Once you have a starting category list, you can add and delete categories as you go along.

Finding the Default Category List

Most people may find that using the default category list is the easiest way to start. By using this default list, you have an existing list of categories that you may commonly need. Remember, once you start using this default list, you can easily modify it to suit your lifestyle and spending habits.

Lesson 13.2: Building a Starting Category List

If you're not sure what categories you might need, use the default category list. Follow these steps:

1. Double-click the account in the Account list to which you want to apply the default categories. The account will be selected in the Account list and the filename will appear in the title bar.

2. Click Functions, Add Default Categories. A confirmation dialog box will ask whether you really want to import the default categories. Of course you do.

3. Click Yes and you're ready to make changes to this list.

Editing the Category List

Whether or not you elected to use the default category list, if you want to keep track of where you spend your money, you'll need to use categories. The default category list contains many of the categories that you'll need to record transactions, but you may need to make some changes. If you want to create your own category list, make a list of those spending items that recur frequently and open the Category List.

To open the category list, select Functions, Category List. If you used the default category list, the Category List window will look like the one in Figure 13.4. As you scroll through the list, you'll see categories that you'll use frequently, categories that will be needed only occasionally, and categories that you won't need at all.

13

FIGURE **13.4**

Use categories to track your spending.

Description

Category

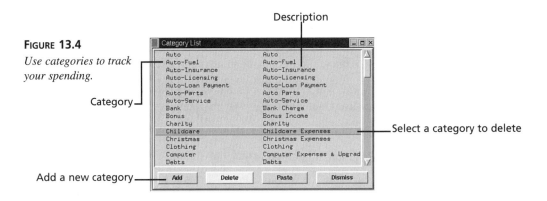

Select a category to delete

Add a new category

If you don't think you'll need a category, highlight the category and click the Delete button. You'll be asked to confirm your choice. If you need to add a category to the list, click the Add button and fill in the information to describe the new category.

Lesson 13.3: Creating a New Category

If you want to keep track of where you spend your money, you'll need a category for each type of spending. You may also want to create separate categories for your different income sources. Follow these steps:

1. Open the Category List.
2. Click the Add button to display the Add New Category dialog box shown in Figure 13.5.

FIGURE **13.5**

Create additional income and expense categories.

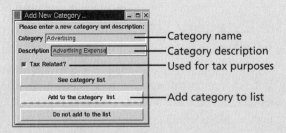

Category name
Category description
Used for tax purposes

Add category to list

3. Type a name for the category that describes the type of income or the type of expense.
4. You may want to add a few words to remind you what the category is used for in the Description text box.
5. If the category is an item that you claim on your tax return, select the Tax Related? option.

6. When you've finished, click Add to the category list. The new category will appear in the Category List in alphabetical order.

If you are entering transactions and need to add a new category to the list, you can create categories on the fly. Just type a title for the category in the Category field of the entry area. You'll be asked if you want to add the category to the list.

Recording Transactions

Once you have set up CBB by entering a starting date for transactions, setting up your accounts, and creating a custom category list, it's time to start entering all those checks, deposits, cash machine receipts, and credit card slips.

Recording Checks

Probably the most common transaction is for checks you write to pay bills. You'll find that the transaction entry area in CBB looks much like the lines in your paper checkbook register. If you're familiar with the paper checkbook register, you'll find the CBB transaction entry area very similar. Figure 13.6 shows a simple checking account transaction.

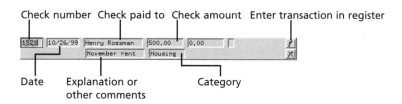

FIGURE 13.6

Create a register entry for bills you pay by check.

To enter the information about the check, click in each of the fields in the entry area and type the check number, date, pay to, and amount information as written on the check. Then add a category. When all the information has been supplied, add the transaction to the register by pressing Enter or clicking the Accept Transaction button.

The first time you record a check, you'll need to manually type the check number. The next time you enter a check, just type a + (plus sign); CBB will display the next check number in sequence.

If you use categories to track your spending, there are a couple of tricks to entering the category type in the Category field. First, no matter which trick you choose, make sure the cursor is in the Category field.

13

- For the first trick, open the Category List, select the category you want to apply to the payment, and click the Paste button. When you go back to the register, you'll see the category in the Category field.

- The other trick is to type the first letter of the category name and press Tab. If CBB can guess the category, it will fill in the rest. If not, type another letter and press Tab. Keep going until the entire category name appears in the field.

> While you are entering transactions, keep the Category List window open. You can use this list to complete the Category field in the entry area.

Lesson 13.4: Assigning Two Categories to a Payment

There may be times when you write one check that applies to two category items. For example, you may go to the supermarket to pick up a few groceries, but while you're there, you buy postage stamps. To assign two categories to a payment, follow these steps:

1. Open the account from which you wrote the check.

2. Type the number of the check in the Chk # field. Or, if you are recording checks sequentially, type the plus sign in the field and the next check number will appear in the field.

3. Type the name of the person or business to whom you wrote the check in the Description field.

4. Type the amount of the check in the Debit field.

5. Place the cursor in the Category field and click the Splits button to open the Category Splits window, as shown in Figure 13.7.

6. Enter the name of the first category to which you want to record a portion of the total payment. You can type the name of the first category in the Category field, open the Category List and paste the category, or type a single letter and press Tab to use the auto-complete feature.

7. Type the amount to be applied to the first category in the Amount field. Since this is a payment, the number needs to be preceded by a minus sign (-).

8. Click in the Category field for the second category. Notice that the amount for this category is already computed for you. Enter the name of the second category.

9. When the total of the categories equals the amount of the payment, click the Dismiss button. The Category Splits window will close and the data you entered will appear in the Category field in the entry area.

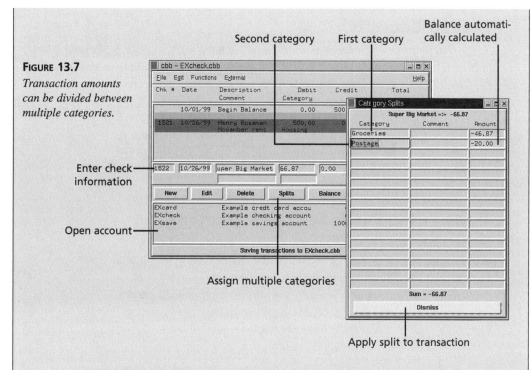

FIGURE 13.7
Transaction amounts can be divided between multiple categories.

10. When the transaction is complete, click the Accept Transaction button. The transaction will appear in the account register and the account balance will be reduced by the amount of the check, as shown in Figure 13.8.

FIGURE 13.8
If you've been following the example, this is how your checkbook register should look.

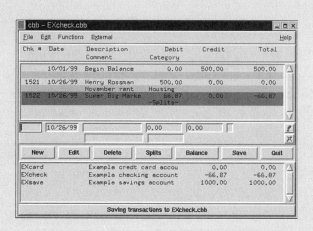

13

Posting Deposits

You'll find that entering a deposit into CBB is much the same as entering a check. The only difference is that you don't use a check number, and the amount is entered in the Credit field. You do want your balance to increase, don't you? The example in Figure 13.9 shows a simple deposit.

FIGURE **13.9**

Debit means decrease; credit means more cash!

Deposit amount

Transferring Funds Between Accounts

For those times when you need money and it isn't in the right bank account, you'll need to make a transfer. A transfer is actually two transactions in one. First it is a withdrawal out of one account. Second, it is a deposit into another account. If your bank allows you to transfer money between accounts, and those accounts are set up in CBB, you can complete both these transactions in one easy step.

Keep your eyes open when making changes to a transfer. The change should appear in both the account from which the money was withdrawn and the account to which the money was deposited. You may want to check the transaction in both accounts to make sure it was handled properly.

Lesson 13.5: Moving Money from Savings to Checking

Let's pretend that it's vacation time once again and you need to buy the train tickets for your Siberian journey. You go to the bank and move money from the savings account to the checking account so that you can write a check to the travel agent who found you this great deal. Follow these steps:

1. Open the account register for a savings account. You will be moving money from this account and depositing it into a checking account.

2. Enter the date on which the transfer was made.

3. Type a description of the transfer; for example, **Vacation 2000**.

4. Type the amount of the transfer in the Debit field.

5. In the category field, select the checking account to which the cash will be

deposited from the Category List (bank accounts are listed at the bottom) and accept the transaction when you are satisfied that the information is correct. Your example should look something like the one in Figure 13.10.

FIGURE 13.10

It only takes one entry to transfer funds between two accounts.

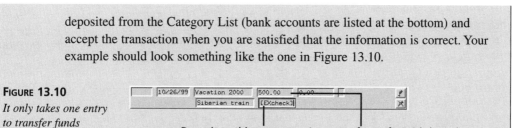

Deposit to this account   Amount of transfer/withdrawal

6. Now open the account register for your checking account. You'll see that the account has been increased by the amount of the transfer and the transaction is listed in date order.

Editing Transactions

When you need to make changes to a transaction that you've already entered, select the transaction in the account register and click the Edit button. The transaction will appear in the Entry Area. Make any changes and click the Accept Transaction button to update the transaction in the register.

Working with Recurring Transactions

There may be a number of bills you pay on a regular basis or types of deposits you make (such as a paycheck) routinely. To avoid the necessity of entering the same information over and over again, you can use CBB's memory function.

Start by entering the check number and the date. Type a few characters of the description and press Tab. CBB will search its memory for the closest match and fill in the rest of the information for you. If the information is correct, click the Accept Transaction button. You can also make any changes to this entry as needed. If you don't want to use the information that was filled in, press Ctrl+Tab (the cursor must still be in the Description field). Only the information that you typed will remain. You will then need to complete the transaction yourself. You can ask CBB to search its memory only once per transaction.

Balancing an Account

At sometime during the month, your bank sends you a statement for your accounts. It's your job to make sure that the information provided by the bank matches what you have stored in CBB. Your first step is to grab that statement, open the corresponding account in CBB, and click the Balance button. After you go through the process of telling CBB

13

the statement ending balance and which transactions appear on the statement, hopefully your records and the bank's records agree. If not, you need to do some investigative research into the cause of this mystery. There are several reports you can run that give you a few clues.

> Once the account has been balanced, the next time you reconcile the account, only the uncleared transactions will appear.

Lesson 13.6: Reconciling an Account

It's that time of the month again; the bank statement has arrived in the mail. Better make sure that your records and the bank's records agree before you go on that next shopping spree. Follow these steps to do so:

1. Open the account that you want to balance and click the Balance button to bring up a list of uncleared transactions.

2. Enter the statement ending balance. You may want to make sure that the statement starting balance in CBB and on your statement match.

3. Double-click those transactions that appear on the bank statement. An asterisk will appear to the left of each transaction that you have marked as cleared. Also, as you select transactions, the difference amount will change, as shown in Figure 13.11.

FIGURE 13.11

The Difference amount is reduced as you clear transactions from the register.

Select cleared transactions

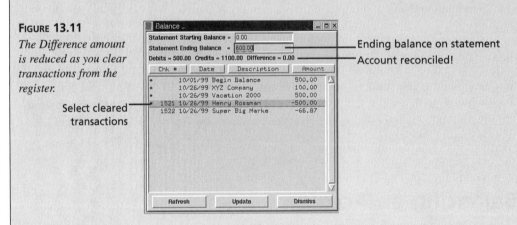

Ending balance on statement

Account reconciled!

4. When all the transactions have been selected, click the Update button. The Balance window will close and you'll notice an "x" to the right of the Credit column in the register next to those transactions that appeared on the bank statement.

If you notice that you've made a mistake entering a transaction and you want to edit the transaction in the register, you can do this while you are reconciling the account. Simply display the CBB window, edit the transaction, switch back to the Balance window, and click the Refresh button.

Creating Reports to Find Reconciliation Problems

There are several reports that you can create to determine why you cannot reconcile your CBB records to the bank's statement. To find the reports, click Functions, Reports.

The Transaction List Report

The Transaction List looks just like the account register for the account. You can see which transactions have cleared your bank (by the "x" to the right of the amount column) and those that have not. You can also use this report to verify that you have entered the correct amounts and that the transactions have been recorded in the appropriate bank account.

There are other variations on this theme. You can also select a Transaction List by Category report. This report sorts transactions according to category and displays a subtotal for each category. If you don't want to see all the transactions, and instead want to view just the category and amounts, select the Short List by Category report.

The Uncleared Transactions Report

This report shows only those transactions that have not cleared your bank. This way you know which checks haven't cleared yet. You can also use this report to make sure that you cleared all the transactions in CBB that were shown on your statement.

The Missing Checks Report

If you need to know whether a check number was not entered in the register, or whether a check number was entered twice, run the Missing Checks Report.

13

Summary

Now that you've had a chance to experiment with the Check Book Balancer, you have hopefully found a new tool that can take some of the stress and strain out of everyday life. By taking advantage of this electronic bookkeeper, you'll no longer have to madly push calculator keys to see how much money is left in your checking account. Reconciling your records to your bank statement is faster because there's no number crunching on your part. After you've worked with CBB to keep track of your basic finances, you may want to use this information to prepare budgets and savings plans.

Q&A

Q I created files for each of my accounts. Now I'm not happy with the way I've named them. Is there a way I can change these names to something more descriptive?

A Open the account and then select File, Save Account As.

Q Is my financial data safe in CBB?

A If your CBB files are stored in your home directory on the system, no one can access those files unless they have access to your user account. You can log out of your user account or use a lock on the screensaver if you don't want others in your user account. Also, make sure that any backups that you keep of your CBB files are stored in a secure place (such as a locked file cabinet or safe deposit box). If you are an encryption expert, you can use CBB's cryptography feature in the Preferences menu.

Q I'd like to make sure I have the latest version of CBB. Is there an easy way to keep the program updated?

A Fire up your Internet connection and let's go take a look. Click External, Install the Latest CBB. CBB will take care of all the business of downloading the package, untarring and gunzipping it, and then take care of the installation. You'll need to restart CBB when finished.

Workshop

You would think that just making you organize your finances would be enough of a test for this hour. No so. We want to get you on your way to becoming lavishly and independently rich! Yes, we dream in mass quantities. So, let's make sure your financial wizardry is in tune and see how well you remember what you learned over the past hour.

Quiz

1. How do you switch between account files when you have separate files for each of your banking and credit card accounts?

2. If you are entering a transaction and you don't have an appropriate category set up, what is the quickest way to create a new category?

3. If there are a number of bills that you pay regularly, such as telephone and car payments, how can you enter these recurring transactions quickly?

4. How do you make sure that your records and the bank statement agree?

Exercises

1. You may have noticed that your CBB window doesn't look the same as the example shown during this hour. Try changing the look of the window by setting different dimensions. To get started, here's the path: File, Preferences, Appearance, Set Dimensions. You'll need to save these preferences changes and restart the program to see the effects.

2. Quicken users can export their Quicken data and import it into CBB. In Quicken, select File, Export, and the account you want to use in CBB. If you want to use more than one account, you'll need to export each account separately. Then, transfer the Quicken QIF file to your home directory in Linux and select File, Import QIF File in CBB. You might also want to try exporting your CBB files into Quicken.

3. Use CBB to do some budgeting. Start by running the Average Monthly Expenses by Category report. This report shows you how you spend your income. Take a look at the report to determine where you can reduce spending. This is a good opportunity to start saving for that rainy day.

13

Hour **14**

Building a Web Site with Screem

Are you looking for a sophisticated Web page-editing program that reminds you of the Web editors from your Windows and Macintosh days? During the last part of Hour 11, "Getting on the Internet," you learned that you could create Web pages with Netscape Composer. Now, there's nothing wrong with Composer, but maybe you're looking for something more—something with more bells and whistles.

Screem differs from Composer in that Screem is designed to create and manage an entire Web site. Screem treats your Web site as a single unit, not as a collection of separate Web pages. Because your Web pages are kept together as a site, if a change is made on one page that affects other pages (such as renaming a page that is linked to other pages in the site), Screem will automatically update hyperlinks and navigation bars.

If you design Web sites, large or small, fire up your Web browser because Screem can't be found on the Linux-Mandrake CD. During the next hour, you will get acquainted with Screem by doing the following:

- Downloading Screem from the Internet and installing it on your computer
- Creating the foundation for a Web site
- Adding text, HTML tags, hyperlinks, and images to Web pages

Getting Ready to Screem

One of the most exciting things about Linux is the availability of software packages. While many of these software programs can be found on the Linux-Mandrake CD, you'll find even more Linux software on the Internet. One of the Linux applications that you need to download from the Internet is Screem.

Now, you may think that downloading a Web page editor like Screem would take all day. Well, the beauty of Linux is that most Linux applications don't require a lot of space on your hard drive or a long download time. Screem weighs in at a mere 1.3MB download.

Lesson 14.1: Installing Screem

Since Screem is not on the Linux-Mandrake CD-ROM, you need to download the RPM file from Screem's Web site. Here's where to get Screem:

1. It's time to get Screem. Navigate to www.screem.org to find the Screem RPM. Scroll down the page until you get to the Download section. You need to download the file named screem-0.1.98-1.i386.rpm.

2. Install the Screem RPM on your system. Open a file manager and display the RPM file you just downloaded. To upgrade the package from KDE, click the file to display the installation window. In GNOME, right-click the file and select Upgrade.

If you need a refresher course on how to install packages, turn to Hour 9, "Managing Applications."

3. When the installation is complete, you can open an X terminal window, type **screem**, and press Enter. The Screem Web site creation program will open, as shown in Figure 14.1.

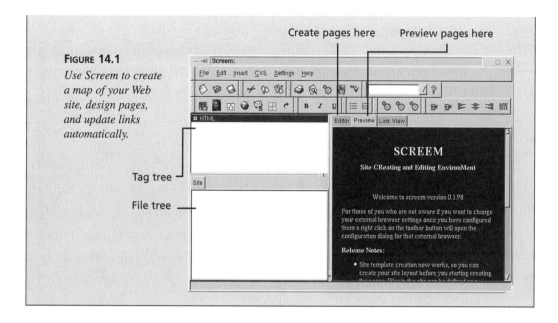

FIGURE 14.1

Use Screem to create a map of your Web site, design pages, and update links automatically.

Create pages here   Preview pages here

Tag tree

File tree

SCREEM

Site CReating and Editing EnvironMent

Welcome to screem version 0.1.98

For those of you who are not aware if you want to change your external browser settings once you have configured them a right click on the toolbar button will open the configuration dialog for that external browser.

Release Notes:

- Site template creation now works, so you can create your site layout before you starting creating

Starting Your First Web Site

From your experience with other operating systems, you may be familiar with the concept of *wizards*. Wizards make your life easier by walking you through a task and asking appropriate questions.

NEW TERM Screem also contains a number of wizards, except you will find that they are called *druids*. No matter what you call them, these wizards/druids are smarter than us mere mortals and already know everything you need to do in order to get a job done.

The easiest way to get started on your Web site is with the assistance of the Site druid. The Site druid walks you through the process of setting up a structure for your Web site and then collects all the information needed to upload your Web site to your ISP's Web server when you are ready to reveal your site to the wired world.

14

Lesson 14.2: Organizing Your Web Site

Before you can start designing Web pages, you need to tell Screem where you want to save the Web site on your computer and to what Web server the site will be uploaded when you are ready to publish your site on the Internet. To use the Site druid to help you start your site, follow these steps:

> Before you begin this lesson, you may want to check with your ISP and get directions for uploading your Web site to its Web server.

1. Click the New Site button to display the opening screen of the Site druid. Read the opening message and click Next to display the next screen of the druid.

2. Type the path for the directory in which you want to save your Web site in the Site Pathname text box. For example, if you want to save it in a subdirectory of your user home directory, the path may look something like

   `/home/username/website`

3. Type a name for the Web site in the Site Name text box. This is the name that will appear in the title bar of the Web browser. An example of this first screen appears in Figure 14.2. When you are finished, click Next.

FIGURE 14.2

The Site druid needs to know where to save your files and what you want to title your Web site.

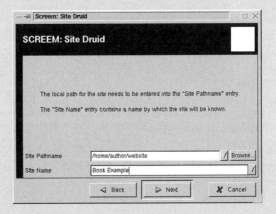

4. The next screen asks whether you want to use a template to create a directory structure for the site or to create a uniform look for your Web pages. Click Next since you have not created any templates.

5. The druid then asks whether you want to use a version control software program to keep track of updates to the Web site. If you know about version control software, select this option and enter the path to the program. If not, click Next to move to the next screen.

6. Type the address where your Web site host requires that you upload your Web pages in the Remote Address text box. You also need to add the URL address from which your site can be accessed. An example is shown in Figure 14.3. When you are finished, click Next.

FIGURE 14.3

Tell the Site druid where to upload your Web site on your ISP's Web server.

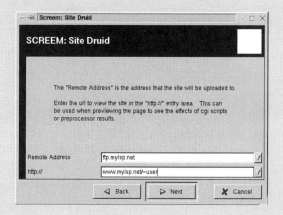

7. The next screen needs to know how you will be uploading your Web pages to the Web server. Select the method required by your ISP from the Remote Method drop-down list. Many ISPs use FTP. You will also need to enter the directory path (in the Remote Path text box) where the Web site is stored on your ISP's Web server. Click Next when you are ready to move to the next step.

8. Enter the username and password provided by your ISP that are needed to access the Web server so that you can upload your files. Click Next when you are finished.

9. Your site is ready to go. Click Finish and you will see the beginnings of your new site in the File tree.

If you need to make any changes to the information you entered into the Site druid (such as where the Web site will be published), select Settings, Site.

14

Adding Web Pages to Your Web Site

Once you have built a structure for your Web site, it is time to start adding pages. It's pretty easy to insert pages into the site; the Page druid does all the hard work for you. The Page druid not only adds pages to your Web site, but it can also set the text, link, and background color or image.

If your Web site will contain a large number of pages, you may want to create a directory structure in which to store different types of pages. For example, if your site will contain information about your products, a corporate profile, and pages for your employees, you may want to place each group in a separate subdirectory such as the following:

```
/home/username/website/products
```

```
/home/username/website/profile
```

```
/home/username/website/employees
```

The use of subdirectories makes it easier to manage a large Web site by allowing you to place information in logical groupings. You can use a file manager to create these subdirectories. For help using file managers, go back to Hour 6, "The Marvelous, Mystical Filesystem Tour."

Lesson 14.3: Creating a New Web Page

Part of building a structure for your Web site is to add the pages you want contained in the site to the Site tree. When you create a page, the only content that is contained in the page is the title and color information. You will add content (such as text, hyperlinks, and images) after the pages have been created. To add a page to your Web site, follow along with this lesson:

1. Click File, New, New Page to start the Page druid.

2. Click Next to get to the first screen of the Page druid.

3. Type the directory path and filename for the new page in the Page Path text box. Following the example in Lesson 14.1, the path may look something like

   ```
   /home/username/website/pagename.html
   ```

   You should also type a title for the page in the Page Title text box. This title will appear in the Title Bar of the Web browser when the page is visited. An example is shown in Figure 14.4. Click Next to move to the next screen.

4. You are then asked to select colors for the different elements of the Web page. To change a default color, click the option button for the element you want to change and then click the corresponding color button to display a color picker. After you have selected colors, click Next.

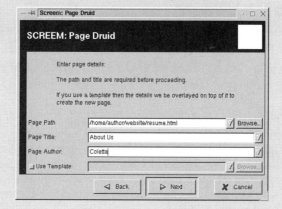

FIGURE 14.4
Provide the Page druid with the directory path and filename, title, and author of the page being created.

5. If you want to use an image file for the page background, select the Use background image option and then type the directory path and filename for the image that you want to use. When you are satisfied with your choice, click Next.

6. You're now finished creating the page. Click Finish and you'll see the new page added to the File tree, as shown in Figure 14.5.

FIGURE 14.5
The Web page is added to the File tree and is ready for you to add content in the Editor area.

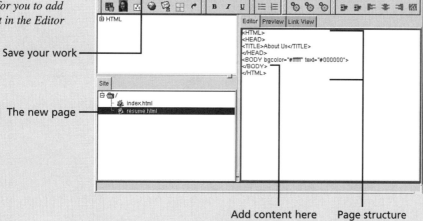

Save your work

The new page

Add content here   Page structure

14

Remember to save your Web pages often. When you click the Save button, every page in the Web site is saved. There's no need to save each individual page.

Designing Web Pages

Your site structure is complete and you've added a few pages. It's time to start adding content to those pages. To display the page to which you want to add text, hyperlinks, and pictures, double-click the file in the File tree. This displays the page in the Screem Editor. From here, it's up to you to design a great looking page.

> The Screem Page druid creates the HTML tags required in every Web page. These tags indicate the beginning and end of the page (the <HTML> tag), heading information (the <HEAD> tag), the title of the page (the <TITLE> tag), and the part of the page that appears in the Web browser (the <BODY> tag). Just remember that your content needs to be placed between the <BODY> tags.

Formatting Text with HTML Tags

Adding HTML tags to text is a simple matter of typing the text into the Editor, selecting it, and then browsing through the Tag tree to find an appropriate HTML tag. Figure 14.6 shows an example of a first level heading inserted into the body of a Web page.

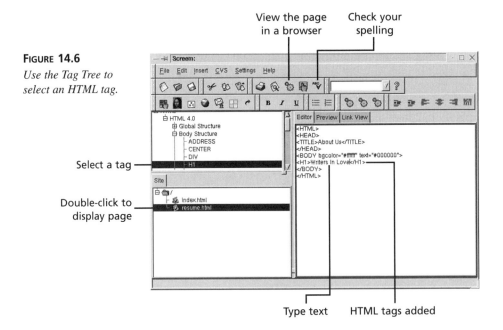

FIGURE 14.6
*Use the Tag Tree to
select an HTML tag.*

You can also select an HTML tag before you type the text. When you do this, the beginning and ending tags appear and the cursor will be located between the tags. You can then type the text.

> If you want to see how the page will look in a Web browser, you can either click the Preview tag or click the View button.

Hyperlinking to the Wired World

Hyperlinks are the transportation carrier of the Internet. Hyperlinks take your visitors from page to page within your Web site, direct visitors to Web sites outside your own, and make it easy for visitors to communicate with you.

There are several ways to create a hyperlink. You can just type the code in the Editor. You can use the Tag tree to help you out. Or, make life easy and start the Link Wizard. You can get to the Link Wizard (shown in Figure 14.7) by either clicking the Link Wizard button on the toolbar, or by selecting Insert, Link.

Start the Link Wizard   The finished hyperlink

FIGURE 14.7

Select the type of hyperlink you want to create and provide the Wizard with the link information.

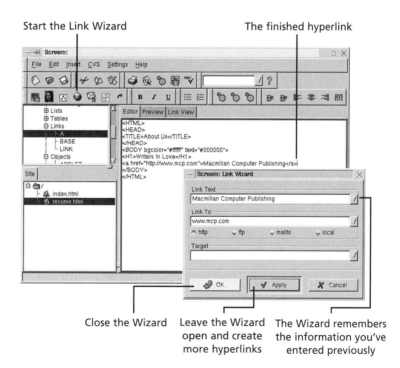

Close the Wizard   Leave the Wizard   The Wizard remembers
                    open and create   the information you've
                    more hyperlinks   entered previously

14

Inserting Images

For our last wizard trick of the hour (see Figure 14.8), click the Image Wizard button on the toolbar (or select Insert, Image). You can use this wizard to add images to your Web pages.

FIGURE **14.8**

The Image Wizard is self-explanatory. Hold the mouse over a text box to display a screen tip.

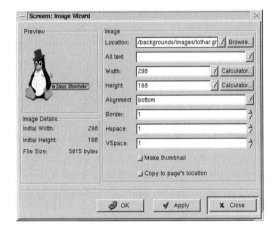

Summary

In this hour, you learned how to begin creating a Web site with Screem. Screem is more than just a Web page editor. With Screem, you not only can create HTML code, but also can manage every aspect of your Web site. Screem will automatically update your site if you rename or rearrange pages in the site.

Q&A

Q **I have Web pages that I created in another Web page editor. Can I use these pages in Screem?**

A It's quite simple to open these files in Screem. Click the Open Site button and navigate to the directory in which the Web pages are stored. Screem will ask you to enter the site information once the files have been imported.

Q **I'd like to learn more about how to write HTML code. Can you recommend any good sources?**

A There must be tons of books that will teach you how to create Web pages by writing your own HTML code. One of the better books that we've come across is *Sams Teach Yourself Web Publishing with HTML in 21 Days* by Laura Lemay.

If you want to surf the Internet for HTML help, check out About.com. About.com is a Web portal that contains information for everyone. There are two areas of About.com that Web designers will find most useful: html.about.com and webdesign.about.com.

To go straight to the HTML authorities, visit the World Wide Web Consortium HyperText Markup Language Home Page at www.w3.org/MarkUp.

Workshop

It's now time to check up on your Web site design skills. Here are a few quiz questions to test the knowledge you gained over the past hour. There are also a couple of exercises to help you create an even better Web site.

Quiz

1. What is a druid?

2. Name two ways in which a druid can make your life easier.

3. Which HTML tags provide the basic structure of a Web page?

Exercises

1. If you have a large Web site with several pages and several people working on different pages, you may want to use the To Do feature to keep track of tasks that need to be accomplished for each page, who is responsible for completing the task, and when the task needs to be completed. To access the To Do List, click the View Site To Do List button.

2. One of the easiest ways to make your Web site look good is with graphics. Your job is to collect images that look good together and give your Web site a unifying theme. There are several Linux programs that you can use to create your own graphics. In Part VI, "Going for the Graphics," you'll learn about The Gimp, KIllustrator, and a host of other graphics utilities that can help you create good looking artwork. You can also download images from the Internet; use a search engine to find free Web graphics. You'll also find images on your computer. (Look in /usr/share/wallpapers for background images in .jpg format.)

14

HOUR 15

Printing and Faxing Documents

Even though it is an ecologically sound idea to work in a completely paper-less office, there is still a need for paper documents because there are times when an electronic file just doesn't cut it. You may find that not all comput-ers are set up to handle the types of files you create, and not everyone wants their email box filled with file attachments. If you have a hard time editing documents on the screen, you may want to print a copy of the file. In these cases, you'll need to attach a Linux-compatible printer to your computer and then tell Linux how to use the printer.

Another hindrance to the paperless office is the fax machine. Fax is still a popular way to transmit documents (not everyone uses email). One way to reduce paper usage with the fax machine is to use one of the fax software programs. This will cut your paper use in half—the fax you send is saved as an electronic file and only the recipient receives a paper copy.

During the next hour, you learn how to use your computer to print and fax documents. Specifically, you learn how to do the following:

- Determine whether a printer is already configured for your system
- Configure a local printer
- Change printer settings for Hewlett-Packard LaserJet printers
- Send faxes with KVoice

Getting Ready to Print Your Documents

During the Linux-Mandrake installation, you were given the option to set up a printer. If you didn't do this during the installation, you need to configure a printer before you can print any of your files.

NEW TERM First, check to see that your printer is attached to the parallel port, plugged into a power source, and turned on. If you use a *pass-through parallel port cable*, this is not a problem. Pass-through parallel port cables allow you to attach a device (such as a CD-ROM drive, scanner, or ZIP drive) between the computer and the printer. You will find that you won't be able to use your printer while you're using a device attached to a pass-through cable.

If you don't know whether a printer has been set up for your computer, try the exercise in Lesson 15.1.

Lesson 15.1: Is a Printer Configured for Linux?

Before you try to set up a printer, test to see if any devices are configured on the computer's parallel port. To begin, you need to be logged in to the root account. Once you are there, open an X terminal window. Then, follow these steps:

1. At the command prompt, type the command

   `ls > /dev/lp1`

   where *lp1* is the name of the parallel port where the printer is attached. This sends a directory listing to the parallel printer port.

   If a printer is configured, a number of stair-stepped lines appear on the printed page. Don't worry how this looks, it just means you can use the printer.

   If the printer does not print, a response similar to the following will appear:

   `bash: /dev/lp1: Device not configured`

2. If a printer is not configured, use the *printtool* to set up the printer (discussed in the next section).

Using the Red Hat Linux Print System Manager

A quick way to set up a printer to work with your Linux system is to use the Red Hat Linux Print System Manager. This tool (also called *printtool*) manages any printers that are attached to your computer. Not only can you add and delete printers, but you also can limit the size of the files that are sent to a printer.

NEW TERM The *printtool* can configure about 60 printer types for use as the local or network printer. A local printer is attached directly to a computer workstation (usually through a parallel port); only that workstation can send jobs to that printer.

If your computer is attached to a network, you may have access to a printer through the network. And, you may have to walk down the hall to pick up your printed document. Easy for you because the system administrator is responsible for setting up new equipment on the network and making sure everything is configured and working correctly.

To get to the Red Hat Linux Print System Manager, you must first be logged into the root account. Then, type **printtool** in an X terminal window.

> You can also access the Red Hat Linux Print System Manager from DrakConf. Select the Printer Configuration option. You'll find that the DrakConf printer configuration method looks slightly different from the Red Hat print tool.

A series of Error windows will appear. Don't worry about these. These errors let you know about packages that are not installed on your computer. You won't need these to configure a local printer. The opening printtool window appears, as shown in Figure 15.1.

FIGURE 15.1
Configure printers that are attached to the computer with the printtool.

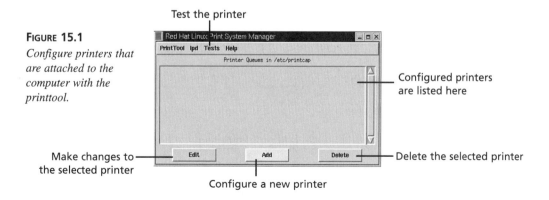

Test the printer

Configured printers are listed here

Make changes to the selected printer

Configure a new printer

Delete the selected printer

Lesson 15.2: Configuring a Local Printer

Before you begin this lesson, you may want to dig out the user manual for your printer. If your printer is not on the printtool list, you need to select a printer that closely matches your printer's settings. Follow these steps to configure a local printer for use with your Linux system:

1. Click the Add button to display the Add a Printer Entry dialog box.

2. Select the Local Printer option button and then click OK. The printtool looks for any parallel printer devices and lists the detected ports in the Info dialog box. You may want to make a note of the detected parallel port. Click OK to get to the Edit Local Printer Entry dialog box (shown in Figure 15.2), where you will configure the printer.

FIGURE 15.2

Set the information the printtool needs to drive your printer.

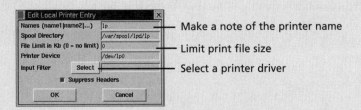

— Make a note of the printer name

— Limit print file size

— Select a printer driver

3. Click the Select button to open the Configure Filter dialog box shown in Figure 15.3.

FIGURE 15.3

Either select a printer that closely matches yours, or select one that your printer can emulate.

Select a printer

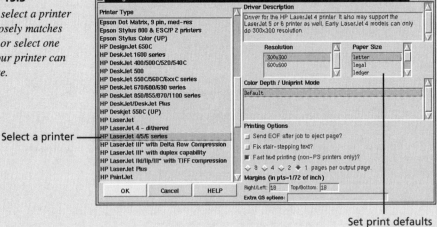

Set print defaults

4. Scroll through the Printer Type list and select your printer (or a printer that is close to it). Then click OK. You are returned to the Edit Local Printer Entry dialog box. Notice that the printer appears in the Input Filter text box.

5. Click OK again. You are returned to the printtool and the printer will be listed there.

6. To test the printer, select the printer from the list and click Tests, Print Postscript test page. An Info dialog box will tell you that the test page printed. Did the page print correctly? If not, you may want to make changes to the printer. Just select the printer and click the Edit button.

7. When you are finished, click PrintTool, Quit. You're ready to print away.

Working with HP LaserJet Printers

Those of you with a Hewlett-Packard LaserJet printer can use a utility that lets you manage your HP LaserJet printer from your desktop. This tool allows you to change the paper size and orientation, print resolution, and a number of other options.

To find this utility, open the KDE main menu and select Utilities, HP LaserJet Control Panel. You can also type `kljettool` from an X terminal window.

The HP LaserJet Control Panel opens to the Paper tab. From this tab you can change the paper orientation, the number of copies to print, and the paper orientation. The Printer tab (shown in Figure 15.4) changes the print resolution and density, and selects a different printer (if one is set up on the system).

FIGURE 15.4

Use the Printer tab to change the print resolution and density settings.

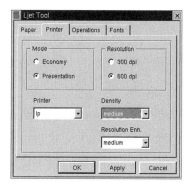

After you make changes in the HP LaserJet Control Panel, those changes will appear on all the pages that you print. When you want to change the default print settings again, open the utility and change the settings.

Sending Faxes from Your Computer

If you want to send a fax from the convenience of your computer screen, you must first have a fax-compatible modem attached to your computer. Then, you must decide which fax program you want to use. During the last part of this hour, we look at KVoice, which sends simple, one-page faxes or can fax files stored on your computer.

Getting Started with KVoice

Although KVoice is capable of much more than just sending faxes, you must also have a modem that can answer incoming voice calls. With the right kind of modem, KVoice can be a full-fledged answering machine and fax system.

Before you get started using KVoice, the root account will need to set up Kvoice to send outgoing faxes. To start KVoice, select Applications, Voice Mail & Fax from the KDE main menu. You can also type **kvoice** in an X terminal window.

The first time you open KVoice, a notice appears that states that KVoice has never been run before. The program will try to determine your system configuration when you click OK. Even though KVoice insists that it was configured correctly, you should still check the setup options to make sure everything will work as planned.

Once everything is ready, the KVoice window shown in Figure 15.5 appears on your screen.

FIGURE 15.5

If your home or business needs a fax and answering system, try KVoice.

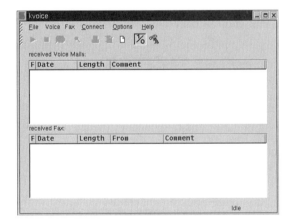

Lesson 15.3: Checking the KVoice Configuration

15

Even though KVoice checks its own configuration, you still need to do some configuration tasks. To make sure that KVoice is set up properly to send faxes, follow along with this lesson:

1. Click Options, Setup to open the Setup dialog box.
2. Click the Modem tab shown in Figure 15.6. You have several tasks to perform from this dialog box.

FIGURE 15.6

KVoice needs to know the modem port, its speed, and the manufacturer.

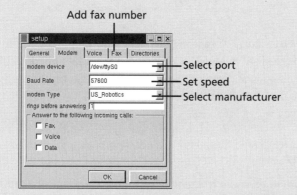

Here are the configuration tasks you need to perform from the Modem tab:

- Select the port to which the modem is attached from the Modem Device drop-down list.
- Select the modem speed from the Baud Rate drop-down list.
- Select the modem manufacturer from the Modem Type drop-down list.

3. Click the Fax tab and replace the small x's in the phone number text box with the phone number to which the computer is attached.
4. Click OK when you are finished making your changes. You can now send a fax with your new fax program.

Creating a Kvoice Fax Job

KVoice allows you to send a fax that contains plain text, or you can send a fax cover sheet with a file that is stored on your computer. To start a new fax, select Fax, New Fax. This opens the fax window displayed in Figure 15.7.

FIGURE 15.7

Fill out the KVoice cover sheet and attach any needed files.

Send the fax

Attach any files to be sent with the fax

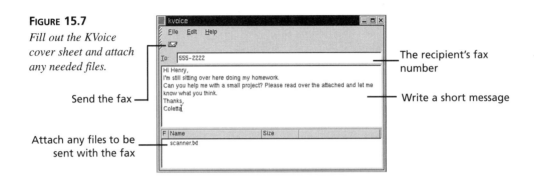

The recipient's fax number

Write a short message

It's easy to send a fax. Just type the recipient's fax number in the To text box and write a short note in the space below that. If you need to attach any files, select File, AddFile. A dialog box will open and you can search the filesystem for the file you want to attach. When you're done, click the Send Message button. The fax will be placed in the fax queue until you select Fax, Send spooled.

Summary

Since it's hard to get away from the need for paper documents, printing and faxing are still popular ways of communicating with others. In this hour, you learned how to set up your Linux computer to print from all your favorite applications. You also learned how to fax those documents to others using KVoice.

Q&A

Q Is there any way to get quick access to printing files?

A You may want to place a printer icon on the desktop or the panel. To place a printer icon on the panel from the GNOME main menu, select Panel, Add applet, Utility, Printer Applet. When you want to print a file, open a file manager window, select the file you want to print, drag it to the printer icon, and drop it. The file will print automatically.

In KDE, use the KDE Configuration Wizard (found in the Utilities menu) to place an icon on the desktop. You can also drag a file from the file manager and drop it on the printer icon to print a file.

Q **The header line for faxes that I send through Kvoice doesn't contain the right information. How do I fix this?**

A Here's the answer everyone loves to hear. You need to edit the /etc/mgetty+send-fax/faxheader file. The easiest way is to open a text editor (such as gEdit, GXedit, KEdit, or Emacs which is covered in Hour 16, "Text Processing with Emacs"), and then open the file. Replace the text between the asterisks with your name or your company name and change the numbers that follow to your fax telephone number. Your completed file will look something like the following:

```
FAX FROM:  **C. Witherspoon** 1 555 555 1212  TO:@T@ Page @P@ OF @M@
```

Workshop

Questions, questions, questions. Why do we always ask so many questions? Well, we want to make sure that you are comfortable with the information you learned over the past hour. If you're not, go back and read those parts you missed the first time around.

Quiz

1. What is the difference between a local printer and a network printer?

2. What are some of the more popular printers supported by Linux?

3. How much information should be included in a KVoice outgoing fax?

Exercises

1. Test some of the documents that you've created so far as you've followed along with the lessons in this book. Did you create a word processing file with KLyX? Maybe you've started using the Check Book Balancer to manage your finances? Try your printer setup by printing files of some of your favorite Linux programs.

2. Give yourself a challenge. If your modem can accept incoming voice calls, set up Kvoice as a telephone answering system.

Part V

The Beginner's Guide to Emacs

Hour

HOUR 16

Text Processing with Emacs

Emacs is one of the most powerful applications found in any Linux distribution. And the really amazing thing is that Emacs is available for nearly every operating system in existence. Emacs can be anything you want it to be. It is a text editor, a programming tool, an appointment book, and a collection of Internet utilities. You'll also find a few time-wasting games hidden away. And this is just the start. All this makes Emacs complex and intimidating. But don't let that stop you.

During the next three hours, you learn how to unravel the Emacs maze by doing a few familiar tasks. This hour shows you how to move around Emacs and work with text files. The next hour shows you how to customize Emacs. The last hour of this beginner's guide to Emacs shows you how to keep appointments and a diary with the calendar tools.

After you've finished this three-hour tour, begin using Emacs for some every day tasks, read the help files and search the Web for Emacs help, and gradually you'll learn a little more about the program as you go along. To get you going, during the next hour you work with Emacs and learn how to do the following:

- Navigate between several open files
- Create new files and open existing files
- Work with files containing formatted text
- Build outlines

Getting Started with Emacs

One way to learn a new software application easily is to apply what you've learned by working with similar applications. Well, this hour puts a twist on this theory and introduces you to Emacs by using XEmacs. XEmacs is GNU Emacs with a graphical interface and a few added applications. Even though it is easier to work with the XEmacs menus and toolbars, this hour shows you how to move around XEmacs using standard Emacs commands.

You'll want to memorize these commands for a few reasons. You can easily use Emacs on different operating systems if you know the commands. By using the commands introduced during this hour, you'll have a basis for understanding other Emacs commands that you may come across in the future. And, if you like to spend more time on the keyboard and less time with the mouse, the commands consist of just a few keystrokes.

Starting XEmacs

There are several flavors of Emacs found on the Linux-Mandrake CD. We'll start with XEmacs because it is installed by default. But you can still follow along during this hour if you wish to use the GNU Emacs version or the Emacs for X Windows version. If you can't find Emacs in the GNOME or KDE menus, type **emacs** from an X terminal. If XEmacs was automatically installed on your system, use Table 16.1 to get started.

TABLE 16.1 Locating XEmacs

When Starting From Here	Use This Method
GNOME Main Menu	Move the mouse pointer to Editors, XEmacs
KDE Application Starter	Click on Applications, X Emacs
X terminal window	Type **xemacs** and press Enter

When XEmacs first opens on your screen (as shown in Figure 16.1), you see the splash screen that shows the version of XEmacs you are using and some commands for accessing help.

FIGURE 16.1
The XEmacs splash screen.

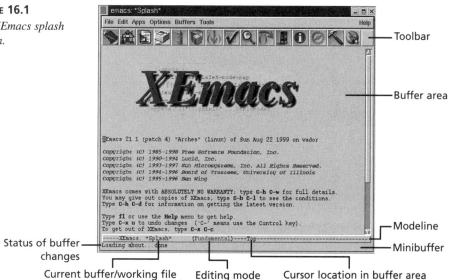

16

Before getting started, take some time to look around XEmacs. You may notice some screen elements that are unfamiliar and in other instances screen elements have names that you may not recognize. Here's a quick rundown of what you'll see on the screen. You'll learn more about these screen elements as you progress through the hour:

- The *toolbar* contains buttons that execute a number of common tasks. To find out what a button does, hold the mouse pointer over the button. A description will appear in the minibuffer.

- The *buffer* is the area in which you work with files and applications. Each open file and application is contained in a separate buffer. Figure 16.1 shows one buffer displayed in the XEmacs window. A window can be split so that multiple buffers can be viewed at one time.

- Think of the *modeline* as a status bar. The modeline tells you the name of the file contained in the buffer and whether changes to the buffer have been saved.

- The *minibuffer* is the Emacs command line. If Emacs thinks you are typing a command, the command will appear in the minibuffer. The minibuffer also prompts you to enter information that may be needed to complete the command.

Emacs assumes you are using a three-button mouse. So, if you are using a two-button mouse, here's the deal—click the right and left mouse buttons simultaneously when told to click the middle mouse button.

Switching Between Multiple Buffers

NEW TERM Every time you open a file, the file is placed in a *buffer*. The buffer keeps track of any changes that may have been made to the file while it is in the buffer. The buffer will store the changes, but you need to save the files to make the changes permanent.

When you have several files open, you can use the Buffer menu to display a buffer when you need it. When you are finished working with a file in a buffer, save the file and then close the buffer. Follow along with Lesson 16.1 to open a couple of buffers, look around them, and close a buffer that you don't need.

Lesson 16.1: Displaying the Emacs Tutorial in a Buffer Window

Emacs contains an extensive help system. Much of this help can be accessed from the Help menu or by entering a simple command. A good place to start is with the Emacs Tutorial. The tutorial not only contains good information, but you can use this file to practice moving around a text file and to edit text. Try these steps:

1. Open the Emacs tutorial in a buffer. Select Help, Basics, Tutorials, English from the menu bar. You can also press **Ctrl+H T**. The tutorial will appear in a buffer and you'll no longer see the splash screen. Notice the name of the tutorial file in the modeline.

2. Click on the Buffers menu. The menu list shows all the open buffers. You should see buffers for the tutorial, the splash screen, and a scratch. These are all the active buffers.

3. Click the Splash buffer to make the splash screen the active buffer.

4. To close the Splash buffer and to close the splash screen file, click File, Delete Buffer *Splash*. There should no longer be an open file or buffer for the splash screen and the tutorial buffer should now be the active buffer.

5. Click the Buffers menu again. The menu should only list the tutorial and scratch buffers.

> To find more Emacs help, use the Ctrl+H A command. It accesses the Hyper Apropos function. You supply a keyword and Emacs will list functions, variables, and commands that match your keyword. Press Enter or click the middle mouse button on one of the listings for more information. Typing Q will exit Hyper Apropos.

Working with Files

NEW TERM When you open existing files or create new files, you can either open the file so that it appears in the entire *frame*, or you can open the file in a *split window* so that it shares the frame with another file. Windows are an easy way to compare the information in two documents, or a way to browse one file while working in another.

Since you are working with XEmacs, moving between windows is as simple as clicking in the window that you want to make active. You can then use the scrollbars to move through the file.

Creating a New File

When you need a blank file, you can't just tell Emacs to give you a blank buffer. New files must be created before an empty buffer file will appear in the window. To create a new file, use one of the file commands:

- To open the file in a separate frame, click File, Open in New Frame or use the command Ctrl+X 5 F.

- To open the file in a window, select File, Open in Other Window. You can also use the command Ctrl+X 4 F.

Using the menu to create a new file opens a Find File dialog box like the one shown in Figure 16.2. Use the dialog box to navigate to the directory where you want to store the new file and then type a name for the file. An empty file appears in the frame or the window—whichever you chose. This file does not really exist until you save the file; it is stored in a temporary buffer until then.

16

FIGURE **16.2**

Create a blank file that you can edit in the buffer.

Use the middle mouse button to select directory

Type a name for the file

Lesson 16.2: Opening a File in a Split Window

Opening a file in a split window allows you to work with two files at one time. You should still have the Emacs tutorial open from the first lesson. You'll now open an empty file and learn how to navigate between the two windows:

1. Use the Ctrl+X 5 F command to create a new file. As you type the command, you'll see the command displayed in the minibuffer. When you finish typing the command, the minibuffer will display this message:

    Find file in other frame: ~/

    You are being asked for the directory in which you want to store the file and a name for the file. The default location is the home directory of your user account.

2. Type the directory path (if needed) and a filename, and press Enter. The frame will be split in two and a new file will be created in the bottom window, as shown in Figure 16.3.

FIGURE **16.3**

Splitting a window is an easy way to view the contents of several files at one time.

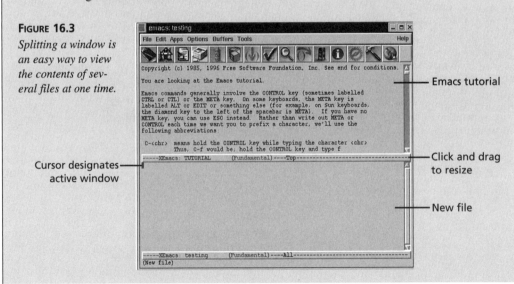

Emacs tutorial

Cursor designates active window

Click and drag to resize

New file

3. To move the cursor between windows, use the Ctrl+X O command. If the cursor was located in the new file, it will move to the tutorial file. Use the Ctrl+X O command to move back to the new file. As the cursor moves between windows, it remembers its last location in the window and will return to that location when you switch back to the window.

4. If you want to work in one window (to add or edit text) and scroll through the other window to read the information in the file, use the Esc Ctrl+V command to scroll the inactive window. You can only go forward, not backward, through the other window. Or, you can just use the mouse and drag the scrollbar.

5. To close a split window, place the cursor in the window you want to close, and then use the command Ctrl+X 0. This command leaves all other windows open.

16

Saving Files

After you've created a new file or made changes to a file in a buffer, you need to save the changes. When you want to save the contents of the buffer to the actual file, select File, Save [FILENAME] from the menu or use the Ctrl+X Ctrl+S command. The minibuffer will display a message that looks something like

```
Wrote /home/user/filename
```

When you want to save the contents of the buffer to a different file, you need to save the file under a new name. From the menu select File, Save As; or use the Ctrl+X Ctrl+W command. You need to specify the directory in which you want to save the file and a file-name.

To verify that your changes have been saved, look at the first four characters of the modeline. If there are no changes, "-----" appears in the modeline. If the text in the buffer has been edited and not saved, you'll see "--**" in the modeline. Read-only files use "--%%" in the modeline and when you make changes to a read-only buffer, you see "--%*" in the modeline.

When you switch between buffers, any work that is unsaved in the first buffer will remain unsaved when you are in the second buffer. If you don't want to switch back and forth to save the files, click File, Save Some Buffers (or use the command Ctrl+X S). For each buffer that contains unsaved changes, you are asked if you really want to save the file.

Opening Files

Earlier you learned how to close a file contained in a buffer. What do you do when you've closed a file and later want to work with it again? Use Table 16.2 to decide how to open the file.

TABLE 16.2   Opening Files in Either Frames or Split Windows

To Open a File	Use this Menu or Command
In a new frame	File, Open in New Frame
	Ctrl+X 5 F
In a new window	File, Open in New Window
	Ctrl+X Ctrl+F
As read-only	Ctrl+X Ctrl+R

The menu commands open a Find file dialog box (similar to the one shown in Figure 16.2). Click the middle mouse button to select a directory and also to select the file. The commands will display a prompt in the minibuffer where you supply the directory path and filename.

Working in Enriched Text Mode

NEW TERM   Now that you've learned how to move around Emacs, it's time to learn about a few different Emacs working modes. *Modes* are used when doing certain tasks, such as text processing or programming. By putting Emacs into a mode, the program can help you do your job easier. Emacs contains several major modes that function independently of each other, as well as a number of minor modes that can be used in conjunction with a major mode.

This section shows you how to work with formatted text in Emacs by using Text mode (a major mode) and Enriched mode (a minor mode). By using a combination of these two modes, you can create documents that contain formatted paragraphs and text, colored text and highlighting, and bold and italics.

Lesson 16.3: Starting a Text File

Before you begin entering and formatting text, you need to make sure that Emacs knows that you want to work with enriched text. Let's get in the mode by creating a new file and typing a few commands.

1. Create a new file in a new frame. Use the Ctrl+X 5 F command or choose File, Open in New Frame.

2. Select the directory in which you want the new file stored and type a name for the file. You can use the .doc extension for enriched text files.

3. Turn on Text mode by typing Alt+X text-mode and pressing Enter.

4. Turn on Enriched mode by typing `Alt+X enriched-mode` and pressing Enter. Be sure that you enable Text and Enriched mode before you begin entering text. To make sure you are in the right mode, look at the modeline. The editing mode should be Text Enriched.

5. Type a few words in the buffer, such as a title for your document.

6. Save the buffer contents to the file. You can use the `Ctrl+X Ctrl+S` command to do so.

16

Entering Text

Now that Emacs knows that you want to work with formatted text, you can begin typing in the buffer area. As you type, the cursor automatically moves to the next line in a paragraph when you get to the right edge of the window. At the end of each line, you'll see a continuation character like the one shown in Figure 16.4.

FIGURE 16.4

Type text in the buffer just as you do in a word processing program.

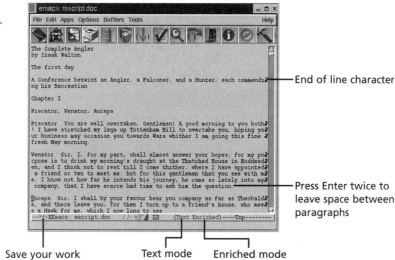

End of line character

Press Enter twice to leave space between paragraphs

Save your work   Text mode   Enriched mode

Notice that words do not always appear correctly at the end of lines. And, if you change the width of the Emacs window, the width of the text lines will change. If you want to use the default line width, use the Auto Fill mode. By using this minor mode, words will break when there is a space or return character. To use the Auto Fill command, use `Alt+X auto-fill-mode` and press Enter. Any text you type after applying the Auto Fill mode will fit within the default line width.

If you typed text before applying the Auto Fill mode, this text will not change. To change the rest of the paragraphs to fit in the default line length, use the Fill paragraph command. Place the cursor in the paragraph you want to refill and press Alt+Q. You'll find that the text is much easier to read. The text in the lesson example has been refilled and now looks much neater, as shown in Figure 16.5.

FIGURE 16.5

Use Auto Fill to refor-
mat paragraphs that
are longer than the
default line width.

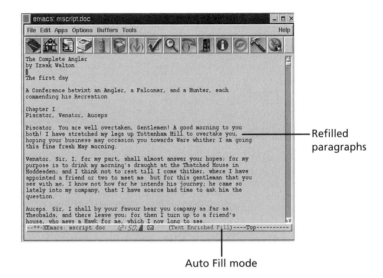

Refilled
paragraphs

Auto Fill mode

Inserting Repeating Characters

▼ SYNTAX

There may be times when you want to repeat a single character several times within the text. You sometimes see repeating characters as delimiting characters in a table of information (such as the table of contents of a book). The following code shows the syntax for repeating a single character multiples times in sequence in text:

```
Ctrl+U number character
```

Ctrl+U is the command that tells XEmacs that you will be using a numeric argument, number is the number of times you want to insert the character, and character is the key on the keyboard that you want to appear in the text.

For example, the command

```
Ctrl+U 12 ~
```

would produce

    ~~~~~~~~~~~~

Moving Around a Document

Emacs uses two methods to move around text in a buffer window. First there is the mouse/keyboard method. You can use the familiar mouse to work the scrollbar, and to move the cursor to a different position. There are also a few keys on the keyboard that move the cursor around—the arrow keys, Page Up, Page Down, Home, and End.

The other method involves typing commands. This isn't as hard as you think. Cursor commands involve holding either the Ctrl key or the Alt key while pressing another key on the keyboard. Table 16.3 lists some common commands that you can use to move the cursor around in a buffer window. It's also a good idea to learn these cursor commands if you want to become a more advanced user of Emacs.

NEW TERM In the Linux world, the Alt key on a PC keyboard is referred to as the *Meta key*. The Meta key terminology is a holdover from the UNIX world. Not all types of computer systems use the same keyboard keys. An alternative Meta key is the Esc key. But, use the Alt key, if it's on your keyboard.

TABLE 16.3   Using Cursor Commands to Move Through Text

Cursor Direction	Command
Down one screen	Ctrl+V
Up one screen	Alt+V
Up one line	Ctrl+P
Down one line	Ctrl+N
Left one character	Ctrl+B
Right one character	Ctrl+F
Center cursor position in window	Ctrl+L
Right one word	Alt+F
Left one word	Alt+B
Beginning of a line	Ctrl+A
End of a line	Ctrl+E
Beginning of a sentence	Alt+A
End of a sentence	Alt+E
Beginning of buffer file	Alt+<
End of buffer file	Alt+>

Using Numeric Arguments with Cursor Commands

SYNTAX ▼

Let's make things a bit more complex. You can move a specified number of character spaces, lines, words, or sentences. You don't have to move one line at a time or one screen at a time. The following code shows the syntax for using numeric arguments with cursor commands.

```
Ctrl+U [number] [cursor command]
```

Ctrl+U is the command that tells Emacs that you will be using a numeric argument to perform a cursor command, the `number` is the number of units you want to move, and `cursor command` indicates whether you want to move forward or backward, by characters or by sentences.

▲

The exceptions to this syntax are the `Ctrl+V` and `Alt+V` commands, which control screen movement. The numeric arguments that you use with these commands will not scroll the entire screen; the screen moves by the number of lines specified.

Let's pretend you want to move the cursor down five lines. You use the command `Ctrl+U 5 Ctrl+N`. As you type this key combination, you'll see the command in the minibuffer. To move forward in the text by eight sentences, for example, you use `Ctrl+U 8 Alt+E`.

> If there is no response to a command or the command is taking too long to execute, type the command `Ctrl+G`. You can also use `Ctrl+G` to discard a command that you do not want to finish.

Editing Text

NEW TERM   When you are trying to organize text in a document, you'll probably move things around a lot before you're satisfied with the final result. Emacs uses the good old cut and paste method, better known in the UNIX world as *kill* and *yank*.

When you want to move a block of text, first select the text with the mouse. Then click Edit, Cut; or for you keyboard fans, use the command `Ctrl+W`. Then position the cursor where you want to insert the text and select Edit, Paste. Table 16.4 lists other editing commands that you can use to rearrange your words.

> If you want to place text on the X clipboard, perhaps to use it in other applications, select the text and click Edit, Cut. The text can be pasted to another place in Emacs or into another application.

TABLE 16.4 Edit Commands

To Perform this Edit	Use this Key Combination
Delete one character to the left	Delete
Delete one character to the right	Ctrl+D
Cut (kill) word to the left of cursor	Alt+Delete
Cut one word to the right of cursor	Alt+D
Cut from cursor to end of line	Ctrl+K
Cut from cursor to end of sentence	Alt+K
Cut a specified number of lines	Ctrl+U [number] Ctrl+K
Paste (yank) deleted text	Ctrl+Y
Undo edit	Ctrl+X U

16

To display a help file for a command, use Ctrl+H K [command]. If you want to know more about the Yank command, use Ctrl+H F Ctrl+Y. For general help, use the Ctrl+H Ctrl+H command.

Enhancing a Document

After you have entered and organized the text in the file, it's time to format the text. You can apply bold and italic text formatting, change paragraph alignment, and make other formatting changes from the menus, or you can use a number of formatting commands.

Before you can perform any formatting commands, text or paragraphs must be selected. You can select a paragraph by placing the cursor inside the paragraph. To select text, click and hold at the beginning of the text and drag to the end of the text.

Another way to select a block of text is to place the cursor at the beginning of the text and press Ctrl+Spacebar. This sets a Mark in the document. Then, hold down the Shift key while you use the arrow keys to move the cursor to the end of the block of text. Once the block of text is selected, you can perform the command, such as making the block of text bold.

To change formatted text back to the default text style, select the text and choose Edit, Text Properties, Remove Properties from the menu.

Formatting Text

There are a number of formatting attributes that you can apply to text. Before you can apply the attribute, you need to select the text. Text formatting attributes can be found in the Edit menu under Text Properties, Face.

You have two options for using commands to format text. If the text that you want to format already appears in the buffer, select the text and then use one of the formatting commands listed in Table 16.5. If you want to set the text formatting before you enter the text, place the cursor where you want the next text to start, use the formatting command, and then begin typing the text.

TABLE 16.5 Applying Text Formatting

Text Format Attribute	Command
Default text format	Ctrl+X Shift+F D
Bold text	Ctrl+X Shift+F B
Italic text	Ctrl+X Shift+F I
Bold and italic text	Ctrl+X Shift+F L
Underline text	Ctrl+X Shift+F U

To view text formatting, select the text and click Edit, Text Properties, List Properties.

Lesson 16.4: Changing the Default Tab Positions

If you want to line up text in rows and columns, the easiest way is to use tabs. By default, Emacs sets tab positions every 10 spaces. Follow along and change the tab stops for your document:

1. Place the cursor in the document at the place where you want to use tabs.

2. Use the Tab Stops command by typing **Alt+X edit-tab-stops** and pressing Enter. This displays the Tab Stops buffer shown in Figure 16.6.

3. To delete a tab marker, you must first select it by either using the Right Arrow key to highlight the marker, or by clicking on the tab marker. Then, press the Spacebar and the marker will disappear.

4. To create a tab marker, move the cursor to the position where you want to place the marker and type a colon (:) character.

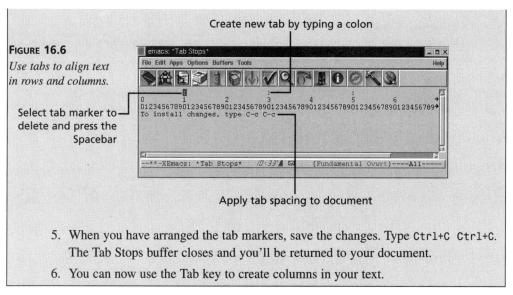

16

FIGURE 16.6
Use tabs to align text in rows and columns.

Create new tab by typing a colon

Select tab marker to delete and press the Spacebar

Apply tab spacing to document

5. When you have arranged the tab markers, save the changes. Type Ctrl+C Ctrl+C. The Tab Stops buffer closes and you'll be returned to your document.

6. You can now use the Tab key to create columns in your text.

Formatting Paragraphs

You'll want to align paragraphs in different order to make them appear differently on the page. To change a paragraph's alignment, select the paragraph and then choose an alignment from Edit, Text Properties, Justification. You have these choices:

- *Center* places every line in the middle between the left and right current margins.
- *Full* justifies the text so that the left edge of the text is on the left margin and the right edge of the text is on the right margin. This alignment is difficult to read in large blocks of text.
- *Right* aligns each line along the right margin. The left edge of the paragraph is jagged.
- *Unfilled* aligns each line along the left margin. The right edge of the paragraph is jagged.

> You can indent paragraphs to add emphasis. Select the entire block of text that you want to indent, and then choose Edit, Text Properties, Indentation, Indent More.

Adding Color to a Document

There are two ways to add color to text. You can change the color of the text characters—the foreground color. You can also apply a color to the area behind the text—the background color.

Before you begin applying color to your text, display the list of colors from which you can choose. From the menu, select Edit, Text Properties, Display Colors. The Colors buffer will appear in a split window at the bottom of the frame, as seen in Figure 16.7.

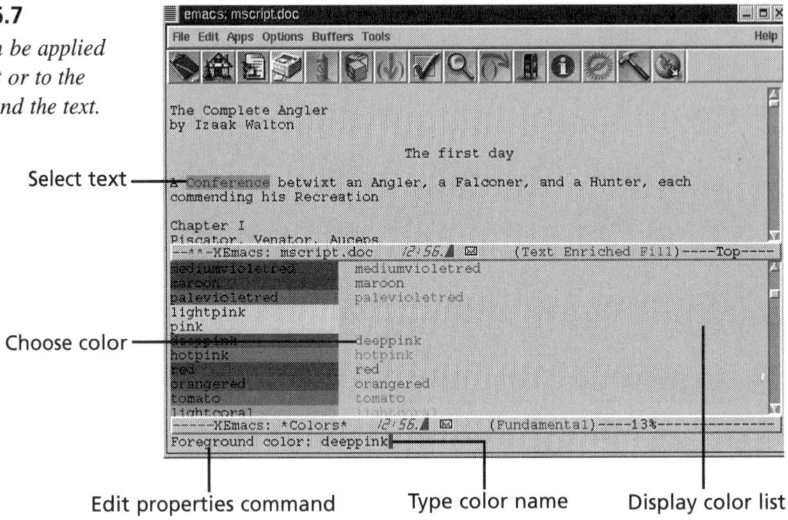

FIGURE **16.7**

Color can be applied to the text or to the area around the text.

FIGURE **16.7**

Color can be applied to the text or to the area around the text.

Your next step is to select the text to which you want to apply a color, and decide whether you want to use a foreground color or a background color. Now, go back to the Edit, Text Properties menu and select either Foreground Color or Background Color. The final menu that appears does not list any colors, it only lists an Other option. When you select Other, you are prompted to type a color name in the buffer. Here's where the Color buffer comes in handy. Scroll through the list until you see a color and then type the name in the buffer. When you press Enter, the color will be applied to the text.

The next time you go back to the Foreground Color and Background Color menus, colors that you've selected previously appear in the list. To reuse a color, select the color from the menu instead of typing the color name in the buffer.

Creating an Outline

The most important tool used by writers is the outline. An outline helps you arrange your thoughts about a subject in a logical order. It also shows the relevance of one topic in relation to the other topics. Outlines aren't just necessary for lengthy manuscripts (such as this book). You'll find it much easier to write a short term paper, a research report, or a memo to the boss if you start with an outline.

Before you begin your outline, open a new file and turn on Enriched Text mode. If you need a refresher course, go back to Lesson 16.3. To this mode, you'll need to add the Outline minor mode. Type Alt+X `outline-minor-mode`. The editing mode in the mode-line will read

```
(Text Enriched Outl)
```

Your outline will consist of two types of lines—heading text and body text. A heading represents a specific topic level and is preceded by a series of asterisks. A single asterisk is a first level heading, two asterisks represent a second level heading, and so on. Body text is any information that supports the heading above it. Body text does not use an asterisk. The following is an example of how headings and body text are represented in an outline file:

```
* First level heading
Regular text appears within the outline.
Don't use the asterisk before the line of text.
** Second level heading
** Second level heading
Regular text can add descriptions and notes to your outline.
*** Third level heading
*** Third level heading
* First level heading
Another first-level topic with its header line.
```

If you need to move text around in your outline, use the `kill` and `yank` commands discussed earlier. You can also expand and collapse your outline to see how things are progressing.

You may have noticed that three new menus appear on the menu bar when you added the Outline minor mode—Headings, Show, and Hide. Use the Headings menu to jump from level to level in the outline. If you'd rather use the commands, you'll find the commands listed at the right of the menu. The Hide menu will collapse the outline so that body text disappears, or so that body text and lower outlines levels will disappear. To bring these hidden items back into view, use the Show menu.

Be sure to show the entire document before editing the outline. If you delete a visible line, all the following invisible (or hidden) lines will also be deleted.

16

Summary

There you have it, your first hour on the Emacs tour. We hope you had a good time looking around this most powerful program. You've just barely scratched the surface with Emacs. You may want to go back and commit some of the Emacs commands that you've learned to memory. These commands make it easier to create files, move around within a buffer, and edit and format text. You may also want to play around with split windows and frames. Split windows and frames come in handy when you need to work with multiple files; or, as you'll find out over the next two hours, windows and frames are great for working with multiple Emacs applications.

Q&A

Q How do I create split windows that are side by side, not one on top of the other?

A Use the `Ctrl+X 3` command.

Q I want to change the margins for my Emacs file. How do I do this?

A You can't exactly change the margins, but you'll change the number of characters that display on a line. By default, Emacs is set to display 70 characters per line. To change this, use the command

`Ctrl+U [number] Ctrl+X F`

Where `[number]` is the number of characters that you want to appear on a line.

Q How do I use Emacs to search for text and replace it with text I specify?

A You can use two methods to get to the search and replace command. From the menu, select Edit, Replace; or use the `Alt+%` command. Both of these display the following in the minibuffer:

`Query replace:`

Type the text you want replaced and press Enter. The minibuffer will contain the following:

`Query replace [text] with:`

Type the text that you want to use as a replacement and press Enter. Emacs will search the buffer for the text and when it finds the first instance, you'll see the following in the minibuffer:

`Query replacing [text] with [text]:`

You'll also see that the first occurrence of the text is highlighted in the buffer. If you want to replace the text, type `Y` and press Enter. Type `N` if you don't want to replace the highlighted text. Emacs will then find the next occurrence. Type `Q` to stop the search and replace.

Q Can Emacs display the cursor position as a line number instead of as a percentage of the document?

A Use the `Alt+X line-number-mode` command. This will display the line in which the cursor is located in the modeline. You can also display the column where the cursor is located by using the `Alt+X column-number-mode` command. These two commands act as toggle switches. When you no longer want to see the line and column positions in the modeline, type the command a second time.

16

Workshop

Here you are, at the end of another hour. Standard operating procedure says it's time for another workshop where you can test the skills you've acquired. If you can breeze through the Quiz and Exercises, jump right on over into the next hour. If you stumble a bit, don't worry; no one will ever know if you read the lesson a second time.

Quiz

1. Where is the modeline located in the Emacs window and what purpose does it serve?

2. How do you start a new file in Emacs?

3. Which commands move the cursor to the beginning of the buffer file and to the end of the buffer file?

4. How many asterisks precede a third level heading in an outline?

Exercises

1. Get on the Internet and learn a bit more about Emacs and XEmacs. Visit the GNU Web site and see what they have available for Emacs (`www.gnu.org/software/emacs/`). The XEmacs site (`http://www.xemacs.org/`) also contains a few user manuals. For help on the Gnus newsreader, go to `www.gnus.org`. To find out more about the VM mail reader, try `www.wonderworks.com`. If you like newsgroups, check out `gnu.emacs.help`, `comp.emacs`, `comp.emacs.xemacs`, `gnu.emacs.gnus`, and `gnu.emacs.vm.info`.

2. Before you print any document, you want to make sure that everything is spelled correctly. Try the Emacs spell checker. You'll find it under Apps, Spell-Check Buffer.

HOUR 17

The Emacs Help System

Now that you've had a chance to get acquainted with Emacs and learn about it's text-processing modes, it's time to use Emacs to learn more about Linux, Emacs, and other GNU applications.

To help you understand some of the concepts and commands that were covered in Hour 16, "Text Processing with Emacs," you'll use the Emacs help commands.

You may also want to spend some time learning about the programming language that keeps Emacs running. Emacs, and some of the other programs that you've seen that run under Emacs, use the Lisp programming language. If you understand what makes Emacs tick, you can create your own applications that will work with Emacs. You will also be able to customize Emacs to fit your needs.

During the next hour, you learn how to do the following:

- Read Linux man pages with Emacs
- Search for GNU documentation
- Find documentation on commands and Lisp functions

Reading the Linux man Pages

Remember the Linux man pages from Hour 3, "Troubleshooting the Linux-Mandrake Installation"? Well, guess what. They're back! Only, in Hour 3, you learned how to read the man pages from the command line. You can also read man pages in Emacs.

Depending on which flavor of Emacs you installed, the menu sequence to the man pages varies. To access the man pages in Emacs for X11, select Help, Manuals, Read Man Page. In XEmacs, go to Help, Manuals, UNIX Manual. The following command appears in the minibuffer:

```
Manual entry: (default buffer.)
```

If you want to display the man page that describes how the man pages work, type **man** and press Enter. This is the same as using the brief syntax for man at the command line as follows:

```
man man
```

The man page appears in a buffer window, like the example in Figure 17.1.

 You can save the man page to your user directory and then use the text modes and editing tools you learned about in Hour 16 to work with the files.

FIGURE 17.1

Display man pages in a separate frame or a split window.

Scrollbar ┘

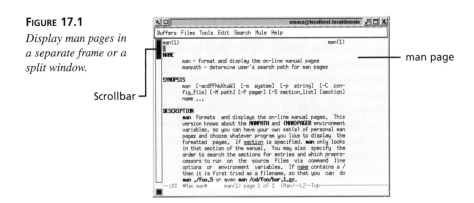

man page

Using the Texinfo Documentation System

One way to learn more about Emacs and other GNU programs is to browse through the Texinfo documentation system. This documentation is read using a program called Info. To display a list of the major topics (shown in Figure 17.2) that can be accessed by Info, use the Ctrl+H I command.

FIGURE 17.2

The Texinfo documents appear in the Directory node.

Select a topic —

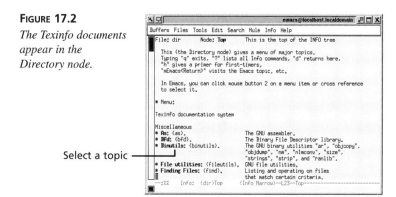

You can move through these Info pages using the cursor commands discussed in Hour 16. The topics are listed in bold along the left. When you hold the mouse over a topic, it is highlighted. To view the documentation for a topic, middle-click (or click the right and left mouse buttons simultaneously) the topic. Figure 17.3 shows the Info page for the `tar` command.

17

If you'd like to learn more about Info, use the Ctrl+H I H command to display the Info Getting Started manual.

FIGURE 17.3

You can navigate through Info pages much like you navigate Web pages.

Select a menu topic —

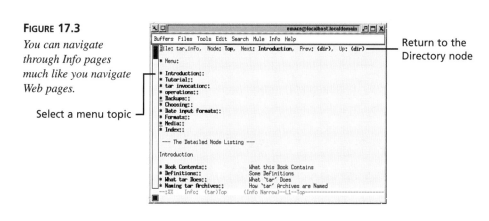

 Return to the Directory node

Each Info file contains a menu that you can use to move around in the Info file. To display a menu topic, middle-click the topic name.

You can use the middle button with the Node:, Next:, Prev:, and Up: navigation tools at the top of the page to jump from page to page in the Info file, and back and forth to the Directory node where you can middle-click to select another topic.

Displaying Command Documentation

The first Emacs command that was discussed in the last hour was the Ctrl+H T command. When you pressed this series of keys, the Emacs Tutorial appeared in a buffer window.

From that point, you saw long lists of these commands that performed tasks such as moving the cursor, editing text, and working in text modes. These commands were all shown as a series of keystrokes.

If you'd like to know more about these commands, you use the Describe Key command.

The Syntax for the Describe Key Command

The following code shows how to find information about a command:

```
Ctrl+H K [command key sequence]
```

where Ctrl+H K is the command that displays the help documentation and [command key sequence] is the command (typed as a series of keystrokes) for which you are requesting the documentation.

For example, to view the documentation for the save command, type the following:

```
Ctrl+H K
```

This displays the following in the minibuffer:

```
Find documentation for key:
```

Then, type the key combination for the save command, which is

```
Ctrl+X Ctrl+S
```

The documentation for the command (shown in Figure 17.4) appears in a buffer window.

Command   Lisp function name

FIGURE 17.4

Learn about commands with the Describe Key command.

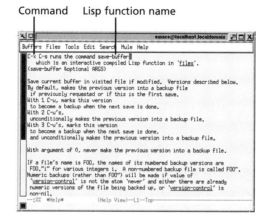

Introducing Lisp Functions

In the last hour, you learned how to work with formatted text in Text mode. If you remember, the command that enabled Text mode is `Alt+X text-mode`. The `text-mode` portion of the command is the Lisp function. You may have also noticed the Lisp function name on the first line of the documentation displayed by the Describe Key command.

NEW TERM   The GNU Emacs text editor is written in the *Lisp* programming language. Lisp stands for LISt Processing. This programming language uses code that is written in lists of instructions. These instructions tell the computer what to do when a command is presented.

Lisp keeps these lists in order by marking the boundaries of a list with parentheses. This makes Lisp code look odd to the non-programmer.

> If you want to learn more about Lisp programming, check out the Programming in Emacs Lisp Web page at `www.gnu.org/manual/emacs-lisp-intro`.

If you want to customize Emacs, a basic background in Lisp programming is essential. If you want to use Emacs as an electronic mail reader, you need to write a short Lisp function so that Emacs knows where to pick up your mail.

The Describe Function command displays the documentation for a requested Lisp function. Type **Ctrl+H F** to display the following in the minibuffer:

```
Describe function:
```

Type the function name and press Enter. If you want to know more about the function associated with the Text mode command, type the following:

```
text-mode
```

and press Enter. The documentation for the function appears as shown in Figure 17.5.

FIGURE 17.5

Learn about Lisp functions with the Describe Function command.

To read the documentation for the mode in which you are currently working, type **Ctrl+H M**.

Summary

After working with the man pages and the Info files, you should have a better understanding of how Linux operates and how to use some of the commands and programs that are installed on your Linux system. If you have an interest in programming, you may want to use Emacs as a programming environment.

Q&A

Q Where can I learn more about Emacs?

A The best place to start is at the Emacs Web site (`www.emacs.org`).

Q I typed a few commands and something strange happened to Emacs. And...I don't remember what I did. Is there some way to see what commands I used?

A Use the `Ctrl+H L` command to display the last 100 commands you entered. Then use the `Ctrl+H K` and `Ctrl+H F` commands to learn more about the commands displayed by the `Ctrl+H L` command.

Workshop

This past hour was spent learning how to use Emacs to learn more about Emacs and Linux. It's up to you to continue your education. Test your knowledge and then see if you can teach yourself a new Emacs trick or two.

17

Quiz

1. Where do you find the `man` command?

2. How do you find documentation on a command?

3. What is Lisp?

Exercises

1. Create your own Linux help manual. As you browse through the man pages, Info pages, and other help files in Emacs, copy information that you find useful and that will help you understand Linux and Emacs. You can also add your own notes and directions.

2. Teach your computer to speak. Emacspeak (available at `cs.cornell.edu/home/raman/emacspeak`) is a speech interface designed for the visually impaired. You may want to check out the Emacspeak FAQ at `www.emacs.org/Emacspeak-HOWTO.html`.

HOUR 18

Time Management with Emacs

Trying to keep your life and business organized can sometimes get confusing if you don't keep track of important dates and meetings. You'll find many calendars in the Linux-Mandrake distribution, such as Ical and the GNOME Calendar.

There's also a calendar application that works inside of Emacs. This calendar can be used to record appointments and set reminders so that you don't miss meetings, to keep track of important dates such as birthdays and anniversaries, and to help remind you of things you need to get done. Before you start this hour, you may want to read Hour 16, "Text Processing with Emacs," if you are not familiar with how Emacs works. This hour helps you organize your time by introducing you to the Emacs calendar. You learn how to

- Flip through the months of the calendar and select dates
- Look up holidays and moon phases
- Keep a list of important dates and appointments
- Set reminders so that you won't miss any meetings with the boss

Trying the Emacs Calendar

You'll find that the Emacs calendar lacks the slick graphical interface found in some other calendar programs. Don't let this keep you away. The Emacs calendar can keep your life organized quite nicely and you'll get a chance to learn more about Emacs. As you work through this next hour, you learn how to use lots of commands for navigating around the calendar, in addition to using the mouse. And, as we've said before, the more you use Emacs, the more you'll find out about it, and then you'll want to learn more.

Before you get started, make sure Emacs or XEmacs is displayed on your computer screen.

Starting the Calendar

The easiest way to get started is to display a three-month calendar that includes the current month, the previous month, and the following month. From the menu, select Apps, Calendar, 3-Month Calendar. You can also use the Alt+X calendar command. The calendar will show in a buffer at the bottom of the frame like the one shown in Figure 18.1. You'll notice that the current date is highlighted.

FIGURE **18.1**

The Emacs calendar displays the current three months. Scroll through the calendar to display other months.

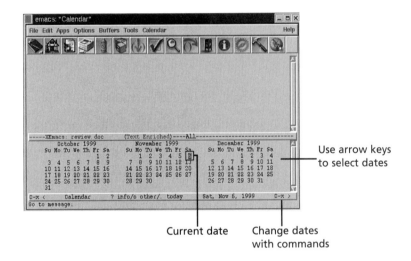

Use arrow keys to select dates

Current date   Change dates with commands

If you want to display a different three-month period, you'll need to use the Ctrl+U Alt+X calendar command. The minibuffer will prompt you for a year (the current year displays by default and you can edit this date) and then a month. Type the month that you want to view and press Enter. You'll see the month you requested and the previous and following months.

Moving from Date to Date

Before you can add diary information to a date (such as appointments and birthdays) or view other information for a specific date, the date on the calendar must be highlighted. You can move around the calendar by using the Arrow keys on the keyboard or the Page Up and Page Down keys. An easier way is to use the commands found in Table 18.1 to travel through the days, weeks, months, and years.

TABLE 18.1 Using Commands to Select a Date on the Calendar

To Select This Time Period	Use This Command
Next day	Ctrl+F
Previous day	Ctrl+B
Beginning of the week	Ctrl+A
End of the week	Ctrl+E
One week forward	Ctrl+N
One week backward	Ctrl+P
Beginning of the month	Alt+A
End of the month	Alt+E
One month forward	Alt+}
One month backward	Alt+{
Beginning of the year	Alt+<
End of the year	Alt+>
One year forward	Ctrl+X]
One year backward	Ctrl+X [
Go to a specified date	G+D
Go to current date	. (Period)

18

A Few Fun Features

Before we get into the mundane, calendar-keeping tasks, let's play around with the calendar a bit. There are ways to display holidays for a specific day or for a range of days. Or, if you need to know the phases of the moon so that you can plan your summer garden, the calendar can give you those dates also.

Displaying Holidays

The Emacs calendar knows the dates of all holidays recognized in the United States, the major religious holidays, and the occurrence of solstices and equinoxes. You can use the menu to display a list of holidays, but the commands in Table 18.2 give you more control over which holidays are displayed.

TABLE 18.2 Commands for Displaying Holidays

To Show Holidays For	Type This Command
Selected date	H or click middle mouse button
Months displayed in calendar	A or pick Apps, Calendar, Holidays from the menu
Previous, current, and next months	Alt+X holidays
Specified month and year	Ctrl+U Alt+X holidays
Specified range of years	Alt+X list-holidays
Highlight holidays in calendar	X
Unmark highlighted holidays	U

Need a short break? Look in the Apps, Games menu. You'll find a number of time wasters, fun games, and rudely humorous quotations.

It's Full Moon Again

When you need to know when the next full moon is coming around, you can ask the calendar to display the dates of each phase of the moon. The calendar will also show the time for each phase (using your local time zone). Table 18.3 lists the commands used to display the dates and times for the moon phases for a period of time that you select.

TABLE 18.3 Use the Moon Phase Calendar to Decide When to Plant that Vegetable Garden

Display Moon Phases For	Use This Command
Calendar period displayed	Shift+M
Previous, current, and next month	Alt+X phases-of-moon Apps Calendar, Phases of the Moon, from menu

Dear Diary

Do you need to keep track of things that need to be done, places to be visited, birthdays and anniversaries, or what you've done? Create a diary file in Emacs and write to your heart's content. The diary file stores your thoughts, appointments, and important dates. Emacs can search the diary to help you find a specific event in the volumes of words that you've stored away. For those that need a gentle reminder that it's time to leave for a dentist appointment, Emacs can take the place of the string you keep tied around your pinky finger.

Lesson 18.1: Starting Your Diary

The first time you make an entry in the diary, you'll also create a file in which all your diary entries, appointments, and reminders are stored. This file is actually just in the buffer until you add something to the buffer and then save the file. This lesson shows you how to start a diary file, add a simple diary entry, and then save the file. Follow these steps:

1. Display the month in the calendar that contains the date for which you want to create a diary entry.

2. Click with the middle mouse button (or if you don't have a middle mouse button, click the left and right buttons simultaneously) on the date you want to create the diary entry. A menu will appear.

3. Click Insert diary entry. A new window will appear in the top of the frame and will be named "diary." The date you selected will appear in the diary buffer. You'll also notice that there is a blank space between the date and the cursor. There must always be a space between the date and the beginning of each entry.

4. Begin typing the diary entry. An entry can consist of one or more lines. If you use multiple lines, you'll need to leave at least one blank character space at the beginning of each line after the date. By leaving a blank space, you are telling Emacs that this is just one entry. Emacs ignores lines that do not begin with a date or a blank space. Figure 18.2 shows how a diary entry might appear.

5. Save the diary file using the Ctrl+X Ctrl+S command. You now have a diary file that can be closed when it's not needed.

When you want to read your diary, you'll need to open the diary file. Select any date on the calendar and use the S command. Yes, just press the S key on your keyboard.

18

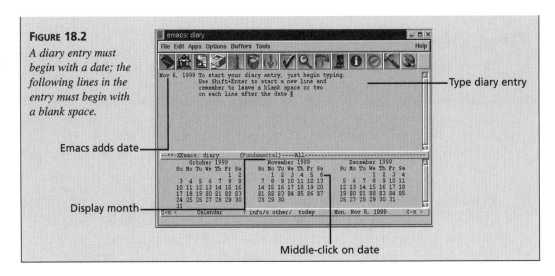

FIGURE 18.2

A diary entry must begin with a date; the following lines in the entry must begin with a blank space.

Keeping Track of Appointments

In addition to just keeping a diary, you can use the diary file to keep track of appointments or tasks that need to be done on specific dates. The diary can track an appointment or task that occurs on a single date in the future, or it can keep track of items that recur on a regular cycle. After you enter your appointments, you can have Emacs send you a reminder sometime before that important meeting or deadline.

Entering an Appointment

When an appointment is expected to occur only once, you can create a simple diary entry by selecting the appropriate date and using the I+D command. When you press the I key on the keyboard followed by the D key, the selected date will appear at the end of the diary file. You can then type a short description of the appointment (see Figure 18.3).

Don't worry about the order in which you see these entries in the file. You'll learn about search commands later so that you can find the information you need.

When you enter the time of the appointment, make sure you indicate the time in terms of morning or afternoon. And be sure there is no space in the time. For example, use a format such as 9:15 a.m. or 6:00 p.m. Emacs uses this time format to set reminders.

FIGURE 18.3

Enter the time of the appointment and a short description.

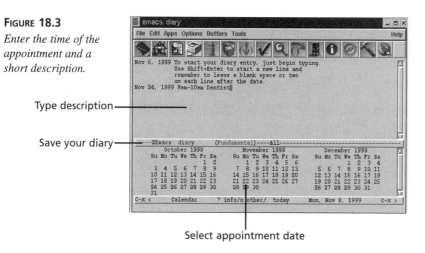

Type description—

Save your diary—

Select appointment date

Remember that the same rules apply when entering appointments. If you want to use more than one line, all lines following the date must begin with a blank space. You'll also want to save the diary file after adding an entry.

Lesson 18.2: Keeping Track of Birthdays and Anniversaries

When you need to remember special dates and the year on which they occurred, create a special diary entry to record the date and year of the event. Follow these steps to do so:

1. Display the calendar for the year and month for which you want to record the birth, marriage, or other event.

2. Select the date on which the event occurred.

3. Use the I+A command to create the diary entry.

4. Type the information about who was born or who got married. You'll have an entry that looks something like

   ```
   %%(diary-anniversary 1 22 1901) Grandma Goodie's birthday
   ```

   This entry will appear on January 22 of every year after Grandma's birth in 1901.

5. Save the diary file.

Entering Recurring Appointments

You may have meetings or things to do on a regular basis; whether that be weekly, monthly, or yearly. If an event occurs regularly, there's no need to select each day the event occurs and make separate entries. You can tell Emacs how often the event occurs and Emacs will make all the necessary entries. The diary file in Figure 18.4 shows an example of each of the commands used to keep track of recurring events.

FIGURE **18.4**

*Emacs uses a special
date format to keep
track of items that
occur on a regular
basis.*

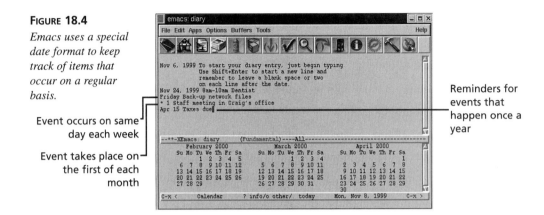

Event occurs on same
day each week

Event takes place on
the first of each
month

Reminders for
events that
happen once a
year

- When an event occurs on the same day each week (such as backing up your computer files every Friday), you'll first need to select any date that falls on that day of
  the week, and then use the I+W command. The day of the week will appear at the
  end of the diary file. All you need to do is type yourself a note about what needs to
  be done.

- For meetings that occur on the same date each month, select the date and use the
  I+M command.

- To keep track of events that happen on the same date each year, select the date (the
  year you use is not important), and use the I+Y command.

Lesson 18.3: Scheduling Vacation Time

There may be times when you need to block out a range of dates for a vacation, confer-
ence, or when the kid will be off to summer camp.

1. Middle-click the first day of the vacation and select Mark date. The first day of the
   vacation is remembered by Emacs and you'll see the message "Mark set" in the
   minibuffer.

2. Click the last day of the vacation and then use the I+B command. The beginning of
   the diary entry will be placed at the end of the diary file and will look like this:

   %%(diary-block 12 19 1999 12 31 1999)

   This shows a vacation that is scheduled for December 19, 1999 to December 31,
   1999.

3. Type a description of the vacation.

4. Save the diary file.

Setting Appointment Reminders

In order for Emacs to automatically remind you of appointments a few minutes in advance, you'll need to add a few lines to your .emacs file. If you think you want to tackle this task, go to Lesson 18.4 and do a little customization work.

Lesson 18.4: Customizing Your .emacs File

Before Emacs can notify you of upcoming appointments, you'll need to customize the file that controls how Emacs works. Follow these steps to do so:

1. Open the .emacs file by using the `Ctrl+X Ctrl+F` command.

2. Type `.emacs` and press Enter. The Emacs configuration file will appear in a window.

3. Scroll to the bottom of the file and type the following:
   ```
   (display-time)
   (add-hook 'diary-hook 'appt-make-list)
   (diary 0)
   ```

4. Save the file and then close it.

5. You can now go back to the calendar and diary and enter any appointments that you have scheduled. When you are finished, save the diary file.

6. At some time after midnight each night, Emacs updates the appointment list so that it is ready for you the following morning.

7. First thing each morning, display the diary file in an Emacs window. You can use the `D` command if the calendar is selected, or use the `Alt+X diary` command. During the day, Emacs will give you a reminder 10 minutes before the scheduled appointment.

18

Searching the Diary File

Now that you have added tomes of text, appointments, and birthdays, you may be wondering how you are going to search through a large diary file. Emacs can do this for you. You just need to give Emacs a date. Table 18.4 lists several commands you can use to display diary entries for a date you select. If you want to know whether a date has entries, use the highlight dates command to highlight the dates on the calendar that have entries.

TABLE 18.4 Display Diary Entries According to Your Needs

To Display This	Use This Command
Diary entries for selected date	D
Diary entries for current date	Alt+X diary
Entire diary file	S
Highlight dates with diary entries	M
Remove highlight on calendar	U
Print the diary buffer	Alt+X print-diary-entries
Email reminders to yourself	Alt+X diary-mail-entries

Summary

After spending some time with the Emacs calendar and diary, you've hopefully found at least one way in which you can use these tools to organize your time and keep you on schedule. One of the benefits of using calendar tools to make better use of your time is having more time for fun stuff.

Q&A

Q **I want to edit some of the entries that I've made in my diary. What's the best way to do this?**

A First, you need to display the entire diary file. Do this by selecting any date in the calendar and using the S command. This will display the entire diary file. If you don't edit the entire diary file, you may inadvertently delete something that you'll need later. After you make your changes, you need to save the diary file with the Ctrl+X Ctrl+S command.

Q **Is there an easy way to remind myself to change my contacts every three weeks?**

A Use cyclic diary entries to keep track of events that occur on a regular basis but do not occur on the same day each month or week. To create this type of entry, select the first date on the calendar on which you want to set the event (such as the day you started a new pair of contacts) and then use the I+C command. The minibuffer will prompt you for a number of days. For a 3-week interval, type **21**. You'll see a diary entry that looks something like this:

```
%%(diary-cyclic 21 11 6 1999) Change contacts
```

Workshop

Emacs may not look like the classic diary with the lock and key, but it does make a suitable electronic substitute. Use the Emacs calendar and diary to keep your life organized and to record your personal history. To get yourself motivated, stick around for the workshop.

Quiz

1. What is the quickest way to move to a date that is several months or years away from the currently selected date?

2. How do you keep track of appointments and other events that happen on certain days of the week, month, or year?

3. How do you display your appointment list and other diary entries for the current date?

Exercises

1. Sit down at the end of the day when life has quieted down and spend time with your diary. Tell your diary what you did during the day, your goals and aspirations, your grumps and gripes, successes and failures. Once in a while, go back in time and read your diary.

2. Find out when the sun is going to rise and fall on certain days in your hometown. Before you begin, you need to know the latitude and longitude of your location. You can find the sunrise and sunset times by going to the Apps menu and selecting Calendar, Sunrise/Sunset. You can also select a date on the calendar and use the Shift+S command. The minibuffer will prompt you for the information it needs in order to give you the times.

18

Part VI

Going for the Graphics

Hour

HOUR 19

The Gimp

One of the more popular and most sophisticated programs in the Linux lineup is The Gimp. The Gimp is the all-purpose graphics tool that can handle everything from simple drawings to heavy-duty photo editing. Everyone—from the budding artist to the graphics professional—will find the tools they need to create spectacular artwork in The Gimp.

There is so much that you can do with The Gimp, that we can barely touch the surface of this cool graphics tool in just an hour. But, what we can do is help you set up your computer system so that you can use The Gimp according to your needs as well as show you a few photo editing tricks.

To help you get started with The Gimp, you learn the following during this hour:

- Hardware requirements for running The Gimp and where to get help using scanners and graphics tablets
- How to work with the brushes and paints in The Gimp's toolbox
- A few tips and pointers for enhancing photographs and performing quick touch-ups

Getting Ready for an Art Adventure

Before you begin exploring The Gimp, you may want to sit down and decide how you plan to use it. Do you want to create simple illustrations for use in a report or term paper? Do you want to create images for your Web site? Do you just want to make your photographs look better? Are you a starving artist in need of a high-end graphics application that will run on your low-end workstation?

Depending on your needs, take a look at how much computer power you will need in order to run The Gimp efficiently. You can also use scanners, digital cameras, and graphics tablets in your quest for better art. But, before you hook up your scanner to your Linux system, you need to check the hardware compatibility list and make sure you have the additional drivers and software to make these peripherals work with The Gimp.

System Requirements

Since The Gimp can handle any graphics job (from creating a simple illustration to editing a high-resolution photo scan and handling pre-press production), it is important to know just how much hardware is required so that you can use The Gimp to fit your needs.

At a minimum, The Gimp will run on a 486-66/DX2 computer with 16MB RAM and a 40MB Linux swap partition. You will also need space on your hard drive to work with image files. Ideally, you should keep a minimum of 200MB hard drive space available. A computer with this configuration can produce simple illustrations and handle low-resolution (and small file size) photo images. But, be warned, The Gimp may perform slowly in this environment.

 Although The Gimp will run with an 8-bit (256 color) display, you may not always like the results. The Gimp prefers a color depth of 16-bit or greater.

Like many software applications, if you want more performance, get more RAM. More RAM also means larger swap space, which means that you can create larger images with less drain on your system.

Web graphics work requires a beefier computer. A Pentium-133 with 32MB RAM and a 64MB swap partition will perform admirably. Most home users and many small businesses will find this setup adequate for creating greeting cards, brochures, and GIF and JPEG images.

The professional artist or photographer will require more from The Gimp in terms of the capability to handle large file sizes, perform more complex image editing, and prepare photos and graphics for the printing press. If this is where you want to go with The Gimp, you need at least a Pentium-200 with a minimum of 64MB RAM. You may also want to have 500MB or more of free hard drive space.

> If you have a Wacom graphics tablet that supports the Wacom IV or Wacom V protocols, look for the Wacom XInput driver at www.lepied.com/xfree86.

Scanning Photographs

SANE (an acronym for Scanner Access Now Easy) is an application programming interface which provides access to raster image scanner hardware. With SANE, you can capture images from flatbed and hand-held scanners, video and still-cameras, and frame-grabbers.

Before you decide to hook up your scanner to your Linux system, you should make sure that the SANE (Scanner Access Now Easy) interface is installed on your system.

To determine whether your scanner is compatible with Linux and The Gimp, go to the SANE Backend Drivers Web page at www.mostang.com/sane/sane-backends.html. This page lists the drivers that are supported by SANE and the hardware with which the drivers work. You'll find that most of the scanners on this list use a SCSI interface.

19

> There are SANE drivers that can operate digital cameras. For example, sane-qcam provides a driver that operates Connectix QuickCam cameras. You can then use the xcam application to grab pictures from your digital camera.
>
> You can use gPhoto to preview images stored on a digital camera and then select images to download to the computer. gPhoto will resize, color correct, and print your digital photographs.

There are several programs that you can use to capture images from a scanner. Here are two of the programs you can use to scan photographs and other artwork:

- The original graphical scanner interface for the SANE environment is xscanimage. xscanimage can acquire single images from flatbed scanners, slide and film scanners, and cameras. xscanimage is included on the Linux-Mandrake CD and is installed automatically when you install the SANE package.

- If you want to use your scanner as a scanner/fax machine/copy machine, check out Xsane. You can download Xsane from `www.wolfsburg.de/~rauch/sane/sane-xsane.html`. Xsane allows you to save scanned images in a number of useful formats (including .png and .jpg).

And Here's...The Gimp

You're probably excited to start drawing. The best way to get acquainted with a drawing program is to look at all the brushes, paints, and selection tools available to you. The Gimp comes equipped with quite an arsenal.

Lesson 19.1: Starting the Gimp for the First Time

This lesson shows you how to open The Gimp for the first time. Once you have The Gimp on your screen, you may want to take a look at some of the available Gimp help. Follow these steps to start your art adventure with The Gimp:

1. If you can't find The Gimp in the KDE or GNOME menus, or as an icon on your desktop, type `gimp` in an X terminal window and press Enter. An installation dialog box lets you know that before the program can start, several files need to be installed in your user home directory.

2. Click Install to load the necessary files. When the installation is complete, the User Installation Log tells you that the files were installed in your home directory.

The files that are stored in your user home directory are initialization files and modules. This design makes it possible for each user on the system to customize The Gimp for their individual user account. Other user accounts are not affected.

3. Click Continue, and The Gimp splash screen appears while the program and plug-ins load.

4. When The Gimp appears, you see the Toolbox and a Tip of the Day message.

5. Read through a few of the tips by clicking the Next Tip button. When you're finished with the tips, click Close.

You may want to download the latest Gimp User Manual from manual.gimp.org.

Getting Started

The Gimp toolbox (shown in Figure 19.1) contains tools that help you draw objects and select areas of an image. The toolbox also contains menus that open and save files, display options for brushes and colors, and run scripts that create objects.

FIGURE **19.1**

The Gimp toolbox contains all the art tools you need to draw and edit graphics.

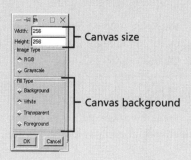

Select an area of the image

Work with text
Add color to objects

Draw and edit objects

Foreground color

Color picker
Background color

Hold the mouse pointer over a toolbox tool to display a short description.

Lesson 19.2: Creating a Blank Canvas

Now that you have a toolbox, it's time to set up a canvas so that you can experiment with the toolbox tools. Here's how to open a new file and save it in the native Gimp file format:

1. Click File, New to display the dialog box displayed in Figure 19.2.

19

FIGURE **19.2**

Set the size and background fill for the drawing area.

Canvas size

Canvas background

2. Set the size (in pixels) for the drawing area in the Width and Height text boxes.

It is recommended that you work in RGB. You can convert your drawing to grayscale later.

3. Select a fill type for the canvas background. Choose one of the following options:
   - The Background option uses the background color from the color picker as the canvas color.
   - The White option gives you a white canvas.
   - The Transparent option is great when you are creating transparent GIFs or when you do not want any color for the background.
   - The Foreground option uses the foreground color from the color picker.

4. Click OK. The drawing area will appear on the screen in a separate window.

5. Right-click the drawing area and select File, Save As to display the Save Image dialog box.

6. Navigate to the directory in which you want to save the file.

7. From the Determine file type list, select XCF. This is the Gimp native file format. Use this file format when you are working on files with The Gimp.

 This file format supports all The Gimp's tools and features. When you are finished with a drawing, you can save the file in a variety of image file formats.

8. Type a name for the file in the Selection text box. You do not need to add an extension. The Gimp will add this for you. Click OK when you are finished. You're now ready to start playing with the drawing tools.

Selecting a Drawing Tool

Now that you have a blank canvas, it's time to experiment with some of the drawing tools. You can create a variety of shapes in every color imaginable.

 You can change the way a tool operates by double-clicking the tool button and changing the options.

Lesson 19.3: Drawing Lines

There are quite a few steps you need to perform before you can draw an object on the canvas. You need to decide what colors you will use and decide on a number of other options. Follow along and create a simple line:

1. Click the Pencil tool button to select it.

2. Click the foreground color in the color picker to display the Color Selection dialog box shown in Figure 19.3.

FIGURE 19.3

Choose colors for lines, fills, and gradients from the Color Selection dialog box.

Select a shade ──

── Pick a color

3. Click and drag the slider in the color bar to select a color. The various shades of the color (from darkest to lightest) appear in the area on the left of the color bar.

4. Click the color shade you want to use for the line. Notice that the foreground color in the color box changes to the shade you selected.

5. Click File, Dialogs, Brushes to display the Brush Selection dialog box shown in Figure 19.4.

19

FIGURE 19.4

Select from a variety of brush sizes and patterns.

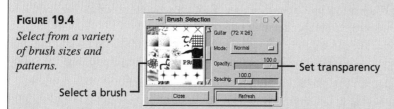

── Set transparency

Select a brush ──

6. Click the brush style that you want to use and change the opacity and spacing options if needed.

7. Draw the line on the canvas. Click and hold the pointer over the place where you want to start the line, move the pointer to the end of the line, and then release the mouse button.

Enhancing Photographs

Because your photographs don't always turn out just exactly the way you had hoped, it's great to have the help of a good photo editor. There are a few easy ways to fix over- and under-exposed pictures, change the color imbalance, adjust brightness and contrast, crop out unwanted areas of a photograph, and hide blemishes. Here are a few tricks to make your photographs look better:

- If your photographs are under- or over-exposed, try adjusting the dynamic range (right-click the drawing area and select Image, Colors, Levels).

- When colors don't appear as they should, try the Curves color correction tool (Image, Colors, Curves). You can select the color you want to correct (red, green, or blue).

- To add warmth to a picture, change the color saturation (Image, Colors, Hue-Saturation). Select the color that you want to change and adjust the hue, lightness, and saturation.

As you apply these enhancements, you'll see the changes in the photograph. If you don't like the change, right-click on the image and select Edit, Undo.

- If an image is too dark, change the brightness (Image, Colors, Brightness-Contrast). You can make an image lighter or darker and change the contrast.

- When you don't want to make changes to the entire picture, use one of the selection tools to draw an outline around an area. You can separate areas so that each area can be worked on independently.

- You can also apply filters to a photograph to give it a different effect. If you want your photograph to look more like a painting, use the Canvas filter (Filters, Artistic, Apply Canvas). If your photo is blurry, sharpen it (Filters, Enhance, Sharpen).

- To get rid of unsightly blemishes, scratches, or any other object that you don't want in the picture, try the clone tool (you'll find it in the toolbox).

There are some every good Gimp tutorials on the Web. Start your search at the official Gimp Web site (www.gimp.org).

You may also want to check out *Sams Teach Yourself Gimp in 24 Hours*.

Summary

The Gimp is the all-purpose graphics tool for almost every need. During this hour, you learned how you could set up your computer to handle different graphics jobs. You then played with the drawing tools (you'll need to supply the creativity) and scored a few tips for making photographs look better than life.

Q&A

Q **Where can I find more brushes, patterns, and gradients that I can use with The Gimp?**

A If you look on the Linux-Mandrake CD, you'll find a package that you can install that adds more brush and pattern files to The Gimp directories. You'll want to install the package named gimp-data-extras-1.0.0-6mdk.noarch.rpm.

You can also download brushes, patterns, gradients, and patterns from `www.gimp.org/data.html`.

Q **I understand that there is a scanner plug-in so that images can be scanned from The Gimp. Where can I find out how to do this?**

A We're going to send you back to the Web to find help on this. If you want to use Xscanimage as a Gimp plug-in, point your browser to `www.mostang.com/sane/man/xscanimage.1.html`. You'll find directions on how to use `xscanimage` in conjunction with your scanner and how to use `xscanimage` as a Gimp plug-in.

If you want to use Xsane as a Gimp plug-in, navigate to `www.wolfsburg.de/~rauch/sane/sane-xsane-gimp-doc.html` for directions.

Q **I don't want to spend a lot of time on a drawing. Can you recommend any quick starts?**

A Take a look in the Xtns menu under Script-Fu. You'll find quite a selection of logos, Web page elements, and pattern generators.

You may also want to look around in the Linux filesystem for images that you can change. You also can download free graphics from the Internet. You may also find clip art in some of the other graphics applications you have stashed around the workplace.

19

Workshop

There's so much that you can do with The Gimp that no one book or tutorial can cover it all. This hour gave you a very brief introduction to The Gimp's tools. If you find The Gimp to be a useful tool, take a little time out of each day to learn one new task or trick. This workshop provides a few suggestions to get you started.

Quiz

1. What file format should you use when working on images and photographs in The Gimp?

2. How do you change the color that's applied to a drawing object?

3. What are some of the basic photo enhancements you can use to correct the quality of your photographs?

Exercises

1. Get artistic with your photographs and experiment with filters. Open your photograph in The Gimp and save it under a new filename using the .xcf extension. This way you retain your original photograph. Then, right-click the photo and select one of the filters from the Filters menu. If you don't like the effect, press Ctrl+Z to undo the change.

2. Experiment with the color palette (File, Dialogs, Palette) instead of the color selector to change the foreground and background colors in the color picker.

Hour **20**

KIllustrator

Do you ever wonder whether your doodling could be turned into fine art?
Do you need to create charts for a staff meeting? Is your small business in
need of a logo? Do you want to create your own Web page graphics? Well,
if your answer to any of these questions is yes, welcome to KIllustrator.

Unlike many drawing programs, KIllustrator is a vector drawing program.
Now, what makes a vector drawing program so special? These types of
drawing programs allow you to create objects (such as lines, rectangles, circles, and multisided shapes) without using tons of memory or slowing down
refresh rates.

How's this done? Each shape is described in mathematical terms using
angles, coordinates, and distances. The program knows at what point on the
screen the object starts, where it turns, how long it goes in one direction,
and where it ends. It doesn't have to store each point in between (like a
bitmap program does).

This means that no matter how much you reduce or enlarge an image, you
retain image resolution and quality. If you think this is good stuff, take 10
steps, turn, and draw! During the next hour, you learn how to perform the
following tasks with KIllustrator:

- Create basic shapes (circles, squares, and lines)
- Organize your drawing and save your work
- Change the appearance of drawing shapes
- Add text to a drawing

Getting Started with KIllustrator

KIllustrator is one of the many graphics programs found in the Linux-Mandrake distribution. If you need a graphics program with the power of Adobe Illustrator or CorelDraw!, you'll want to give KIllustrator a try.

Chances are that you'll find KIllustrator in the KDE Application Starter under Graphics. If you can't find KIllustrator in the GNOME or KDE menus, type **killustrator** from an X terminal window. If you still can't find it, you may need to go back to Hour 9, "Managing Applications," and install the program from the CD.

Another vector drawing program that you may want to try is Sketch. You won't find any help files for Sketch, but you'll find that the skills you'll acquire during this hour can be helpful when working with Sketch. The advantage to Sketch is that it can import more file types than KIllustrator. Its disadvantage, it doesn't do layers.

Exploring the KIllustrator Window

When you first open KIllustrator, you may notice some familiar screen elements and drawing tools. The menu bar and the standard toolbar can be found along the top of the window (as seen in Figure 20.1). Along the left side of the window are the drawing tools and along the right side is the color picker.

Any objects you create start from a drawing tool. Drawing tools help you create lines, circles, squares, and multisided shapes. Hold the mouse pointer over a drawing tool to read a description of the tool. The color picker lets you change the color of the outline and interior of each shape you create.

Toolbars can be moved to any location on the KIllustrator window or they can be removed from the window. Click and hold the right (or top) of a toolbar and move it to any location on the window or off the window. Or, you can click a toolbar to hide it, leaving behind only a small icon. Click on this icon to make the toolbar reappear.

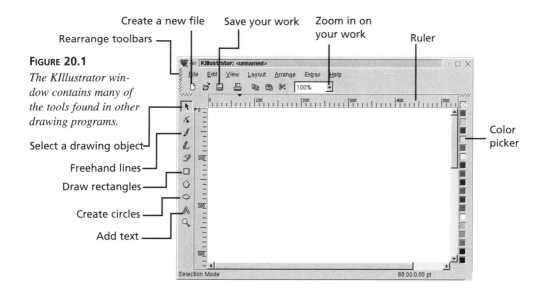

Create a new file   Save your work   Zoom in on your work

Rearrange toolbars

Ruler

FIGURE 20.1

The KIllustrator window contains many of the tools found in other drawing programs.

Color picker

Select a drawing object

Freehand lines

Draw rectangles

Create circles

Add text

Lesson 20.1: Drawing Basic Shapes

There are three shapes that you may use more often than other shapes found in the KIllustrator toolbox—freehand lines, rectangles, and circles. This lesson shows you how to create these shapes and how to use the color picker to select a color for the shape before you begin. Here's how to create colorful basic shapes:

1. Right-click a color in the color picker to set the line color for the shape. A warning dialog box appears telling you that the default color will be changed. Click Yes.

2. If you will be creating a square or circle, click a color in the color picker that you want to use as a fill color. Another warning box appears telling you that the default color will be changed. Click Yes.

If you do not want to use a color for the line or the fill, find the color box that appears crossed out. This is the transparent color box.

20

3. Select the drawing tool for the shape you want to create (either the Freehand line, rectangle, or ellipse tool).

4. Click and hold the place where you want the shape to begin, and then drag the mouse pointer away from that point. Notice that the shape appears as you draw with the mouse. When the shape appears on the page as you want, release the mouse button. Your shape may look like those displayed in Figure 20.2.

If you want to draw a perfect square or circle, press and hold the Ctrl key while you draw the shape.

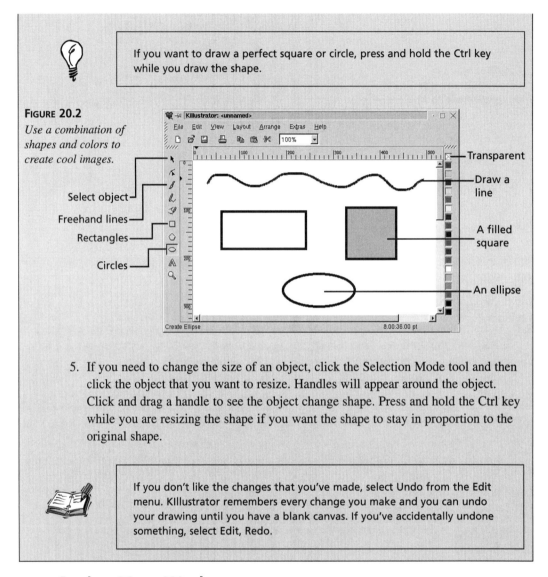

FIGURE 20.2

Use a combination of shapes and colors to create cool images.

Select object

Freehand lines

Rectangles

Circles

Transparent

Draw a line

A filled square

An ellipse

5. If you need to change the size of an object, click the Selection Mode tool and then click the object that you want to resize. Handles will appear around the object. Click and drag a handle to see the object change shape. Press and hold the Ctrl key while you are resizing the shape if you want the shape to stay in proportion to the original shape.

If you don't like the changes that you've made, select Undo from the Edit menu. KIllustrator remembers every change you make and you can undo your drawing until you have a blank canvas. If you've accidentally undone something, select Edit, Redo.

Saving Your Work

Saving your work soon and frequently can never be stressed enough. And, since we're on a soapbox, frequent backups are a necessity also. So, if you don't have a regular backup system in place, go to Hour 8, "Backing Up the Filesystem."

The first time you need to save your work, click the Save Document button. You are presented with the Save As dialog box. Select the directory in which you want to store the file and type the filename at the end of the directory path in the Location text box. This saves the file in the KIllustrator native file format (.kil). You will want to keep one of these .kil files around so that you can use KIllustrator to change the drawings. The .kil file format preserves any special KIllustrator functions such as layers.

Once your drawing is complete, you can then save it in a variety of formats depending on your needs. If you plan to use your drawing on the Web, try GIF, JPEG, or PNG image formats. KIllustrator can save image files in several more file formats (see Table 20.1). When you are ready to convert your drawing to another format, select File, Export.

TABLE 20.1   Export KIllustrator Drawings to a Variety of File Formats

Supported Image Formats	File Type
Graphics Interchange Format	.gif
Joint Photographic Experts Group	.jpg
Portable Network Graphics	.png
Encapsulated Postscript	.eps
X11 Pixmap	.xpm
Portable Pixmap	.ppm

Setting Up Your Drawing

Now that you've had the quick tour, it's time to plan your first drawing. Where do you start? With a pencil and a piece of paper. Before you begin your computer-generated drawing, you may want to make a few sketches and jot down a few notes. Figure 20.3 shows the design phase for a brochure cover. Different elements of the brochure cover are placed on different layers so that text can be changed to create covers for different products.

You've already seen that KIllustrator does a great job at creating basic images. It also contains tools that help you lay out your design and keep things in order.

One way to create balance in your drawings is to use a *grid*. A grid separates your drawing area into a series of rows and columns.

Select Layout, Grid if you want to use a grid to help arrange your drawing. The Grid dialog box shown in Figure 20.4 is where you will set up the dimensions of your grid.

20

Create balance with grids

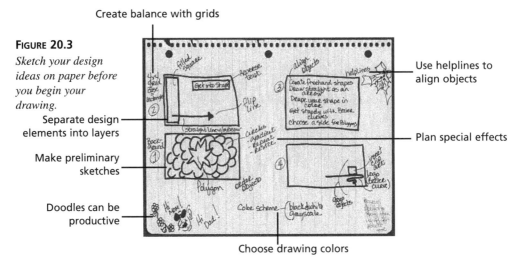

FIGURE 20.3

Sketch your design ideas on paper before you begin your drawing.

Separate design elements into layers

Make preliminary sketches

Doodles can be productive

Use helplines to align objects

Plan special effects

Choose drawing colors

FIGURE 20.4

Grids help organize your drawing into logical sections.

Align objects to closest gridline

Show gridlines onscreen

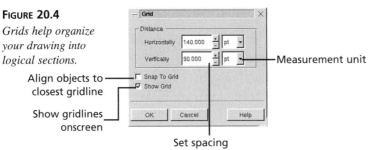

Measurement unit

Set spacing

Set the distance between each grid marker, for grid lines that appear across the page and grid lines that appear from top to bottom. Since this grid will help you position objects on the page, select the Show Grid option to display the gridlines on your canvas. If at any time you want to hide the gridlines, select View, Show Grid.

NEW TERM Another method used to organize a drawing is the use of *layers*. Layers are a way of combining several drawings into one drawing. When you use layers, different parts of the image are placed on separate layers. When the different layers are arranged, images on one layer may cover an image on a lower layer.

There are many advantages to using layers. The most obvious is that you can rearrange the order of the layers to make the drawing look different. That is, you can move objects out from behind other objects by changing the order of the layers. Another advantage is that you may hide some parts of a drawing when certain elements of the drawing are not needed. For example, you may have a slogan that you don't always want to appear with a logo. Put the slogan on one layer and the logo on another layer.

Lesson 20.2: Working with Layers

You may have parts of your planned drawing that you may not want to use each time you print a drawing or export it into another file format. Or, a part of your drawing may need to be a different color for different purposes. When a drawing needs separate elements that you can easily display and hide based on your needs, use layers.

Before you begin this lesson, you need a new canvas for your drawing. If you do not have a blank page displayed in the KIllustrator window, click the New Document button or select File, New. Here's how to organize your drawing so that different elements can be placed on separate layers:

1. Click Layout, Page to display the Page Layout dialog box. Use this dialog box to set the page size for your drawing.

2. To add layers to your drawing, click View, Layers. The dialog box shown in Figure 20.5 appears.

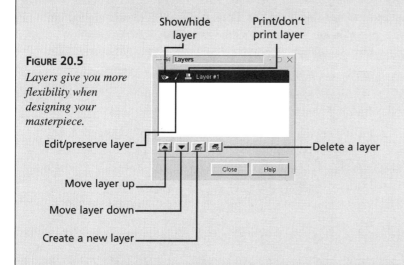

FIGURE 20.5

Layers give you more flexibility when designing your masterpiece.

Show/hide layer

Print/don't print layer

Edit/preserve layer

Move layer up

Move layer down

Create a new layer

Delete a layer

Keep the Layers dialog box open while you work on your drawing. By doing this, you can easily change the order of the layers and whether or not changes can be made to the layer.

20

3. To create a new layer, click the New Layer button. The new layer will appear at the top of the list.

4. To change the order in which the new layer appears, make sure the layer is selected and then click the Down button. The new layer will now be located beneath the first layer.

5. To change the name of a layer, double-click the layer name. The cursor will appear at the end of the name. Use the backspace key to delete text and then type your own text. To accept the change, press Enter.

6. The three buttons to the left of the layer name control how the layer can be used. These buttons work as toggle switches. If you can see the button icon, the function is on. If you can't see the button icon, the function is off.

   • The Visible button determines whether you can see the layer in the KIllustrator window. Click the Visible button to hide the layer in the drawing. The button icon will also disappear. Click the Visible button a second time and the artwork on the layer will become part of the drawing again.

   • The Editable button allows you to make changes to a layer. When this button is off, you cannot make any changes to any element on that layer.

   • The Printable button decides whether a layer will be printed along with the rest of the drawing.

7. When you are ready to draw on a layer, select the layer (from the Layers dialog box) on which you want to create the shape, and then move back to the KIllustrator window and begin drawing.

8. Switch to another layer by clicking the layer, and draw another picture.

9. Hide the first layer on which you created an object. You should only see the objects you drew on the second layer.

Another way to limit the amount of canvas that you see is to use the Zoom tool. By using the Zoom tool, you can magnify the part of the drawing with which you want to work. The Zoom tool works very well when you need to see the fine print.

Colorizing Drawing Objects

Earlier in this hour you learned how to select colors for a drawing object before drawing the object on the canvas. What do you do if you don't like the color you chose? Well, change it. And while you're at it, you can also change the thickness of the shape's outline.

To change the color of a shape, click the Selection Mode tool and then click the shape to which you want to make changes. With the shape selected, right-click the shape and select Properties from the menu. The dialog box that appears (see Figure 20.6) shows you the type of shape and its coordinates on the canvas.

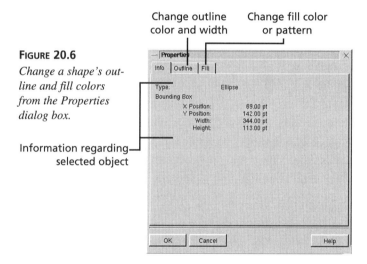

FIGURE 20.6
Change a shape's outline and fill colors from the Properties dialog box.

The outline is the line that appears around the outside edge of a shape. This line can take on a different color and line style by displaying the Outline tab and making new choices.

The color that appears inside a shape is the fill color. You can make changes to this color also. Display the Fill tab, you have several choices of fill colors:

- *Solid* fills the shape with a single color.
- *Pattern* fills the shape using a pattern consisting of white and another color of your choice.
- *Gradient* uses two colors to fill a shape. Each color in the shape blends into the other color.
- *No Fill* leaves you with a shape that is transparent in the middle.

20

Click the option button for the fill choice you want to apply to the object. When you select an option button, a list of colors or patterns will appear and you can make your selection from there. When you're done making changes to the object's outline and fill, click OK.

Lesson 20.3: Filling a Shape with a Gradient Color

An easy way to add special effects to a drawing object is by filling the shape with a gradient. To begin this lesson, you need to draw a shape (either a circle, square, or polygon). It does not matter what color the shape is filled with. Once you have a shape created, here's how to fill it with a gradient color:

1. Select the drawing object that you want to fill with a gradient color.

2. Right-click the object and select Properties from the menu that appears. This displays the Properties dialog box.

3. To remove the outline from the shape, click the Outline tab to display the Outline properties shown in Figure 20.7. Then click the Style drop-down list arrow and select the transparent option. (It is the first one on the list that is just a blank listing.)

FIGURE 20.7

When using a gradient fill, remove the outline from the shape first.

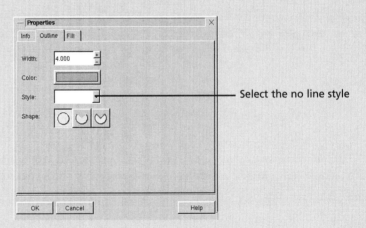

Select the no line style

4. Click the Fill tab to display the fill properties.

5. Click the Gradient option button. The gradient fill options appear on the right side of the dialog box.

6. Click the Color button for the first color to display the Select Color dialog box shown in Figure 20.8.

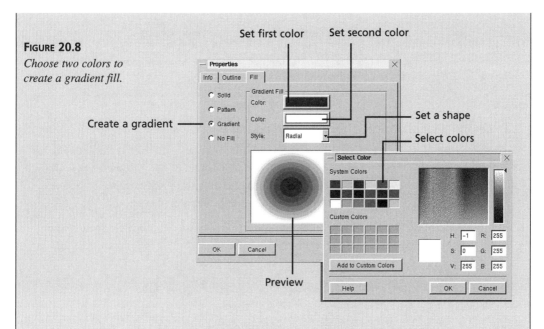

FIGURE 20.8
Choose two colors to create a gradient fill.

Set first color
Set second color
Create a gradient
Set a shape
Select colors
Preview

7. Click a color in the System Colors section and click OK. The color you chose will appear in the color bar for the first gradient color.

8. Click the color button for the second color and select a color from the Select Color dialog box.

9. Click the Style drop-down list and set the shape for the gradient. You'll see what the gradient will look like in the Preview window.

10. When the gradient looks the way you want, click OK. The gradient color and style are applied to the selected object.

Adding Text to a Drawing

20

It has been said that a picture is worth a thousand words; but then again, one cannot live by pictures alone. It is a simple process to add text to your drawing. First, select the layer where you want the text to appear. Then, select the Text tool and click the place on the canvas where you want to place the text. And, finally, begin typing the text.

Once the text is on the page, you can select the text and drag it to a new position. Right-click the text and select Properties from the menu to change the font style and size.

If you want to use text that is stored in another document, copy the text using the Edit, Copy command from the application. To paste the text into your KIllustrator drawing, use Edit, Paste. You can then move the text any place you need it.

Lesson 20.4: Arranging Text Around a Shape

Text does not always have to follow a straight line. You can give your text a little curl or some curves by aligning it with an object. You can use one of several shapes to set the path for the text. Shapes that you can use are freehand lines, polylines, bezier curves, polygons, and ellipses. Here's how to create text that bends or waves:

1. Select the Text tool and type a few words on the canvas. It does not matter where you place the text.

2. Create a drawing object to which you will align the text.

3. Select the text you created in step 1. An example is shown in Figure 20.9.

FIGURE 20.9

Experiment with aligning text along different objects.

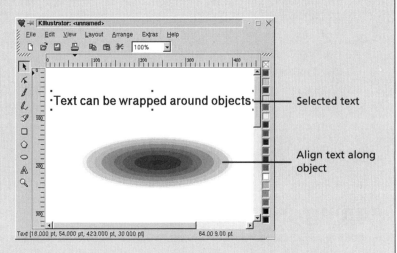

4. Click Arrange, Text along Path. The mouse pointer changes to a heavy right-pointing arrow.

5. Click the shape to which you want to align the text. The text is aligned starting at the left side of the object and follows the contour moving right. An example is shown in Figure 20.10.

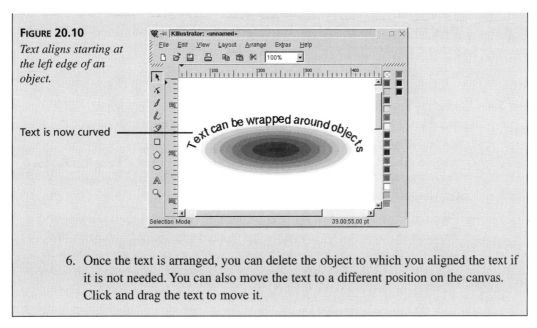

FIGURE 20.10

Text aligns starting at the left edge of an object.

Text is now curved ────

6. Once the text is arranged, you can delete the object to which you aligned the text if it is not needed. You can also move the text to a different position on the canvas. Click and drag the text to move it.

Summary

In this hour, you learned a few of the basic methods for creating drawings in KIllustrator. Although you can create simple, one layer drawings, you can also get as complex as your creativity will allow. You learned how to create simple shapes and add one or more colors to its design. You also learned how to separate your drawing into layers for more flexibility. The one thing you didn't learn was how to be an artist. You need to explore that aspect of your abilities on your own.

Q&A

Q **I have graphics files that I've created in other drawing programs. Can I use any of these files in KIllustrator?**

A A variety of image file formats can be used in your KIllustrator drawings. Most images are inserted into your drawing rather than exported.

If you have Web graphics (saved as GIF, JPEG, or PNG images), these can be added to the drawing by selecting Edit, Insert, Bitmap. You can also add X11 Bitmaps (.xbm format) and X11 Pixmaps (.xpm) from this menu selection. Use the dialog box to navigate to the directory where the image file is stored. These images can then be moved around the drawing, resized, and rotated—whatever you need.

20

Many clipart collections are saved in the Windows Metafile format. You can insert these images by selecting Edit, Insert, Clipart.

Q What if I don't have any image files of my own?

A There are many places to find graphical images. Try the Web; you'll be amazed at what you can find if you ask a search engine for free graphics. Before you download any images, read the rules regarding use of a site's images. You'll also find images in the Linux-Mandrake distribution. Search the filesystem or the CD and see what you come up with.

Q Aligning drawing objects to a gridline is a snap. But what if I don't want the objects on the gridline, but need some other position on which I can make alignments?

A Try using the helplines function. Click Layout, Helplines to access the Setup Helplines dialog box. You can set up one or more helplines that run horizontally, vertically, or both. Type the position on the page at which you want the helpline to appear and click the Add button. You'll find that helplines can be used instead of gridlines, or in addition to gridlines.

Q How do I draw a polygon?

A There are two tools that you can use to draw a multisided shape. The first is the Create Polyline tool. To use this tool, click the place where you want to start the shape, move the mouse pointer, click the place where you want the first line to end, and then click the place where you want each additional line to end. When you want to join the first line to the last line, right-click the place where you want to end the shape.

You can also use the Create Polygon tool. Double-click the Create Polygon tool button to open the Setup Polygon Tool dialog box. From this dialog box, you can select the number of points that you want to appear in the shape, make it a concave polygon, and smooth out the rough edges.

Q I created several objects on one layer and I want them all to line up along the left edge of the canvas. How do I do this?

A Objects can be aligned several ways. Your first step is to select each object that you want aligned. Press and hold the Shift key while you click each object. Once the objects are selected, click Arrange, Align to display the Alignment dialog box. Objects can either be aligned horizontally or vertically from the Align tab. You can also select the spacing between objects from the Distribute tab.

Workshop

If you've worked with other graphics programs (such as Adobe Illustrator and CorelDraw!) you may have found KIllustrator to be a snap. If you haven't, try the exercises in this workshop.

Quiz

1. How do you change the color used to draw a shape?

2. What is the purpose of gridlines and how do you use them in KIllustrator?

3. When is it helpful to use layers in a drawing?

4. Is it possible to add text to a KIllustrator drawing that does not appear on the page in a straight horizontal line?

Exercises

1. Design a card that you can customize for special occasions. Put different design elements on a separate layer. For example, you may want a greeting on one layer, a design on a second layer, and a personalized message for each recipient on the third layer. Look around the Web for free clipart. If you need some design ideas, go shopping at your local card shop or look at some of the electronic greeting cards on the Web.

2. Try exporting your KIllustrator drawing in a variety of file formats. Then experiment using these files as graphics on your Web site or as graphical elements in other application programs, such as a word processing program or another graphics program.

20

Hour 21

Morphing Is for Comedians

Are you a professional artist, or do you plan to be an artist when you grow up? Are you tired of flat graphics that stay in one place? Are you ready to push your art and creative skills to the limit? If you answered yes to any of these questions, you are ready to spend this next hour looking at some of the new and exciting graphics programs being developed by the Linux community.

Particular areas where Linux is quickly gaining ground are animation, 3D rendering, and video editing. This represents a great opportunity for artists on a budget and for those who want to learn about these techniques.

Once again, many of the animation, rendering, and video applications discussed during this hour aren't found on the Linux-Mandrake CD—you need to download these programs from the Internet. But, this is the beauty of Linux. If you can find it on the Web, you can download it for free, test out the program, and keep it if you like it. If not, you can uninstall it, and all you lose is your download time.

During the next hour, you meet a number of video and animation programs. You learn
where to find these programs, how to do the basics, and then use the programs to perform these tasks:

- Animate drawings you've created with other graphics applications
- Create 3D landscapes
- Use morphing techniques to animate pictures
- Edit video

Creating Saturday Morning Cartoons

The art of animation includes a broader world than just the cartoons you may have
watched on Saturday mornings. Animation isn't just for kids. Many independent and
major motion picture studios use animation. Animation doesn't necessarily consist of
cartoon drawings. Some animations appear to be larger than life.

NEW TERM *Animation* describes a sequence of drawings in which each drawing is contained in a separate frame. Each drawing is slightly different from the one
before; this is how motion is added to an animation. An animated film requires 24 drawings for each second of film in order to create smooth animation. Computer animation
may require more than 24 drawings per second.

If you're wondering how to get started with your animations, use some of the drawing
programs you learned about earlier (such as The Gimp in Hour 19 and Killustrator in
Hour 20) to create your cartoon characters and backgrounds. Then, check out the animation programs discussed in this section.

To learn more about how to create animations, visit these Web sites:

- The Animation Learner's Site at come.to/animate provides a good general introduction to creating animations.
- Aimee's Studio at aimee.wyvernweb.com contains a wealth of tutorials. You'll find
  animation articles and tutorials at aimee.wyvernweb.com/anim/animatr.html.
- Animation Meat at www.animationmeat.com/index2.html contains animation
  tutorials, techniques, and tips.
- Royal Frazier's GIF Animation at www6.uniovi.es/gifanim/gifmake.htm shows
  you how to create animated GIFs, but the basics of creating animations are covered.

There are several animation programs that run under Linux. Let's take a look at two different ones—mvComicsMaker and Blender. mvComicsMaker is the easier and less intimidating of the two. Blender will do more than animations and looks more like the animation software used by professional animators and videographers.

Working with mvComicsMaker

mvComicsMaker creates bitmap and vector animations that can be saved in MVA (the mvComicsMaker native file format), FLC, BMP, or PNG file formats. mvComicsMaker imports BMP and PNG file formats for use as backgrounds in your animations.

To get your copy of mvComicsMaker, go to the mvComicsMaker Web page at `members.xoom.com/miishland/9mvCM.html`. You'll want to download the i386 binaries, the tutorial, and the examples. The three files combined are surprisingly small—less than 700KB.

The mvComicsMaker program opens on your screen in four different windows. Each window performs a different function, as explained here:

- The Main window (shown in Figure 21.1) controls files and animations. From the main window, you can start a new animation or edit an existing animation. The controls in this window set up new frames as well as the speed at which animations play in the Edit window.

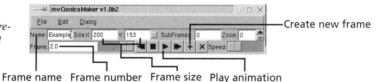

Create new frame

Frame name Frame number Frame size Play animation

- The Edit window (shown in Figure 21.2) is the drawing area. In this window, you'll add background images and work with curves. This window also runs the animation.

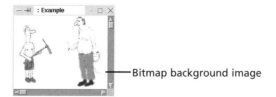

Bitmap background image

21

- The Display Curves window (shown in Figure 21.3) controls and edits vector graphics, adds text to an animation, and controls how curves work in the animation.

FIGURE 21.3

Use curves to work with vector images.

- The Background window (shown in Figure 21.4) controls bitmap graphics and adds these images to a frame. The background is the first object to display in an animation. The Background window is also used to zoom in and out of the animation.

FIGURE 21.4

Use the Background window to place images in a frame.

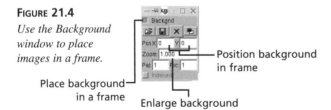

Animating with Blender

If mvComicsMaker won't suit your needs, give Blender a try. Blender is more than an animation program. It will also do 3D modeling, rendering, and perform post-production tasks.

If you are interested in Blender (which is a freeware program), you can find the program, tutorials, and information on purchasing the commercial version at www.blender.nl.

You may find it easier to install an RPM version of Blender. You'll find one at `sunsite.org.uk/Mirrors/ftp.calderasystems.com/pub/openlinux/ contrib./RPMS/libc6`. Download the file named blender-1.70a-1.i386.rpm.

3D Modeling

If you enjoy creating 3D objects, there are several Linux programs that have the look and feel of some of the 3D programs that run under the Windows operating system.

NEW TERM One of the more familiar 3D modeling programs is POV-Ray. Actually, POV-Ray is a ray-tracing program. *Ray tracing* creates computer images that look like photographs. These images are drawn after you specify what objects are to be included in the image, how they are shaped, their color and texture, and from which direction the light reflects off the objects.

The POV-Ray Web site is located at `www.povray.org`. Download the POV-Ray Linux version from `ftp.povray.org/pub/povray/Official/Linux`. You'll need the file named povlinux.tgz.

Go to `www.povray.org/ftp/pub/povray/Official/Docs` to find the POV-Ray user manual.

Another familiar 3D program that runs under the Windows operating system is RenderMan. The equivalent to RenderMan in the Linux world is the collection of Blue Moon Rendering Tools (you'll find them at `www.bmrt.org`). The Blue Moon Rendering Tools are programs that support ray tracing, radiosity, light sources, texture mapping, shading, motion blur, shadows, and depth of field.

Another program that meets the RenderMan specification is GNU GMAN. GNU GMAN supports zbuffer, radiosity, ray tracking, and motion blur. You'll find GNU GMAN at `www.2ad.com/gman`.

Hardware requirements for GNU GMAN are a Pentium 200MHz computer with 64MB of RAM. It will still run on a lesser computer, but the performance may be slow.

21

If you'd like to learn more about creating 3D images on your Linux computer, test out these Web sites:

- 3D Linux dot Org at www.3dlinux.org is a great place to keep up to date on 3D news for Linux.
- Linux 3D at linux3d.netpedia.net contains a long list of 3D environments, renderers, modelers, and other tools that work with the Linux operating system.
- The Linux 3D site at glide.xxedgexx.com lists the hardware and software needed to create 3D images on Linux systems. It also contains a comprehensive list of 3D references.
- An interesting e-zine is *The Rendering Times* at www.spake.org/rtimes. You'll find information to help you create some impressive 3D effects.

Creating Animations with Morphing Software

Morphing is an animation sequence that changes one image into another image. Pixels in the source image are mapped to pixels in the destination image. Distorting both the source and destination images to the same shape, and then dissolving them together, creates the animation. The distortion is reversed and one image transforms into the other image. The number of images (pics) to be saved from this sequence is selected by the user. The morphing program performs its job in increments that are saved as separate images called *pics*. The sequence of pics is then run as an animation.

Understanding the Difference Between Warping and Morphing

NEW TERM   Images can be distorted (*warped*) and then digitally changed into each other (*morphed*). The central idea of morphing is specifying a warp that distorts the first image into the second. Of course, running the process in reverse distorts the second image into the first. As the program moves through the process, the first image is gradually distorted while it slowly fades out. At the same time, the second image begins distorted, and it warps toward the first as it slowly fades in.

Assigning vectors that define influence fields in both the source and destination images creates a warp. The closer a pixel is to the vector, the more the warping effect is influenced. In order to obtain influence fields, you must set the vectors in pairs. One pair of vectors is set in the source image, and the other pair is set in the destination image. The mathematical formulas used by the morphing program control the pixel coordinate-transformations from source image to destination image for each pixel. This means that each pixel is influenced by all vector-pairs, and this is how you get an image to warp.

Early images in the sequence will look like the source image. The image in the middle of the sequence is an average of the source image distorted halfway toward the destination image, and the destination image distorted halfway back toward the source image. As you get to the last images of the sequence, they will look more like the destination image.

The middle image is the key to predicting how it is going to go; if the middle image looks good then the whole animated sequence will probably look good. The common morph process warps two images until they have the same *shape*, and then cross dissolves them into one.

If you want to learn more about the technical aspects of morphing, take a look at these Web sites:

- The Rice University Digital Image Processing course Web site contains project information on image morphing at www.owlnet.rice.edu/~elec539/Projects97/morphjrks/themainpage.html.

- A few Stanford University professors wrote a paper for SIGGRAPH on Feature-Based Volume Metamorphosis which can be found at www-graphics.stanford.edu/papers/morph.

Introducing XMorph

XMorph (shown in Figure 21.5) is an image-warp program that can be found on the Linux-Mandrake CD. XMorph uses Targa (.tga) files as the source and destination images in order to perform a morph.

To start your own morphed pictures, you need to start with two files that are the same size (in pixels). Load one as the source image (from the File menu) and the other as the destination image. Then, click and drag mesh points in both images to shape the morph. Once this is done, you can warp the images so that you either have a single image or a series of morphed images that can be used as an animation.

21

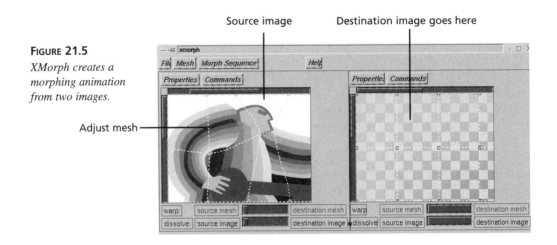

Source image   Destination image goes here

FIGURE 21.5
XMorph creates a morphing animation from two images.

Adjust mesh

Getting Started with XMRM

XMRM is a digital image-morphing program with many possible applications. It is also another of those applications that you won't find on the Linux-Mandrake CD. Here's where you'll find XMRM:

- The XMRM Home page is located at
  `www.cg.tuwien.ac.at/research/ca/mrm/xmrm.html`.
- The XMRM Manual page can be found at `www.cg.tuwien.ac.at/~xmrm`.
- To download the program with your favorite FTP utility, go to
  `ftp.cg.tuwien.ac.at/pub/linux/xmrm` and download the file named
  xmrm20_statuc.tgz. It is less than 1MB.

If you use the KDE File manager, you can right-click the tgz file in the KDE File manager and select Archiver from the drop-down menu. Then use the Archiver utility to extract the files either to your home directory or in the /usr directory. Once the files are extracted, click the XMRM icon in the file manager to start the XMRM program.

The XMRM main window (shown in Figure 21.6) opens when you click the XMRM icon. This main window displays five control panels. When you installed XMRM, a couple of samples files were also installed. They are found in the Samples subdirectory where you installed XMRM. The two files that you can play with are called morph.prj and warp.prj. To open these files, select File, Load Project.

This program will not run at 8-bit color. You may also want to run a screen resolution larger than 800x600.

Number of frames for animation sequence

Calculate warp and morph values

FIGURE 21.6
Load a source and destination image to begin morphing.

Load images

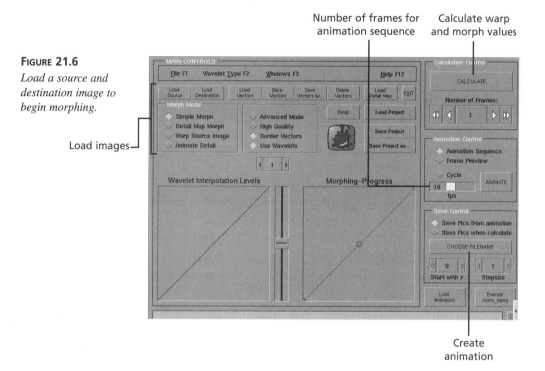

Create animation

Be sure to use the Window menu (at the top-left corner) to close any XMRM windows that are open while the program is running. If you click the close button in the upper-right corner of any of the XMRM windows, the whole program will close.

Going Hollywood

If you have a video camera, you may have an interest in digitizing your home videos, sprucing them up a bit, and preparing them for your Web site. Digitizing video is a great way to keep in contact with friends and family and to showcase your products to potential customers.

21

One of the areas where Linux is just now making headway is in the field of video production. One of the best sources for Linux video techniques is the Video for Linux resource at `www.exploits.org/v4l`. Here, you'll find information on TV cards, radio cards, and QuickCam drivers that are compatible with Linux.

Linux Media Labs LLC (`linuxmedialabs.com`) sells a video capture card for the Linux operating system. This video capture card is bundled with MainActor (`www.mainactor.com`), a multimedia creation package that contains a timeline-based video sequencer and an animation program. You may also want to check out their GNU/Linux Video Capture/Editing/Playback MPEG project at `linuxmedialabs.com/linuxvideo.html`.

Here are a few good places to start if you want to learn more about video editing:

- LinuxPower.org has a series of articles on making movies with Linux. The URL for each part is listed here:
  Part 1 at `linuxpower.org/display_item.phtml?id=120`.
  Part 2 at `linuxpower.org/display.php?id=125`.
  Part 3 at `linuxpower.org/display.php?id=128`.
  Part 4 at `linuxpower.org/display.php?id=134`.
  Part 5 at `linuxpower.org/display.php?id=139`.
- Desktop Video: A Starter's Guide to Video Editing can be found at Hardware Central (`www.hardwarecentral.com/hardwarecentral/tutorials/923/1`).
- If you need a dictionary of video terms, visit the Videonics Video Glossary at `www.videonics.com/video-glossary.html`.

Summary

During the past hour, you were introduced to several multimedia programs that can be used on your Linux system. There wasn't much time to cover any of these programs in detail, but you were provided with places where you can find more information. And remember, you can always use the help files from the program's Help menu.

Q&A

Q What is Qt?

A Qt is a software toolkit that makes it easy to write and maintain graphical user interface applications. Qt is object-oriented and written in C++. When developing software with Qt, you can recompile the code so your program will run on the UNIX and Microsoft Windows operating systems. You can learn more about Qt at `www.troll.no`.

Q Is there one place on the Internet that has a relatively complete list of multi-media applications for Linux?

A Try the multimedia pages at the LinuxStart Web site (`www.linuxstart.com/applications/multimedia.html`).

Q I have been interested in Linux but I haven't seen any applications that are suitable for my business. I produce TV commercials and need a professional-quality video-editing software program. Do you have any suggestions?

A If you aren't in a hurry, the folks at the Free Film Project are trying to organize the Linux community to create a commercial-quality film studio. Their goal is to create a suite of utilities that will produce, manage, design, and publish movies and animations. Information about the Free Film Project can be found at `www.gnu.org/software/ffp/ffp.html` and `www.geocities.com/ResearchTriangle/Facility/6309/index.html`.

You may also want to check out Broadcast 2000 at `heroine.linuxbox.com/bcast2000.html`. This program will capture, render, edit, compose, mix, and master movies and sound.

Workshop

Did you have some fun during the past hour? Hopefully you found a few multimedia applications that started your creativity spinning.

Quiz

1. Which types of software applications create moving pictures?

2. What is animation?

3. What is the difference between warping and morphing?

Exercises

1. Many of the programs covered in this hour have an equivalent program that runs on the Windows operating system. See whether you can determine the Windows look-alike for any of these programs that you'd like to explore. Using help documentation from these Windows programs can provide a good foundation for learning the Linux program.

2. If you have a video camera, try your hand at digitizing some of your favorite film footage. Once you have the video stored on your computer, try one of the video-editing programs and turn your amateur production into the next winner at your local film festival.

21

Hour **22**

Graphics Viewers and Utilities

It's been a graphical whirlwind tour over the past few hours. You've learned how to create your own pictures with some of the best graphics programs that Linux-Mandrake has to offer. But what if your graphics-manipulation needs are relatively simple?

There are several utilities sprinkled around your system that allow you to view a variety of image file formats and to perform simple editing jobs such as sizing, rotating, and papering your desktop. You'll be introduced to several of these utilities in this hour.

You may have other graphics needs that require a special tool. You may want to create your own desktop and panel icons. Then, if you want to show your friends how your new icons look, you can take a picture of your desktop. You'll see a few tools that can get this job done.

During the next hour, you learn how to perform a number of tasks with the following image utility programs:

- Edit images using Electric Eyes
- Sort through image files with GQview
- View slideshows with KView
- Create icons with Icon Editor
- Take a picture of your desktop with KSnapshot

Coloring and Resizing Images with Electric Eyes

Electric Eyes is a rare find. It's an image viewer and a graphics display and editing utility all handily packed into one. Electric Eyes provides many of the tools that most of us are looking for when the crunch hits.

Electric Eyes makes a nice helping hand when you are struggling to resize all the pictures submitted for the company newsletter's "Best Lawn Bowler Trophy Picture of the 1920s" contest. It's helpful at crisis times, such as when you must manage disaster control when all your boss's sales promotion slides turn out to be a strange shade of green and the wrong size.

Electric Eyes can edit the color, brightness, and contrast of your images. You can crop images, edit and resize them, and display them as thumbnails (miniature versions of the original images). You may also display them in a slideshow and save them in a variety of formats.

To start Electric Eyes, look for it in the KDE and GNOME main menus under Graphics or type **ee** in an X terminal window.

When Electric Eyes opens, it displays the splash screen shown in Figure 22.1. The first order of business is to display the Edit Controls window, the Image List window, and the toolbar. You'll find these by right-clicking the Electric Eyes splash screen and selecting the View menu.

FIGURE 22.1
The Electric Eyes
splash screen.

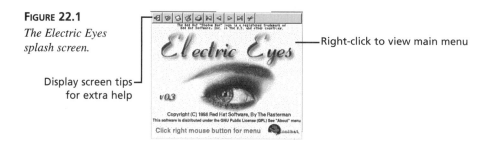

Right-click to view main menu

Display screen tips
for extra help

The Image List can hold a number of files in most any graphics file format (see Figure 22.2). To start adding images to your list, click the Open a New File button. The Select a File to Load dialog box which appears can add a single file to the Image List, or it can add all the files in the selected directory. There is even a preview window to help you find image files.

Once the images are loaded, you can work with a picture by clicking its filename in the Image List. The image file appears in a separate window and a preview appears in the Edit Controls window.

FIGURE 22.2
Use the Edit Controls
to change the image
size and color balance.

Image file   Color controls   Add file to Image List   Thumbnail

Density
Brightness
Contrast

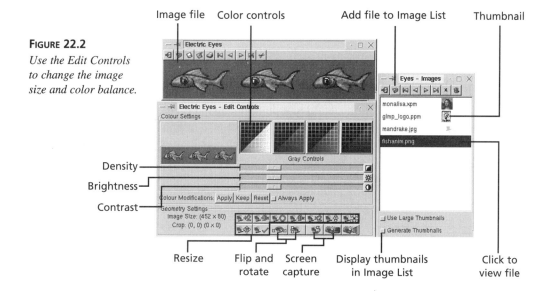

Resize   Flip and   Screen   Display thumbnails   Click to
          rotate   capture   in Image List   view file

All images are composed of three colors (red, green, and blue) and a tone (gray). You can use Electric Eyes to change different aspects of each of these colors. There are four color controls along the top of the Edit Controls window.

To change a color, click the corresponding color control button. You can then use the slider bars to change the density, brightness, and contrast of each color. If you want to keep the color changes, click the Apply button. If you want to go back to the original image, click the Reset button.

If you want to change the size of the image or its orientation, you'll find these controls along the bottom of the Edit Controls window. You can use preset increments to increase or decrease the size of the file, or you can set a custom size.

> If you'd like to use the image file as your desktop background, right-click the image and select File, Set as Desktop Background.

Managing Image Files with GQView

GQView is another handy graphics-management tool like Electric Eyes. GQView can display one image or run a slideshow of all the images in the directory. There are tools to let you zoom in and out and resize the image to the screen.

GQView can filter your images to display only images of a particular format. It also provides a method for you to use your favorite graphics program as an external editor. Just select the graphics program you want to use from a list and GQView will load the program with the image displayed.

You can find GQView in the GNOME main menu under Graphics, or by typing `gqview` in an X terminal window. When GQview appears on your screen, the contents of your home directory appear in the Directory List and the File List, as shown in Figure 22.3.

FIGURE 22.3
Use GQview to manage your graphics files.

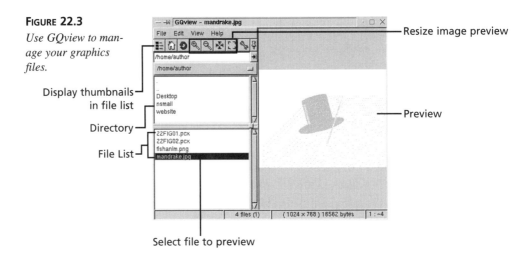

Navigate through the Directory List to display the files with which you want to work in the File List. When you click one of the filenames in the File List, the image appears in the preview pane.

The File menu contains the commands for managing your image files. You can create new directories in your user account in which to store images. You can then make a copy of any file on the system and place it in this new directory. You can also move files from one directory to another, or delete them from the system.

If you'd like to watch a slideshow of all the image files in a directory, click View, Toggle Slideshow.

To use another graphics program as an external editor, all you have to do is open the Edit menu and click your favorite program from the list. The program you select will open on the desktop with the image displayed in its image window.

You can add and subtract external editors from the Edit menu. Select Edit, Options. Click the External Editors tab and type the name and execution command for the editor you want to add to the list.

Watching Slideshows with KView

Just as Electric Eyes is the image viewer for GNOME, KView is the generic image viewer for KDE. You can use KView to crop, rotate, and flip images. KView can also create slideshows.

To open KView from the KDE main menu, select Graphics, Image Viewer. You can also type **kview** in an X terminal window.

You can open several files (select File, Open), one after another, and KView will keep track of them. To view a list of the open files, click Images, List to display the Image List shown in Figure 22.4.

Open an image   Display Image List   Open image files

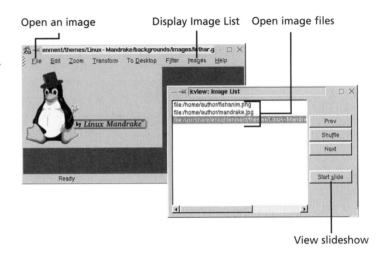

FIGURE 22.4

Display the Image List
to start the slideshow.

View slideshow

When you click a file in the Image List, the selected image will appear in the KView window. If you want the files to appear in a slideshow fashion, click the Start Slide button.

In addition to being an image viewer, KView can rotate and flip images, remove unwanted areas from an image, and use an image as the desktop wallpaper.

Creating Icons with the KDE Icon Editor

The KDE Icon Editor is used to create icons. If you feel creative, you can design icons to use on your desktop. Or, if you're feeling really creative, you can design new icons as part of a desktop theme. But, if you feel you need a little practice, make a copy of an existing icon file and play with it. That way, you can go back to the original version if you don't like your end product.

> Most of the icons you find in your Linux system are in .xpm format.

To open the Icon Editor, display the KDE main menu and select Graphics, Icon Editor (see Figure 22.5). You can also type **kiconedit** in an X terminal window.

FIGURE 22.5

Edit an existing icon file or create an original icon.

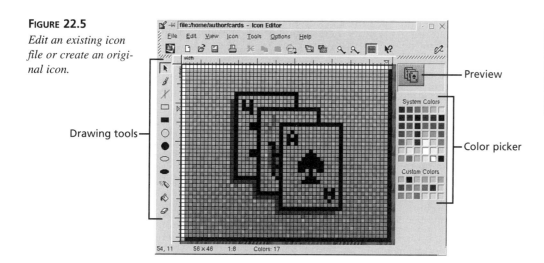

Drawing tools

Preview

Color picker

22

The Icon Editor works like other bitmap drawing programs you've seen. Use the drawing tools to create shapes, apply color, and erase areas on the canvas. Use the color picker to apply color to shapes and pixels on the canvas.

Taking Snapshots of Your Desktop

NEW TERM Have you wondered how the pictures you've seen throughout this book were created? Pretty simple. We used a *screen capture* utility. There are several Linux applications and utilities that will take a picture of your desktop. KSnapshot is one.

KSnapshot (shown in Figure 22.6) is a KDE screen capture utility that can be set up to capture the whole screen or just a selected window. You specify the filename for the image of the desktop and the directory in which it should be saved. You also have a choice of five image file formats in which to save the screen capture.

You can find KSnapshot in the KDE main menu under Graphics, Snapshot. You can also type **ksnapshot** in an X terminal window.

FIGURE 22.6

KSnapshot is an easy way to take a picture of your desktop.

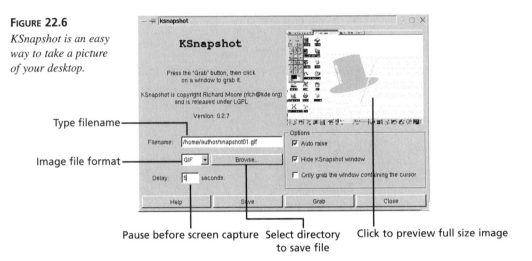

Type filename

Image file format

Pause before screen capture   Select directory to save file   Click to preview full size image

When KSnapshot opens, it captures the screen and displays it in the Preview pane. If you want to keep the screenshot, just type a destination directory and filename in the Filename text box, select a format in which to save the file, and click Save.

If you need a different screen capture image, set an amount of time before KSnapshot takes the picture of the screen in the Delay text box, click Grab, and then set up the screen (within the allotted time) before Ksnapshot takes another picture. If you only want a picture of a specific window, place a checkmark in the Only grab the window containing the cursor checkbox, click Grab, and then click the window that you want to capture.

Summary

You've just seen a few of the added graphics utilities that Linux-Mandrake has to offer. These utilities can be used to make minor changes to image files and to manage these files. If you work with graphics files, you may find yourself in need of some of the programs covered during this hour.

Q&A

22

Q **Where can I find examples of icons?**

A The KDE Icon Editor can open several types of files (.xpm, .gif, and .jpg) and saves files in the .xpm format. You can search the Internet or the Linux filesystem to find some example files. Two directories that contain a number of icon files are as follows:

/usr/share/icons

/usr/share/pixmaps

Q **Are there any other useful image utilities included in the distribution?**

A kuickshow supports the most popular image file formats. It also acts as a file browser and you can look for files that meet your search criteria. kshow can display a series of images in a slideshow and can make copies of files. If you need to convert images from one file format to another format, try xv.

There are also two other paint programs that you may want to try—kpaint and xpaint.

Q **I'd like to create my own mandelbrots (fractal art) to use as desktop backgrounds. Are there any programs that can do this?**

A Use the Fractals Generator (kfract) to create mandelbrots. You can save the images in the .bmp format. You can then use other image viewers described in this hour to use the image as desktop wallpaper.

Workshop

There are many pictures you can draw, photographs you can enhance, and images that you can collect. You'll therefore need a few graphics utilities to help you manage all this artwork. Test your skills and see how well you'll be able to keep up with your ever-growing collection of priceless art.

Quiz

1. Which graphics utility programs can place an image on your desktop and which programs can convert the desktop into an image file?

2. Which graphics utilities can change the appearance of an image file?

3. What are thumbnails?

Exercises

1. In this day, you were introduced to the KDE Icon Editor. You learned that you can make desktop icons with this tool. You may want to go a step further and learn how to create an entire desktop theme. Here are a few Web sites that will get you started:

   `x.themes.org`

   `gtk.themes.org`

   `kde.themes.org`

2. You may have created pictures with the various graphics programs covered in this book. Or, you may have a collection of images you've downloaded off the Web. If your collection is growing large, take some time to organize these files into a directory structure. You can use a program like GQview, or you can work in a file manager.

PART VII

Sit Back and Have Some Fun

Hour

Hour 23

Multimedia

You're almost at the end of a long 24-hour stretch. So, put on some tunes and shake a leg. If you're the couch potato type, pop in a video and stretch back.

In this hour, you learn about a few of the GNU/Linux multimedia players. If you enjoy listening to your favorite melodies while you work, experiment with the different CD players. You'll see three CD players at the top of this hour.

If you share music and video files with friends, or download these files from the Internet, there are players for most of the popular file formats. And, if you like to sing along with the music but are unsure of the words, check out the karaoke player.

Sit back and enjoy the music while you learn how to do the following:

- Create a music CD database
- Play electronic sounds and music
- Sing along with the bouncing ball
- Watch movies on the tiny screen

Playing Music CDs

Noise is a regular occurrence around our office. The whole neighborhood has something to contribute to our work day—dogs barking, roosters crowing, birds screeching, workers talking, tractors backfiring. You get the picture.

To drown out the background noise, we pop some classical music into the CD-ROM drive of one of the office computers and crank up the volume.

If you like to listen to music while you work, check out the CD players listed in Table 23.1.

TABLE 23.1 Choose a CD Player

CD Player	Execution Command
GNOME CD player	gtcd
KDE small/simple CD player	kscd
X Window CD player	xplaycd

The first CD player on the list is the GNOME CD player (shown in Figure 23.1). This is an easy-to-use CD player and has the added benefit of being able to automatically download information about a CD (such as title, artist, and song list) from an Internet database.

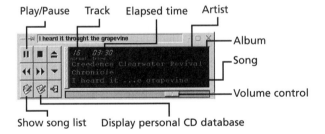

FIGURE 23.1

The GNOME CD player automatically downloads CD information from the Internet.

If you want a CD player with a few more features, take a look at the KDE CD player shown in Figure 23.2. The KDE CD player also downloads CD information from an Internet database, but it does not do this automatically. It does give you more flexibility in how you listen to your CDs.

The song list is located on the CD player itself, which makes selecting a song an easy task. You can also shuffle the order in which songs play or you can play the CD over and over again until you turn it off.

FIGURE 23.2
Shuffle the song list for a little variety.

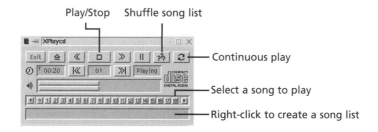

Continuous play

Download CD   Shuffle   Change display   Select a song
information   song list   color and font   to play

Another easy-to-use CD player is the X Window CD player (shown in Figure 23.3). No fancy bells and whistles here. It's easy to play a selected song; just click the track number along the bottom of the player. You can also click the random shuffle button until you find a track order you like. This player does not work with Internet CD databases, but you can enter song information if you want.

Play/Stop   Shuffle song list

FIGURE 23.3
Use the CD album cover to create your own song list.

Continuous play

Select a song to play

Right-click to create a song list

Lesson 23.1: Looking Up CD Information on the Internet

In this lesson, you use the GNOME CD Player to download the album title, artist, and song names from an online CD database. You then learn how to select songs from the playlist. To learn how to keep track of your music CD, follow along with these steps:

1. Connect to your Internet Service Provider.

2. Open the GNOME CD Player and place a music CD into the CD-ROM drive. The player will query the database and display the artist and album title.

3. Click the Open Track Editor button to display a list of the songs on the album. An example is shown in Figure 23.4

4. To play a song from the Track Editor, double-click the title of the song.

If you want to makes notes about a song, you can type information in the text box below the Track Information.

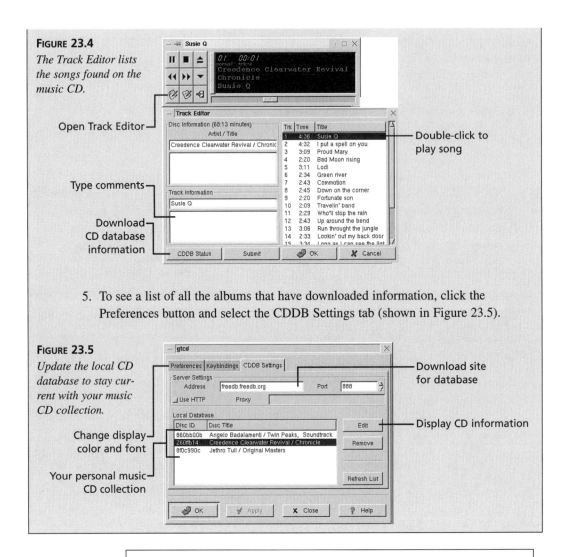

FIGURE 23.4

The Track Editor lists the songs found on the music CD.

Open Track Editor

Type comments

Download CD database information

Double-click to play song

5. To see a list of all the albums that have downloaded information, click the Preferences button and select the CDDB Settings tab (shown in Figure 23.5).

FIGURE 23.5

Update the local CD database to stay current with your music CD collection.

Change display color and font

Your personal music CD collection

Download site for database

Display CD information

If you want to record music CDs (as WAV files), you may want to try out the Grip CD player and ripper.

Listening to WAV and MIDI Files

If you collect sound and music files on the Internet, you'll need a media player to play these files. Two of the most popular sound file formats found on the Web are WAV and MIDI formats.

When you need an easy way to listen to WAV files, open the KDE Media Player (shown in Figure 23.6). You can access this media player from the KDE main menu under Multimedia or by typing **kmedia** in an X terminal window.

FIGURE 23.6

Use the KDE media player to listen to WAV files.

Play

Open a WAV file — Elapsed time   Filename

Another media player that you may find useful is the KDE MIDI player. To find the KDE MIDI player (shown in Figure 23.7), look in the KDE main menu under Multimedia or type **kmidi** in an X terminal window.

FIGURE 23.7

Download MIDI files from newsgroups and play the songs with the MIDI player.

Create a play list   Volume control   Shuffle through play list

If you are using the KDE Desktop, you can open WAV and MIDI files from the file manager. Open the file manager and click the file you want to play. The appropriate player will open and begin playing the file.

Karaoke in Your Own Backyard

Do you like to sing but don't always know the words to the songs you hear on the radio? Do you and your friends have a garage band and need more material? One of the easiest ways to learn new songs is to download karaoke files (they have a .kar extension) from the Internet. Then, find a karaoke player and begin memorizing those tunes.

To find the KDE MIDI and karaoke multimedia player (shown in Figure 23.8), look in the KDE main menu under Multimedia or type **kmid** in an X terminal window.

You can also play .mid files with the karaoke player.

Create a play list   Change musical instruments

FIGURE 23.8

*Learn to sing with the
KMid karaoke player.*

Open a karaoke or
MIDI file

Sing along with the
flashing words

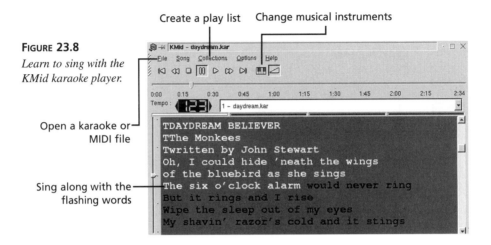

Watching Videos

For all you television and movie addicts, there are several movie players included in the
Linux-Mandrake distribution. The most versatile of these video players is aKtion (shown
in Figure 23.9). You'll find action in the KDE main menu under Multimedia or you can
type **aktion** in an X terminal window. aKtion can handle .avi, .mov, and .mpg video file
formats.

FIGURE 23.9

*aKtion will play most
video file formats.*

Summary

Multimedia is some of the latest news in application development for the Linux operating system. This hour shows you a few of the music and video players available in the
Linux-Mandrake distribution. You'll find these players extremely easy to use. If you want
to learn more about Linux multimedia, keep your ear tuned to the Internet for the latest
in Linux news.

Q&A

Q **I've tried playing WAV and MIDI files, but I can't hear any sound. What can I do?**

A Your sound card is probably not configured correctly. You can use the sound configuration tool to correct this, but before you begin, make sure you know the I/O port and IRQ and DMA settings for the sound card.

To configure the sound card, log into the root account and type `sndconfig` at the command prompt. This runs the sound configuration tool. If your sound configuration tool does not detect your sound card, you'll need to select from the list.

You can also use the soundcard configuration tool found in DrakConf. Open DrakConf and select the Hardware configuration option. DrakConf will try to detect the soundcard and other devices. From the list of devices, select the soundcard and run the configuration tool to test the sound.

Q **Which players can I use if I want to play MPEG files?**

A If you want to play .mp3 format files, try the KDE MPEG audio player (`kmpg`). The KDE MPEG audio player not only plays MP3 files, but you can listen to broadcasts off the Internet. There's also the Kmp3 player.

23

Workshop

With all the singing and dancing going on during this hour, you may have thought we would forget to test what you've learned over the past hour. We'll skip the talent show, but here are a few questions that test your performance skills.

Quiz

1. What is the easiest way to keep a database of all your music CDs?

2. What are some of the popular sound file formats that are found on the Internet?

Exercises

1. You may find that you have other multimedia needs than those covered during this past hour. There are other media players that you can download from the Internet. There are also TV tuners so that you can watch your favorite television shows on your computer screen. Do some research on the Internet and see what else you can learn about using multimedia applications with Linux.

2. Organize your own karaoke sing-along. Get on the Internet and download your favorite songs. There are quite a few sites that contain archives of .kar files. After you've collected a few tunes, use KMid to create collections of the karaoke files. This will make it easier to manage the sing-along. You can also print the words (File, Save Lyrics) in case your friends need a lyric cheat sheet.

HOUR 24

Games

Congratulations! You've made it to the final hour. It's time to have a party, so let the games begin! Linux has lots of games. In fact, plenty of interesting little distractions come with your Linux distribution.

In addition to those games that are already on the system, Linux provides an excellent platform for some of the popular multiplayer games that are beginning to catch on with Internet enthusiasts. After you play with some Linux games, you'll have a chance to try one of the commercial games ported into Linux.

You'll also spend some time finding out where you can get more games on the Internet, and find out about playing games from some other popular operating systems on Linux.

During the next hour, you learn how to

- Search through your Linux system for some fun games
- Install commercial games designed for Linux
- Find games on the Internet
- Determine whether your Windows games will run on Linux

Fun Stuff that Comes with Linux-Mandrake

Let's go back to the beginning for just a few minutes and go over some of the components you may have selected during the installation. By installing the KDE and GNOME interfaces, a number of games tagged along just for fun. There were also a couple of game components (console games and X games) that you had an opportunity to load along with Linux-Mandrake.

How do you find all these games? Well, first, flip through the KDE and GNOME menus.

Looking at What KDE Has to Offer

If you start at the KDE Application Starter button, there is a Games submenu where several games are stored. You'll find a number of card games (such as Poker), many board games (such as Abalone, Mahjongg, Minesweeper, and Reversi), and a few puzzles (remember the Rubik's Cube?).

Maybe the most exciting game you'll find in the KDE Game menu is the GnuLactic Conquest (shown in Figure 24.1). If you can't find the game, open an X terminal window and type **konquest**. GnuLactic Conquest is a game in which two or more players compete against each other to take over the universe. To set up the game and the player list, click the New Game button along the left side of the window. You may also want to read the Help file before you begin.

FIGURE 24.1

If you can't really take over the universe, you can at least pretend you are that powerful.

Start a new game

Competing players

Add more players

Let the game begin!

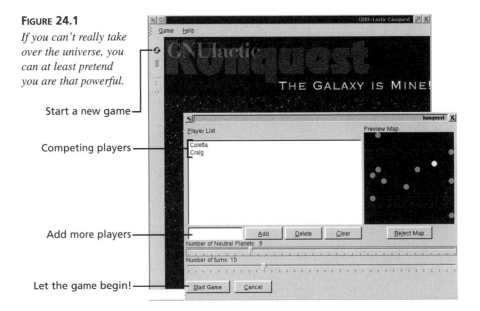

Finding Games in GNOME

The GNOME main menu also contains a Games submenu where you'll find plenty to keep you entertained. You may also notice some of the same games listed in the KDE menus.

> Both KDE and GNOME have a version of Mahjongg that is identical to the classic tile game. But the KDE version has three other tile layouts that vary from the standard game.

If you are a fan of dice games, get out your dice cups and gather around GNOME Tali (see Figure 24.2). GNOME Tali is a takeoff of the Yahtzee dice game that was so popular in the 1970s. If you want to try out a little wrist action, select Game, New Game and see how well you score against the computer players. If you'd rather play with a real friend, click Settings, Preferences and choose a different class of players.

24

Select number of players

FIGURE 24.2
GNOME Tali is a strategy game for dice players.

Select your score

Click the dice to re-roll

Roll the selected dice

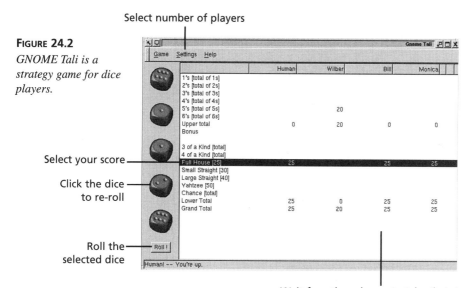

Wait for other players to take their turns

Playing X Strategy Games

There's another menu in GNOME that lists a number of X games. The X games are games that run on the X server that you configured for your Mandrake system during installation. If you want to test your strategy (and your patience), give a few of these games a try. Start at the GNOME Main menu and move the mouse pointer to AnotherLevel menus, Games, Strategy.

Here you'll find some of your favorite board games, such as backgammon and chess, and other games where you try to solve the puzzle in the shortest amount of time possible. One of the best chess games available is the GnuChess chess engine. GnuChess is played using XBoard (shown in Figure 24.3) as the graphical user interface. To start XBoard, look for it in the AnotherLevel menus, or type **xboard** in an X Terminal window.

FIGURE 24.3

When you want a quiet, comfortable game of chess, open the XBoard.

White's move

Drag and drop chess pieces into position

Keep track of moves

Pause the game

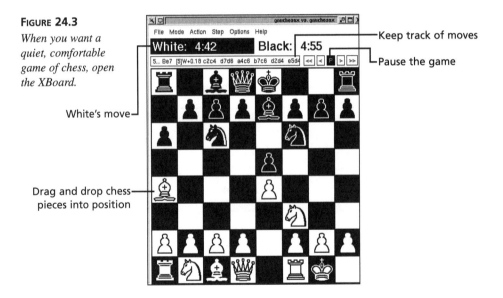

Playing X Video Games

If you'd rather have some action along with your games, try some of the X video games. You'll find these games in the AnotherLevel menus under Games, Video.

For those of you who enjoy blasting tiny Martians to smithereens, XKobo is another bang-bang, shoot 'em up, outer space game. If you'd rather just go for a leisurely cruise, try the XPilot flight simulator. And, no video game arcade would be complete without some version of Tetris. The Linux version is called Xtrojka (seen in Figure 24.4).

Start a new game   Change the pace

FIGURE 24.4

See how well you can line up the colored blocks.

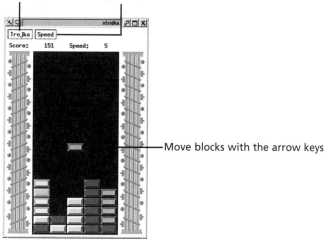

Move blocks with the arrow keys

Playing Linux Games

You'll find a number of popular games being ported to the Linux operating system. A couple of the forerunners in this category are the Quake games from ID Software and Civilization from Activision. If you would like to purchase these games, visit

`www.macmillansoftware.com/catalog/software_results.cfm`.

> Before you install any of these programs, carefully check the system require-
> ments. Many of these games require a significant amount of hard disk
> space. You may also find that if you run your screen at a lower resolution
> (such as 800x600) or if you do not have a 3D accelerator graphics card, you
> won't get the display you dreamed about.

To install most of these games, you either need to find a Readme file on the CD or a printed user manual that tells you how to install and play the game. Make sure you read the instructions carefully.

Lesson 24.1: Installing Civilization

If you are looking for a game that installs just as easy as any game that runs on the Windows operating system, Civilization may be your answer. Before you can install the program though, you must first be logged into the root account.

Civilization is an animated strategy game that gives you a unique opportunity to build and shape your own civilization (and rule it) through several levels spanning time. You will build and guide your civilization from primitive beginnings in an ancient world all the way to colonizing a planet in a future of 3000 AD. Actions and decisions, outcomes of wars, and other factors in the earlier world reflect in the future one. Civilization can be played as a multiplayer game or just you against the machine.

1. Place the Civilization CD-ROM in the computer's CD-ROM drive.

2. At the command line, type **mount /dev/cdrom** and press Enter to mount the CD-ROM so that the contents of the disk can be read by the system.

3. Type **sh /mnt/cdrom/install** and press Enter. The Civilization: Call To Power setup screen will appear. Notice that along the left side of the window, there are three buttons.

4. Click the Install button. The Welcome to Civilization: Call To Power install dialog box appears on the screen (see Figure 24.5).

If you later decide you do not want this game on your computer, mount the CD-ROM drive, display the setup window, and click the Uninstall button.

FIGURE 24.5

Select a mount point that contains plenty of free space.

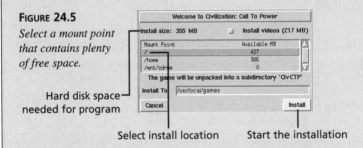

Hard disk space needed for program

Select install location   Start the installation

5. Click the mount point where you want to install the program.

6. If you have enough space on your computer, you can install the display videos on your hard drive by selecting the Install videos option. If you don't have enough space, don't select this option. Instead, you'll need to mount the Civilization CD-ROM when you play the game. The program will play the videos from the CD-ROM.

7. Click the Install button. The installation process will begin (as seen in Figure 24.6). As the installation progresses, you'll see the status at the upper-left corner and a status bar along the bottom of the window. You can also read the callouts on the graphics for some technical details about the game pieces.

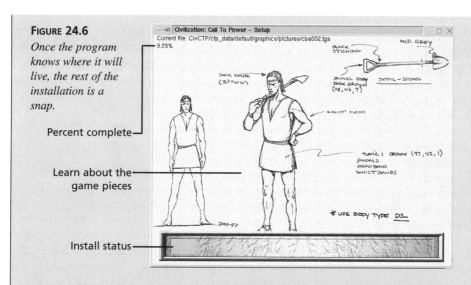

FIGURE 24.6
Once the program knows where it will live, the rest of the installation is a snap.

Percent complete—

Learn about the game pieces—

Install status—

8. After the installation is complete, you'll be asked if you want to create a symbolic link in several directories. Click the No to All button. You are then returned to the initial setup screen.

9. Click the Installation Complete button at the bottom of the window.

10. After you close the initial setup screen, you can log into your user account and begin playing the game. To start the game, open an X terminal window and type

    `/usr/local/games/CivCTP/civctp`

    and press Enter. The game loads and you will see the opening screen.

You can also place a link to the Civilization game on your desktop. Open a file manager and navigate to the /usr/local/games/CivCTP directory. In KFM, drag the civctp file to the desktop and select Link from the menu that appears when you release the mouse button.

Finding Games on the Internet

So, you haven't had enough fun yet? Looking for more ways to spend your free time? Time to hook up that Internet connection and take a look at what's available for Linux in the games department.

The Linux Portal site provides over 350 games at `www.linuxlinks.com/Software/Games`. The games are organized by category. There are also links to many of the Web sites of these games.

One of the largest collections of Linux games is the Linux Game Tome at `www.happypenguin.org`. There are over 300 games available for downloading. This site also contains news about new game releases and a database where you can search for a game by name, type, or date released.

Tucows also hosts a number of Linux applications at `linux.tucows.com`. Tucows contains a number of games along with a host of other applications for many purposes.

The LinuxApps Web site at `www.linuxapps.com` contains more software than just games. You'll find about every software category imaginable. The software is arranged by categories.

The Linux Archives Web site at `www.linuxarchives.com` has a few games and a good selection of other Linux software. You'll also find links to other archive Web sites that have collections of software for other operating systems.

To keep up on the latest happenings in the Linux game arena, cruise over to the Linux Games Web site at `www.linuxgames.com`. This site has a daily update of Linux game news with links to a variety of other gaming sites. You can also download games from the Linux Games site at `ftp.linuxgames.com`. Many of the game programs are available as RPM files and can be installed on your system using Gnome-RPM or KPackage.

Another source of Linux game information is GameSpot's Linux page at `www.gamespot.com/features/linux`.

Playing Windows Games with Wine

Many of you may have a favorite game that you play on the Windows operating system. It is not an easy task (and most times, impossible) to get a program to work on an operating system for which it was not intended. But, there may be hope. Currently, a Windows emulator called Wine is in development that allows you to run your Windows programs on Linux. Wine is still in development and not recommended for everyday use, but you may want to take a look at Wine to see if it is something you want to tackle.

The Wine Development Headquarters (at `www.winehq.com`) contains a variety of resources for people who want to run Windows-compatible software under a UNIX/Linux operating system. If you want to find out whether an application will run under Wine, check out the Wine application database at `www.winehq.com/Apps/query.cgi`. This is a searchable database and you can limit the type of applications that are displayed. As of this writing, the database contained over 1900 applications.

Another source of information about running your favorite Windows-compatible games under Linux using Wine can be found in the Wine success stories at `www.linuxgames.com/wine`.

Summary

Over the past hour, you learned how to find a number of games which are either installed on your system or can be installed from the Linux-Mandrake CD. Hopefully you had some fun while you were looking through the menus and deciding which games you might enjoy. After you get bored with these games, you can find a number of commercial games or you can download games from the Internet.

Q&A

Q I know there must be more games installed on my Linux computer than I can see in the KDE or GNOME menus. Is there some way I can find out what other games are installed?

24

A To see what is installed on your computer, open either Gnome-RPM or KPackage. On the left side of the window, you'll see a list of package categories. Expand the list to see all the installed packages.

If you want more information about a package, click it. In KPackage, a description of the application will appear on the right side of the window. To do the same thing in Gnome-RPM, click the Query button to see a description of the game or other application.

Q What's the best Solitaire game?

A Try xpat2. This Solitaire game contains 14 card games that you can play by yourself.

Q I'd like to try one of the multiplayer games. Are there any demos I can use first?

A You may find a copy of FreeCiv in the /usr/games directory. Click the file named civ. FreeCiv is another space exploration/conquer the universe game and is a clone of the Civilization game.

Workshop

It may seem crazy to test you on your game knowledge when we just told you to have some fun with this hour. But, hey, you can learn and have fun at the same time.

Quiz

1. Where can you find the games that are installed on your Linux system?

2. There are many games on the Linux-Mandrake CD. Where are other places where you can find Linux games?

3. What is Wine?

Exercises

1. If you installed the Civilization game, you can add a symbolic link to your GNOME desktop that will open the program. The symbolic link needs to point from /usr/local/games/CivCTP/civctp to your desktop directory. You can then use the icon.xpm file in the /usr/local/games/CivCTP directory as the graphic for the desktop icon.

2. Visit some of the game Web sites mentioned in this hour and see if you can find a game that interests you. If you find one, download it and install it on your system. Then, have fun with your new game.

APPENDIX A

Answers

Hour 1

Quiz

1. What does it mean that Linux-Mandrake is optimized for Pentiums?

   The operating system is enhanced to run Pentium class machines and will not run on an i386 or i486 machine.

2. What is a daemon?

   A *daemon* is a system server that works in the background by executing processes automatically without user assistance.

3. What kind of modem is best for Linux-Mandrake to connect to the Internet?

   An external serial modem is best because GNU/Linux doesn't support PCI internal modems.

4. Can you use a ZIP drive with Linux-Mandrake?

   Yes, but only the parallel port connecting version.

Hour 2

Quiz

1. Which installation class allows you to select the packages that you want installed on your computer?

   The custom installation presents you with a list of application types from which you can choose. You probably won't need everything, and you may not have room for everything. If you select too many packages, the installation will let you know that there is not enough room and you will be asked to go back through the list and choose fewer packages. Don't worry if you don't get everything, you can install more applications later.

2. What is the purpose of the startup disk that you created during the installation?

   If, for some reason, you can't get your newly installed Linux-Mandrake to boot, put the startup disk in the floppy drive and reboot the computer. A small version of Linux will load and start up the processes and access your Linux system. Reasons why you would need to use the startup disk include a faulty LILO or BootMagic installation, or when LILO or BootMagic cannot be used on the system.

3. How do you change the operating system that will start by default when BootMagic loads?

   Return to the BootMagic configuration in Microsoft Windows by selecting BootMagic Configuration from the PowerQuest BootMagic program group. Select the operating system that you want to use as the default from the Menu Name list, and then click on the Set as Default button.

Hour 3

Quiz

1. Why do most configuration problems occur in the Linux installation?

   The major contributor to hardware configuration problems is the use of hardware that is not on the Linux hardware compatibility list. If the hardware is listed, chances are that it will be auto-detected during the Linux installation process.

2. Which sound standard does Linux support?

   Computer sound cards that are compatible with the Open Sound System (OSS) will be detected during the Linux installation and you will be able to play sounds and music on your computer. Advanced Linux Sound Architecture (ALSA) is a newer sound system that will be replacing chunks of the present Linux sound architecture as components become as good or better than the existing ones.

3. If you want to read the Linux documentation on your computer, but do not have access to a user interface, how do you do this?

   You can read the Linux man pages from the command line using the man command.

Hour 4

Quiz

1. What tool enables you to easily move back and forth between using a KDE desktop and using a GNOME desktop?

   The Desktop Switching Tool is the easiest way to go back and forth between the two desktop environments. The Desktop Switching Tool also provides easy access to the AnotherLevel desktop environment. If you're using GNOME, you'll find the AnotherLevel menus in the Main Menu. You'll find some applications in these menus that you won't find in the KDE or GNOME menus.

2. You find that you are frequently searching through the application menus looking for the same program. What can you do to make it easier to find and start the application?

   Place an icon for the application on the panel. If you find that your stack of icons is too much for the panel, you might consider placing the icons on the desktop. Open the Main Menu, click and hold on the application you want to launch from the desktop, and drag the icon onto an empty area of the desktop.

3. You can use the window buttons to minimize, maximize, and close windows. Which button do you use if you want to perform some other function to a window?

   The Window menu displays a list of commands that you can perform on a window. It goes beyond just minimizing and closing. You can shade, stick, and remember window states. If you're working in KDE, click the Window Menu button to display the Window menu. In GNOME, you'll need to right-click on the window title bar.

4. Name the different ways you can get a window out of your way and create more desktop space.

   Minimize the window so that it is an icon on the KDE taskbar or the GNOME panel. You can also shade the window so that all you see is the title bar.

5. Explain window focus policy and the different ways you can make a window active.

   Focus policy settings are used to determine the keyboard or mouse actions needed to make a window active. One way to make a window active is by clicking inside the window. You can also set the focus policy so that all you have to do is move the mouse pointer over the window area to make the window active.

A

Hour 5

Quiz

1. Where do you find the navigation controls for the virtual desktops and how do you move from desktop area to desktop area?

   The navigation controls are found on the KDE and GNOME panels. By default, these controls are in the middle of the panel. GNOME calls these navigation controls the pager. It's easy to move from desktop area to desktop area; just click on the icon for the desktop area that you want displayed on the screen.

2. When does it make sense to use sticky windows?

   If you will be working with more than one desktop area, you may want to be able to use certain application windows no matter which desktop you are using. By making the window sticky, the window will follow you from desktop area to desktop area.

3. What options do you have when you want to change the desktop background?

   The simplest background (and maybe the easiest on the eyes) is a solid color background. Two colors can be blended to form a gradient or can be used with a pre-designed pattern. Graphic images can also be used as wallpaper. The image can be centered to take up only a small area in the middle of the screen, it can be tiled to show several small copies of the image in rows and columns, or it can fill the entire screen.

Hour 6

Quiz

1. What command tells you where you are currently working in the filesystem?

   The pwd command. If you are working at the command line and doing file-management tasks, you may want to use the pwd command at regular intervals. It always pays to know where you are working in the filesystem.

2. Which command gives you a list of the contents of your working directory as well as detailed information about each item in the directory?

   The ls -l command displays the long list description of the contents of the working directory. The information in this list tells you the following: whether the item is a file or directory, file permissions, its owner, file size, and the date it was last updated.

3. What does a Linux filename consist of and how long can it be?

   The Linux filename consists of the directory path and the filename. Filenames can be as long as 256 characters. They can contain letters and numbers, as well as characters like the dot and underscore. Filenames cannot contain asterisks or question marks.

Hour 7

Quiz

1. What method do you use to share files with other users on the system?

   You need to create user accounts for each person who will have access to the computer. Once this is done, you'll need to decide which users need to share files and create groups based on file-sharing needs. You can then create a separate directory for each group in which files can be stored and permissions for read and write access to the directory and the file can be assigned.

2. How do you give members of a group the ability to make changes to a file?

   First, every user who is to be a part of the group must be added to the group list. Then, the group must have write permission for the directory and write permission for any files in the assigned directory.

3. Where can you find out how much space is being used on your computer's hard drive?

   There are several utilities that you can use, but the one that gives you the information you need and that also provides other system information can be found in the KDE Control Center under the Information category.

4. When do you need to change the time on your computer's clock?

   If you set the time zone correctly when you installed Linux-Mandrake, your computer's clock should chug away just fine, even when the times change for daylight savings. If you move and change to a different time zone, you have to reset the clock. Sometimes clocks can become off by a few minutes; this is when you'll want to use one of the utilities to adjust the time.

Hour 8

Quiz

1. What are the most important files in the filesystem that should be backed up?

   Configuration and kernel source files should always be backed up before and after any configuration changes are made to the system. You also should back up data files in your user's accounts.

2. Which backup tools can be used to back up and archive important files?

   There are three commands that you can use—tar, gzip, and cpio. You can also use the dump utility.

A

3. What type of media can be used to store backups?

Any type of media that can be separated from your Linux system is potentially a good backup medium. Floppy disks can store a small amount of data. Zip or Jaz drives can be used to store larger amounts of data, such as user account data files. If you want to back up the entire Linux system, use a CD or a separate hard drive.

Hour 9

Quiz

1. What is a package manager and which package managers are available in the Linux-Mandrake distribution?

A package manager is a utility that installs, upgrades, and uninstalls software from your Linux computer. The package manager automates the process of loading the necessary files in the right place and checking the dependencies between files. The package manager takes care of all the hard work of loading new programs.

KPackage and Gnome-RPM are both found in the Linux-Mandrake distribution. KPackage works with the KDE graphical user interface and Gnome-RPM works with the GNOME interface. While both utilities perform the same functions, they approach each task in a different manner.

2. How do you find software programs that are installed on your Linux computer but do not show up in the KDE or GNOME menus?

Open up a package manager (either KPackage or Gnome-RPM) and browse through the list of software categories. To find out how to execute one of these programs, display the package information and look for the execution command. (It is usually the first item listed in the package information.)

3. Where can you find packages that can be installed on your Linux computer?

The first place to start is with the Linux-Mandrake distribution CD-ROM. Unless you elected to install all the components, there are still many programs that are not loaded on your machine.

Another place to look is on the CD for other Linux distributions. Not all Linux distributions are created equally. Some distributions will have software that other distributions do not have, or have a more up-to-date version of that software.

The most complete list of packages available for Linux can be found on the Internet. There are many Web sites that make Linux applications available for downloading. If you want to find Linux software on the Internet, check out the Web sites for the various Linux distributions or look up the Free Software Foundation (www.gnu.org).

Hour 10

Quiz

1. What is the first task you should perform before you start building a network?

    First, you will need to document every piece of equipment (workstation, printer, scanner) that will be attached to the network. Collect as much information about each component as you can. The more you know about your equipment, the better you can plan a network. After you know which pieces of equipment will be used on the network, you can use this information to draw up a plan for the proposed network.

2. Why is it important to design your network on paper before you begin the actual creation of the network?

    One of the major obstacles to overcome when building a network is to make sure that all the equipment is compatible. Since you need to start with the computer equipment that you presently own, you'll want to be sure that everything works together.

    It is also important that you plan for future growth. As your home office or small business grows, you'll want to add more workstations to the network. You need to be sure that there is enough space on the network to add these workstations. You should also plan for new technologies that you may want to take advantage of.

3. Why is the job of network administrator so important?

    The network administrator is responsible for keeping the network up and running. This involves setting up accounts for each user who needs access to the network and creating accounts so that several users can share files in a workgroup. The network administrator is also responsible for backing up the network so that valuable files are not lost. It is also the network administrator who must plan for the growth of the network and keep abreast of changing technologies that could benefit the organization.

Hour 11

Quiz

1. What is the most efficient way to set up an Internet connection that can be used by all user accounts?

    Linuxconf allows you to create one connection that can be used by any person who is logged into a user account. Also, by using Linuxconf, you can use UserNet to connect to the Internet. UserNet is quick at making the connection, and it automatically redials if the connection is lost.

2. How do you set up an Internet connection that is used only by the user who set up the connection? That is, it is not available to other users on the system.

   Use the Kppp dialer. The Kppp dialer looks and acts much like the dial-up connection used by Microsoft Windows. In addition to dialing the modem and connecting to your ISP, the Kppp dialer can keep track of your Internet use.

3. What are the different Internet activities that you can perform with Netscape Communicator?

   Netscape Communicator contains a full suite of Internet tools. The Navigator Web browser can display most any Web page that you may come across. Messenger can send and receive email. Your messages can be composed in plain text, or you can add color and flair and use HTML formatting in your email message. You can also lurk the newsgroups with Messenger. Messenger will store mail and news messages in folders that you designate. Communicator also includes an address book in which you can keep names, email addresses, snail mail addresses, and other information for everyone you know. The address book can be accessed from a new message window so that you don't have to remember email addresses. The final player is Composer. If you want to create Web pages, Composer can handle most of your HTML formatting needs.

4. What is the fastest way to download files off the Internet?

   FTP is the fastest download method. By using an FTP program, such as gFTP, to download files, you don't have to worry about a lost connection. If the Internet connection is broken, the FTP program will save the part of the file that has been downloaded and will pick up the download when the connection is reestablished.

Hour 12

Quiz

1. How do you move text from one location to another in a document?

   First you must select the text that you want to move. Then, you can either select Edit, Cut or click the Cut tool button. Then, move the cursor to the place where you want the text moved and click the Paste tool button (or select Edit, Paste). If you want to place the text in another location in the document, move the cursor to the location you want and click Paste again. The selected text is copied again.

2. If you want to place a border around a single cell in a table, how do you do this?

   Place the cursor in the cell and select one or more of the Border buttons on the Tables toolbar. You can also right-click the table and select either Line Top, Line Bottom, Line Left, or Line Right from the menu.

3. Where can you find special symbols that you can insert in your documents and how do you use them?

    KLyX contains a list of symbols from which you can select. Place the cursor in the location where you want to insert the symbol and click Insert Special Character. Then, just click the symbol from the list.

4. How do you resize graphical images that you've inserted in your document?

    Click the image to display the Edit Figure dialog box. You can change the width and height by selecting a size option and typing the amount in the text box at the bottom of the list of option buttons.

Hour 13

Quiz

1. How do you switch between account files when you have separate files for each of your banking and credit card accounts?

    There are two ways you can go about this one. If the account list is displayed in the CBB window, double-click the account that you want to use. The register for that account will display. If you don't see the account in the account list, click File, Load Account. You'll need to select the account file from the Select File dialog box.

2. If you are entering a transaction and you don't have an appropriate category set up, what is the quickest way to create a new category?

    Type a name for the category in the Category field of the entry area. When you accept the transaction, CBB will ask you whether you want to add the category to the list. If you respond with a yes, the category will be added.

3. If there are a number of bills that you pay regularly, such as telephone and car payments, how can you enter these recurring transactions quickly?

    CBB memorizes every transaction you enter. Each time you pay recurring bills, such as the phone bill, type the check number and the date. Then, type a few characters of the description and press Tab. CBB will fill in the rest of the transaction for you. If needed, you can edit the transaction. Accept the transaction when you are ready to move on to the next one.

4. How do you make sure that your records and the bank statement agree?

    When the bank statement arrives, reconcile the account. You do this by opening the appropriate account and clicking the Balance button. Then, check off each transac-

A

tion that is listed on the bank statement. Hopefully, the ending balance that CBB comes up with will be the same as the ending balance on the bank statement. If not, you'll need to run a few reports to find the discrepancy.

Hour 14

Quiz

1. What is a druid?

   A *druid* provides an automated way to help you perform a task. A druid walks you step by step through the building of your Web site and Web pages. The druid asks questions to which you provide answers and at the end of the process, the requested task has been completed. For those people who are coming to Linux from the Windows operating system, a druid is the same critter as a wizard.

2. Name two ways in which a druid can make your life easier.

   The two tasks that druids perform that make Web site creation a bit easier are creating the foundation for your Web site and adding pages to your site. There are also a few wizards located on the toolbar that make it easy to add images to a Web page, create hyperlinks, design tables, and upload your Web site to your ISP's Web server.

3. Which HTML tags provide the basic structure of a Web page?

   There are four HTML tags that are required for all Web pages—the <HTML> tag, the <HEAD> tag, the <TITLE> tag, and the <BODY> tag. The <HTML> tag indicates that the file uses the HTML language. The <HEAD> tag encloses the header information for the file. The <TITLE> tag is the most common tag you will find within the <HEAD> tag. The <TITLE> tag displays the title of the Web page in the title bar of the Web browser used to view the page. The <BODY> tag encloses the content of the Web page.

   Each HTML tag is enclosed by brackets and needs a beginning and ending tag. The beginning tag turns a feature on and the ending tag turns a feature off. For example, to tell a browser that the text that follows is a title, use the tag <TITLE>. Then, at the end of the title text, you need to tell the Web browser that it has read the end of the title, so you use the </TITLE> tag.

Hour 15

Quiz

1. What is the difference between a local printer and a network printer?

    A local printer is attached to a single workstation and only the workstation can print to the printer. Network printers are not usually attached to any workstation. They are attached to the network with a network interface card and a cable. Any user logged into the network with the proper permissions can access a network printer.

2. What are some of the more popular printers supported by Linux?

    Hewlett-Packard DeskJet and LaserJet printers are high on the list. Most of these printer models can be supported. Even if your HP LaserJet isn't listed, you can try either the plain HP LaserJet driver or try the driver for the LaserJet 4 and 5. Cannon, Epson, and DEC printers are also on the list. If you don't see your printer, you can try either a text-only printer or a PostScript printer.

3. How much information can be included in a KVoice outgoing fax?

    The most important information is the recipient's fax number. Without this, the modem will not dial. You also need to enter a short note for the fax cover page. If you have more information to send, you can attach an electronic file to the fax.

A

Hour 16

Quiz

1. Where is the modeline located in the Emacs window and what purpose does it serve?

    The modeline is located at the bottom of each window and contains status information for the data contained in the buffer. The modeline indicates if there are any unsaved changes in the buffer, the name of the file contained in the buffer, any modes that are used by the buffer, and where the cursor is located in the buffer window.

2. How do you start a new file in Emacs?

    When you create a file, you are actually opening a new buffer. You tell Emacs to find a file, but the name you give Emacs does not yet exist. Emacs creates a buffer for the file. Then, when the file is saved, it becomes an actual file that resides on the computer's hard disk. Once a file is created, you may want to apply one or more major and minor modes—such as Text mode, Enriched mode, or Outline mode.

3. Which commands move the cursor to the beginning of the buffer file and to the end of the buffer file?

The Alt+< command moves the cursor to the beginning of the text in the file. The Alt+> command moves the cursor to the end of the document.

4. How many asterisks precede a third level heading in an outline?

There should be three asterisks before a third level heading. First level headings require one asterisk and second level headings require two asterisks. You also need to make sure that you are working with the Outline minor mode so that you can collapse your outline to show only the headings. You can also expand the outline to show the body text.

Hour 17

Quiz

1. Where do you find the man command?

In the Help menu. There is no command key sequence that starts the man command. In Emacs for X11, select Help, Manuals, Read Man Page. In XEmacs, click Help, Manuals, UNIX Manual.

2. How do you find documentation on a command?

Use the Describe Key command by typing Ctrl+H K followed by the command key sequence. For example, to display the documentation for the Numeric Argument command, type

Ctrl+H K Ctrl+U

3. What is Lisp?

Lisp is the programming language that was used to write Emacs. Lisp code is a series of lists that sends instructions to the computer. The computer then acts on these instructions, and you see the result on your screen.

Hour 18

Quiz

1. What is the quickest way to move to a date that is several months or years away from the currently selected date?

You can go to a specific date by using the G+D command.

2. How do you keep track of appointments and other events that happen on certain days of the week, month, or year?

Use the I+W, I+M, and I+Y commands to create these entries. To use the command, you'll first need to select the specific day on which the event occurs and then use the appropriate command. Emacs will enter the appropriate date format. All you need to do is type enough information so that you'll know what is going to happen on that date.

3. How do you display your appointment list and other diary entries for the current date?

Use the Alt+X diary command. This command displays all the entries in the diary that use the current date. It does not matter which date is selected in the calendar.

Hour 19

Quiz

1. What file format should you use when working on images and photographs in The Gimp?

The Gimp uses the .xcf file format as its native file format. By using this file format, you retain all the Gimp's features in your working files. The .xcf format is needed to retain layers, channels, and other elements that make it possible to work on separate areas of an image.

2. How do you change the color that's applied to a drawing object?

Click the foreground color icon in the color picker. This opens a color selector. Not only can you pick a color, but you can also select a color shade.

3. What are some of the basic photo enhancements that you can use to correct the quality of your photographs?

You can fix poor exposure, color imbalance, color saturation, brightness, contrast, remove blemishes, and apply a variety of filters to your photos.

Hour 20

Quiz

1. How do you change the color used to draw a shape?

Use the color bar located on the right side of the KIllustrator window. When you right-click a color box, you change the default color for the outline. Clicking a color box changes the fill color.

2. What is the purpose of gridlines and how do you use them in KIllustrator?

   Not only do gridlines help you align objects to a straight line, but they are also used to divide the drawing into sections. These sections are used to place objects so that they appear balanced on a page. To set up the gridlines for a drawing, select Layout, Grid and select the distance between each gridline. To show and hide the gridlines, select View, Show Grid from the menu.

3. When is it helpful to use layers in a drawing?

   When there are parts of a drawing that do not need to be displayed or printed for every purpose. By using layers, you can select which elements to view, edit, and print.

4. Is it possible to add text to a KIllustrator drawing that does not appear on the page in a straight horizontal line?

   Yes, you can add text that has some shape to it by aligning the text to either an ellipse, freehand line, bezier curve, polyline, or polygon. You first need to type the text, and then create the shape. When this is done, activate the Selection Mode tool and click the text. Then select Arrange, Text along Path and click the place where you want the text to appear.

Hour 21

Quiz

1. Which types of software applications create moving pictures?

   Animation programs create movement by displaying a series of pictures, each in a different frame. The images used in each frame are created in a drawing program, such as The Gimp.

   Morphing programs create movement by transforming one object into another. The transformation takes place in increments and each change can be recorded so that the entire sequence can be played as one movie.

   Video-editing applications take digitized video and allow you to add animations, text, voice, and other sounds to the video.

2. What is animation?

   Animation describes a sequence of drawings in which each drawing is contained in a separate frame. Each drawing is slightly different from the one before. Displaying the frames in a timed sequence creates the effect of movement, or animation.

3. What is the difference between warping and morphing?

When an image is warped, it is distorted. When it is morphed, the image is changed so that it looks like another image.

Hour 22

Quiz

1. Which graphics utility programs can place an image on your desktop and which programs can convert the desktop into an image file?

Several programs can convert an image into wallpaper for your desktop. Programs that you can use include Electric Eyes and Kview.

If you need to take a snapshot of either your entire desktop or just a single window of the desktop, you can use Electric Eyes or Ksnapshot. You'll even find a screen capture utility in The Gimp (look in the Xtns menu).

2. Which graphics utilities can change the appearance of an image file?

Electric Eyes can change the color, size, and orientation of an image. You can select a file in GQview and use GQview to open the file in graphics editor (such as The Gimp, KIllustrator, or Electric Eyes). Kview can crop images and change the orientation.

3. What are thumbnails?

Thumbnails are miniature representations of images. Thumbnails are often used as previews in file browsers. Thumbnails give you an opportunity to view a file before you open it.

Hour 23

Quiz

1. What is the easiest way to keep a database of all your music CDs?

The GNOME and KDE CD players can download information about music CDs that you place in the CD-ROM drive. You need to be connected to the Internet to download the database information. The information that is downloaded includes the title of the album, the artist, and the song list.

2. What are some of the popular sound file formats that are found on the Internet?

MIDIs and WAV files are found quite frequently. Both file formats are relatively small (which means they transmit quickly) and there are players available for most computer operating systems. Web browsers can also play these sounds automatically.

Hour 24

Quiz

1. Where can you find the games that are installed on your Linux system?

   If you use a graphical interface (such as KDE or GNOME), you can start at the main menu button and navigate to the Games menu. Also found in the GNOME menus are the AnotherLevel menus. You'll find strategy and video games in the AnotherLevel menus.

   Another way to find out what game programs are installed is to open either KPackage or Gnome-RPM and browse through the list of installed packages. You can also mount the Linux-Mandrake CD to find additional games.

2. There are many games on the Linux-Mandrake CD. Where are other places where you can find Linux games?

   Several software publishers have recently begun porting their games to the Linux operating system. These Linux versions are the same as the Windows versions (and cost about the same).

   There are also many places on the Internet where you can download Linux games. Some of these sites are dedicated just to games, others have a wide variety of software packages from which to choose.

3. What is Wine?

   No, it is not a beverage that you serve with dinner. Wine is the Windows emulator that is currently in development. Wine will allow you to run Windows applications on the Linux operating system. Wine is not yet stable and should be used only if you want to experiment.

INDEX

The IT site
you asked for...

It's
Here!

InformIT is a complete online library delivering
information, technology, reference, training, news,
and opinion to IT professionals, students,
and corporate users.

Find IT Solutions Here!

www.informit.com

What's on the Disc

The companion CD-ROM contains Linux-Mandrake 7.0, GPL Edition.

Installing Linux-Mandrake from the CD-ROM

1. Insert the disc in the CD drive.
2. Restart your computer.
3. You may need to change your BIOS settings to boot from the CD-ROM. Typically, you enter your BIOS setup program with the F2 or DEL keys during the boot sequence.
4. Make your changes (if any) and exit the BIOS setup utility.
5. If your CD drive is capable of booting from CD-ROMs, you will boot into the Linux-Mandrake setup program.
6. Follow the onscreen prompts to complete the installation.

Installing Linux-Mandrake from a Boot Floppy Disk

1. Using DOS or Windows, format one 1.44MB floppy disk.
2. Copy two files from the CD-ROM to a temporary location on your hard drive, such as C:\TEMP: D:\IMAGES\BOOTNET.IMG and D:\DOSUTILS\RAWRITE.EXE.

   If your CD drive letter is not D:, substitute the drive letter that corresponds to your system.
3. At the DOS prompt, move to the directory where you copied the two files. Type RAWRITE and press <ENTER>.
4. When prompted to do so, type in the name BOOTNET.IMG and press <ENTER>.
5. When prompted to do so, type in the drive letter of the disk you are going to prepare and press <ENTER>. Since you are going to be booting from this disk, it's typically A:.
6. If you don't already have the boot floppy disk in your disk drive, insert it now.
7. Restart your computer.
8. You may need to change your BIOS settings to boot from the floppy disk drive. Typically, you enter your BIOS setup program with the F2 or DEL keys during the boot sequence.
9. Make your changes (if any) and exit the BIOS setup utility.
10. If your computer is set up properly, you will boot into the Linux-Mandrake setup program.
11. Follow the onscreen prompts to complete the installation.